D1206386

THE PSYCHOLOGY
OF DRIVING

Second Printing

The Psychology Of Driving

FACTORS OF TRAFFIC ENFORCEMENT

By

A. R. LAUER, M.A., M.S., Ph.D.
Professor of Psychology

Director, Driving Research Laboratory
Iowa State University
Ames, Iowa

CHARLES C THOMAS · PUBLISHER
Springfield · Illinois · U.S.A.

Published and Distributed Throughout the World by
CHARLES C THOMAS • PUBLISHER
BANNERSTONE HOUSE
301-327 East Lawrence Avenue, Springfield, Illinois, U.S.A.
NATCHEZ PLANTATION HOUSE
735 North Atlantic Boulevard, Fort Lauderdale, Florida, U.S.A.

First Printing, 1960
Second Printing, 1972

With THOMAS BOOKS careful attention is given to all details of
manufacturing and design. It is the Publisher's desire to present books
that are satisfactory as to their physical qualities and artistic possibilities
and appropriate for their particular use. THOMAS BOOKS will be true
to those laws of quality that assure a good name and good will.

Printed in the United States of America
00-2

FOREWORD

For the past several years we have studied a number of phases of highway safety which have been published in various magazines, scientific journals and other publications. A large number of requests have been made for the papers and it has been suggested that they be brought together into a volume of reasonable size which would be available for anyone having an interest in these specific investigations. Most of the papers are based on experimental studies and the conclusions drawn. We have tried not to include items which are of dubious nature or which are based mostly on opinion.

We are indebted to the Ohio State University Psychological Laboratory for the start in this field and to the Department of Psychology at Iowa State University for the opportunity to pursue these studies through the years. In many cases the results were obtained by collaboration with different persons and in such instances credit will be given. The various studies have been aided by grants from the American Optometric Association, the Allstate Insurance Company, the American Automobile Association, the U. S. Army, the Allied Mutual Insurance Company, the National Research Council, Thomas J. Lipton, Inc., and the Outdoor Advertising Association. The director of the various studies has been responsible for their development into final shape. The titles have been arranged as nearly as possible in a logical order.

Credit is due Dr. Virtus W. Suhr for most of the material in Chapter X on rest pauses. Numerous graduate students have worked on phases of other studies as is indicated in the references at the end of each chapter.

Chapter IX is an adaptation from the *Manual on Motorists' Vision* by the American Optometric Association and the American Association of Motor Vehicle Administrators of which the

v

author prepared the first draft based on researches made in co-operation with the American Optometric Association.

A. R. LAUER
Driving Research Laboratory
Iowa State University*

---

*The name "Iowa State College" was changed to "Iowa State University" in 1959. The research work was carried on prior to that date. Please note when reading text.

INTRODUCTION

The Driving Research Laboratory at Iowa State College has been the natural outgrowth of a demand for research in the field of driving and driving behavior. It was begun by a development of the driving clinic and phases described in this section.

Early investigators, such as Munsterberg, Klamm, Drechsler, Shellow, Viteles, and others in America and Europe, have made earlier studies of like nature. The laboratory has consistently followed out a program of driving research in this area since 1928. At that time the author began a study of driving behavior at Ohio State University in experimental psychology under the directorship of Dr. A. P. Weiss, who was then one of the best known experimental psychologists. Dr. Weiss had been made chairman of the National Research Council's committee to inaugurate a project on psychology of the highway. During the two years which followed, a number of collaborators developed a monograph which was published under the joint authorship of Dr. Weiss and the writer (6).

During this period a number of hypotheses were investigated and certain basic facts revealed which seemed to be worth further investigation. These studies formed a basis for the subsequent work at Iowa State University. It would be impossible to describe all of these investigations in detail and we shall only give the essence of the results as they were obtained.

It must be recognized that the subjects available around a psychological laboratory are not a fair representation of the driving population as far as age, intellectuality, cultural level, experience, and other characteristics are concerned. Consequently it was deemed expedient to carry the validation studies into the field. Industry was very cooperative and drivers from various companies were used as subjects for different investigations.

The approach to the problem was largely that of measuring isolated functions such as sensorimotor, perceptual, intellectual, and emotional characteristics of the driver; to measure composite performance as well as an attempt to quantify certain sociological data which could be obtained from the company records and relate these to patterns of driving behavior. It appeared from these studies that certain well defined antecedent-consequent relationships between levels of performance, personality types, and accident records could be noted.

These early attempts suggested that more specific measuring devices would need to be developed to supplement the conventional psychological laboratory equipment used in universities for evaluation of behavior. In order to motivate the driver to do his best on a test and to enlist his serious cooperation, it seemed advisable to devise measures which would simulate certain types of driving performance. Consequently the drivometer was built as an evaluation device for various phases of the study.

Fig. 1. The Drivometer. This device for simulating driving has been used at Iowa State University for a number of years. Several studies and masters' theses and a doctor's thesis have been done using this as the basic apparatus. A regular car seat is mounted in the mockup car body in the foreground. From numerous studies it is estimated that about 25% of the variance (factors involved in driving) is measured.

WHO HAS ACCIDENTS?

It was also noted that some of these devices which most closely resembled driving performance would not necessarily give a good index of accident susceptibility. Consequently further research was deemed necessary to select suitable techniques which would meet all requirements and be usable for actual driver classification, if possible to do so. It has been found that over a ten-year period approximately 70% of drivers have no accidents. About 25% have one or two accidents during a similar period. Recent studies indicate that about 30% have an accident during a five-year period. From 2 to 4% of drivers apparently have repeated accidents for no verifiable reason. This latter group has been designated as accident-prone, although the term is not universally accepted. Some authorities hold that there is no accident-prone group, but their arguments are usually based on the fact that a large percentage of persons having one accident during a given period will not have one during a similar period of time. This, of course, is to be expected when only a small percentage are designated as accident-prone. Only a few of them could possibly be in a large group that would be studied from one period to the next. Accidents are the result of certain patterns of behavior which may be of temporary or permanent nature. There may be some small anxiety problem which occupies the mind of the person, or even temporary distraction within the car or outside the vehicle. It may be an illness of more or less permanent nature which distracts the driver's attention.

An investigation of cases having more than the average number of accidents indicates that, in most instances, some specific deficiency will account for the individual's difficulty. In some instances it may be a matter of intellectual ability. Some drivers having an IQ (Intelligence Quotient) of 80 or below get into trouble repeatedly without a reasonable explanation. In one case the driver drove off the road twice at a certain turn, driving down through a dry ditch under a bridge to get back on the road. This had occurred at the same point without injury to himself or his vehicle. However, the mishap was potentially very dangerous and it is difficult to see how one would repeat such a performance.

Another driver had considerable trouble running into the rear of vehicles stopping in front of him. It was found that his distance judgment or space perception was faulty; that he not only followed too closely but was unable to detect a change in relative position of two vehicles when one followed the other in time to stop. Of course it could have been due to distraction but the evidence here was strongly in favor of faulty space perception.

One driver had difficulty which apparently was due to excessive speed or speed too fast for conditions. He was more intelligent than the average and somewhat below average age in his position in a utilities plant. Otherwise he was a very desirable employee. The only good reason for his trouble seemed to be his impatience with the job and the desire to get ahead faster than the normal course of events would permit. In other words, a sort of psychological uneasiness or emotional unrest seemed to be responsible for his lack of attention to driving which led him into difficulties on the roadway. His accidents were all quite serious and far too frequent to be explained by chance.

INTELLIGENCE AND ACCIDENTS

The problem of intelligence in driving has been discussed from various angles. Someone has said that a moron makes the best driver. From all the studies we have done, this is not correct. It would be more nearly correct to say that a person of about average intelligence makes the best driver. Apparently the job suits him well and fits his capacity. Persons who might tend to have accidents are those who are about 20% or more below normal and those, again, who are 20% or more above normal. The group below normal apparently are not attentive enough at times or let their attention lapse and get into trouble. Those who are above normal may get into trouble for inattentiveness but for a different reason. They tend to be dissatisfied with what they are doing and inclined to be hasty. Their driving may show this tendency to rush about. The best group in driving ability is found to be in the normal range of intelligence.

Perhaps it might be well to explain what is meant by normal. Intelligence is measured by giving a person a certain number of reasoning problems to solve. These may be arithmetic problems, work problems, or puzzles of different types. Intelligence is figured in terms of mental age. What the average person does at any age is called normal. One who does better or worse than this is above or below normal. It is called an IQ, but is actually merely a percentage. We may use ten years as a basis of comparison. What the average ten-year-old person does would be normal for a ten-year-old person. If a ten-year-old does 20% better than others of his age he has an IQ of 120 or 20% above average. A person who does 20% below average has an IQ of 80 or 20% below the average for ten-year-olds.

In one instance studied, a driver had no mishap for a number of years and was rated as a very safe operator. Suddenly he began having accidents and over a period of seven or eight months he had four or five mishaps. Some of these were rather serious and others were not. It seemed he had run over children at different times but caused no serious injury. At the time of the examination we could find no mental or physical condition which appeared to have a bearing or relationship to such erratic driving behavior. All the tests given were passed with good scores. After the survey had been completed it was noted from a news item that his wife had passed away. Upon investigation it was found that she had been ill for a long time and he had considerable domestic stress during the time in which his accidents increased.

Without going into details, this early period of study established the fact in the minds of the investigators that the causes of accidents for individuals are more or less specific in nature. It also appeared that some persons were more likely to have accidents than others. Thus 25% of all drivers were arbitrarily designated as accident-liable or accident-susceptible. A group of 2 to 5% of the driving population had been conventionally described as accident-prone. However, there is some question as to the existence of an accident-prone group. The writer is firmly convinced that such a group does exist for a part or all of their lifetime. Hence, knowing an individual well and studying his background and performance should establish a sound basis of prognosticating his driving record. Some writers have suggested the accident distribution frequency curve as different from the ordinary normal curve; others contend it best fits a log log or a Poisson type of curve. The latter is a form of curve or distribution in which there is a very slight possibility of an accident happening. Other investigators have found that the curve fits various mathematical formulas. It depends upon the operating conditions, the degree of hazards and the safety measures exerted to reduce accident frequency. We do not accept the notion that accidents happen by chance. There is always some kind of cause in the chain of events which lead to a mishap. Chance happening means that all factors have an opportunity to operate equally or are balanced in their influence on the end effects. This formulation is not reasonable since there is always some one factor which operates more strongly than others due to some influence which may or may not be subject to improvement.

Another observation was made during the early period of investigation. Drivers seem to improve when approached about their difficulties and when these are discussed with them in a semiclinical way. Organizations that have worked with their drivers show a decrease in accidents. One company showed a 52% decrease for the first two years after the study was completed by a research group. It appears that one may compensate for his weaknesses and this may be the important factor in improving his record. An objective check of a driver and a careful and confidential discussion of certain deficiencies noted will result in improved driving behavior with a corresponding reduction in accidents. This phenomenon is being studied at the present time by certain states that have established what is called a driver improvement program. Here the problem cases are taken up by investigators and discussed in a frank manner.

When a road test was given it was noted that a "watched driver" became a careful driver which tends to minimize the value of a road test as such. In other words, to take a driver out for an observation drive does not seem to be entirely valid as a means of rating his performance. It would be better to have a second car follow the driver and observe how well he drives while moving along the roadway. Various studies made since have tended to confirm this belief. However, we have not carried on sufficient controlled research to establish the fundamental facts at the desired confidence level. Much more needs to be done on the matter of driver observation. We do know that with a well devised instrument which has been developed it is possible to get consistent measurements from time to time. In other words, a good rating scale has quite a high reliability or consistency if it can be definitely marked in an objective way and the selection of items is properly made.

DEVELOPMENT OF MEASURING TECHNIQUES

Since 1930 a great deal of attention has been given to developing devices for measuring driver behavior. Not only simulated devices were developed, but outdoor testing fields have been devised. Also standard road performance tests have been used and various states are now employing test areas for this purpose. More effort was put into simulative devices since the drivometer was developed at Iowa State University. The reactometer which was originated by the Aetna Insurance Company was later transformed into what they call a Drivotrainer. The Auto Trainer which is sponsored by the American Automobile Association through the Allgaier Shops in Arlington, Virginia, is another type. During this time there has been much effort put into the development of psychophysical tests as they are generally called. The Porto-Clinic and the Driver Evaluator are examples of such devices which are merely composites of several simple tests such as visual acuity.

Of the various field tests which have been used with several thousand drivers, it appears that perhaps one of the best driver evaluation procedures involving limited time would be a carefully designed parking test such as shown in Figure 2. A parking stall about five or six feet longer than the average car, which would correspond to a vacant space along the street where one could park, can be set up for testing purposes. The routine of parallel parking as conventionally used in driver education courses in the United States can be set up and easily scored, and with little hazard to anyone. This would include extra movements, final placement of the car, etc. The results will give the examiner a fairly good idea of the effectiveness of the operator and certainly will weed out the incompetent quickly. An added feature might be to have the applicant drive to an intersection and turn around while the examiner watches.

Fig. 2. Parallel Parking Stall. Ordinarily 5 feet over the length of the car is needed for satisfactory parking. An ordinary driver should park correctly in 50 to 70 seconds and make no extra hitches or moves. One operator, properly trained, could handle from three to five of these stalls at once, thus speeding up the examination of drivers.

One may not do well in parking for two reasons. Either he has not had experience with a car or lacks knowledge of driving. To determine these two abilities is one of the purposes of a driving test. Another might have to do with aptness or ability to handle a mechanical contrivance. The latter also is one of the objectives of a driver's examination. Whether a person is experienced or whether he is unable to park efficiently for other reasons makes very little difference. The net results are the same and indicate need for more practice.

It should be noted that a driver who is unable to park properly may very well drive down the road or highway without a great deal of trouble under normal conditions. A child can, without training and at a very young age, steer a tricycle down the street on the sidewalk without undue hazard to anyone. It is in emergencies that weaknesses of this type show up and tend to get the operator into trouble. Ordinary driving does not produce emergencies which require a great deal of special maneuvering. It has been calculated that one meets an accident situation only about once in 3,000 hours of driving. This estimate was made early by the author and has been restated by a human engineer of the Ford Motor Company recently and independently calculated. Most of the situations that arise are not real emergencies. It has also been estimated that about one out of three situations which arise are successfully handled by the average driver. The other one-third of accident situations lead to the mishaps which occur.

Thus, a good many drivers may travel considerably without having trouble since a certain amount of so-called "good luck" might avert a mishap and yet one may maneuver very badly. On one occasion two drivers were seen to meet on a highway in Virginia which passed under a bridge. Both swung wide and were on the wrong side of the road. It so happened that they passed in the tunnel, each in the wrong lane and on the wrong side of the road, without injury to anyone. They couldn't possibly have done anything else because they were going too fast to make the turn and keep in the proper lane. However, if a person is inept at handling his vehicle at such times, an accident is likely to occur. These observations tend to raise questions as to the validity of a good road driving test as such. Since the chance of meeting a real danger situation on a short drive is very remote, it remains a matter of doubt as to whether a person can or cannot be sufficiently evaluated or rated in 10 minutes of driving except in a rare instance. The test drive for a driver's license lasts from 10 to 20 minutes; hence, only about 1 out of even 9,000 to 18,000 drivers would get a crucial test of his performance.

Statistical techniques of various types have been used in evaluating the instrumentation and measuring consistency of such devices if a test is given once and then given a second time. A reasonable correlation between the two test results will give one a fair idea of the consistency or reliability of the measures. If the results are identical for both observations, the correlation is very high, showing good consistency. If the two results do not correspond at all the correlation would be zero which would indicate that one device predicts the other no better than chance. The road test should correlate with another test of the same type to the extent of about .8 to be considered satisfactory. A correlation as low as .6 might be passable but it is preferable to have it up near unity or 1.00, if possible.

Low consistency at first is quite discouraging and points to the necessity of improving the techniques or of modifying the entire approach to the problem. From earlier studies in which temporary causes of accidents may vary from time to time, efforts were made to design studies which would utilize more valid criteria against which the validity of the testing instruments could be established. Consequently, a number of commercial studies were made which have not been published as such, since they are the property of industrial organizations developing them. It is hoped that at a later time we may be able to make more detailed studies of lay drivers of a more comprehensive nature such as are now being done at Harvard Medical School.

Considerable has been done on driver evaluation by the Armed Forces, the details of which can be obtained through the Adjutant General's Office of the Army in Washington, D. C. Such activities and their implications will be discussed in a later section.

A second period in the development of the Driving Research Laboratory may be described as being characterized by attempts to develop measuring devices for drivers and to establish the reliability and validity of such measures and procedures. During this time it has become apparent that single measures of any aspect of human behavior will not be likely to correlate highly with traffic accidents as such. By single measures we refer to separate measuring devices such as psychophysical tests including reaction time, distance judgment, field of vision, etc. Even vision does not correlate highly with accidents, which may be expected, since accidents for one period of time correlated against another corresponding period do not show a high relationship. How-

LEARNING TO DRIVE SAFELY

PROFILE OF DRIVING ABILITY

Name _____ Date _____ Age _____ Sex _____

Maximum Score _____ Points Made _____ Percentage _____

Rating / Trait / Letter	Net Score	Profile — Inferior 1 (E) 2 (D) 3 (C-) / Superior 4 (C) 5 (C+) 6 (B) 7 (A)	Estimate of Weighting	Point Score
1. Age			3	1
2. Health and physique			5	2
3. Blood pressure (Systolic)			5	3
4. Blood pressure (Diastolic)			3	4
5. Strength - Grip			4	5
6. Activity - Tapping			5	6
7. Reaction time - Complex			6	7
8. Accidents a year			6	8
9. Car - Years driving			6	9
10. Attitudes toward risk			4	10
11. Attitudes toward law			4	11
12. Knowledge of road law			4	12
13. Mental alertness			6	13
14. Driving speed			5	14
15. Neural stability			4	15
16. Manipulation			6	16
17. Observational capacity			7	17
18. Time for test - score			3	18
19. Color vision			1	19
20. Field of vision			4	20
21. Acuity of vision - R			4	21
22. Acuity of vision - L			4	22
23. Acuity of vision - B			5	23
24. Difference between two eyes			3	24
25. Distance judgement			5	25
26. Stereopsis - score			3	26
27. Eye dominance			3	27
28. Astigmatism			3	28
29. Glare			4	29
30. Phorias			3	30
31. Hearing			3	31
32. Recklessness			6	32

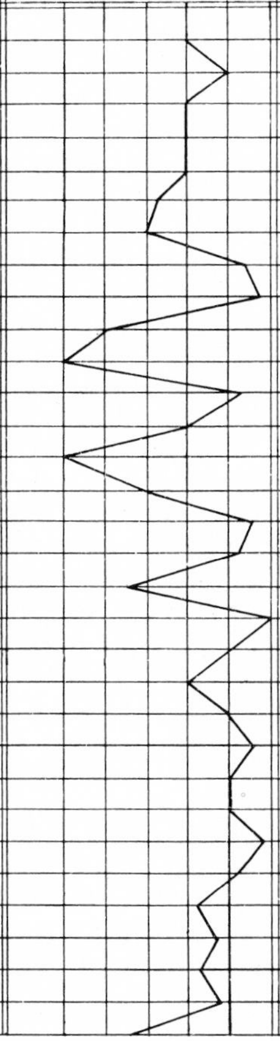

After the Measurements are Made, They are Laid Out
on the Profile Chart for Careful Study

Measured traits are here graphed for a test driver of a large commercial concern. It is to be noted that he is above average in practically all traits and low only in three - attitudes toward risk, attitudes toward law, and driving speed. All three of these traits are in keeping with the nature of his work.

Fig. 3. Profile of a professional test driver.

ever, from data correlated it was found by Allgaier and Lauer (2) that a composite measuring device, such as the drivometer, was more efficient as a prognosticator of driving ability than any single measure of driving behavior taken separately. Conversely, it was found that a profile of abilities might give a better picture and a more valid index of the limitations of a given driver than any one single measure or even a composite measure. By a profile we refer to a list of traits with ratings from high to low on a form of graph. By plotting the standing of the individual on any one trait and connecting the points with a line, a fairly true picture of the person's strong and weak points may be depicted. In a more recent study (4) it was found that a good paper-and-pencil test would do as well or better than a battery of psychophysical tests.

FIELD STUDIES AND VALIDATION

Considerable time was spent in the field in validating studies made in the laboratory. During this time there were several specific studies (1, 2) done which related to driving that have been published in separate papers. Some of these have had to do with the relation between visual defects and accidents and other phases of driving behavior as they were found experimentally. During the validation period studies were made of large groups of lay drivers by using a portable research clinic taken into industrial plants. These studies extended into the late post-World War II period (4).

One of the most extensive and far-reaching studies of drivers was made in cooperation with the Public Roads Administration of the United States in which over 3,000 drivers were carefully examined in the State of Connecticut (1) and the records of several thousands were studied. The accident records were correlated with numerous measurements and other data available. The study was done through cooperation of the Driving Research Laboratory at Iowa State University and the Harvard Bureau of Traffic Research, which was existent at that time. The latter has since moved to Yale and became the Yale Traffic Bureau. The studies were done under the National Research Council as a cooperative project and were published only after a long delay by the principal technician or coordinator of the project (1). Some parts have never been published. Briefly summarized, the results point up the fact that very low correlations are to be expected between any single measure of driving behavior and accident records obtained from the public files. However, a vital finding was made during these studies. It was shown that the reliability of accident records over two trienniums is quite low, being of the order of .20 or lower, and some were in the direction opposite to expectations. Since the correlations as obtained in the Connecticut study were of the order of .10 or below, between tests and accidents, it is obvious that the reliability of the criterion might well spuriously lower these coefficients.

Another fallacy of logic was noted during this series of investigations which extended over several months through a congressional grant. To expect any specific measurement to correlate highly with accidents which might be related to quite remote factors would be unreasonable. Johnson's analysis was investigated to some extent and the classification was not always made entirely to the satisfaction of the experimenters who collected the data. Johnson and his immediate assistants, as coordinators, made the analysis without appreciable consultation or cooperation with those who collected the data. The study, however, does substantiate and verify observations made by the writer and others during the earlier validation period of driving researches as described.

From 1941 to 1946, war years, most of the studies from this laboratory were confined to specific problems of night driving, the effects of flooding the eye with a red light on visibility at lower illumination, development of better highway signs and the improvement of legibility of letters used on signs and markers (5). Early work had been done with license plates during the 1930's. The latter was further investigated by Uhlaner and the results showed that spacing, stroke, width-height ratio, and factors of this type were very important in legibility. Uhlaner's study was somewhat technical and a later paper by Lauer (3) contained the essential features of this research and a license plate study made earlier. A more detailed explanation of the license plate study will be given in a later chapter.

To summarize briefly, this phase of the developmental period was largely devoted to investigation of specific problems of plate legibility, visibility, and seeing as they relate to potential driving performance. The idea of obtaining substantial correlations with accidents was abandoned since previous results did not warrant further efforts in this direction. Instead, the problem was approached more on logical grounds of setting up better conditions for safe driving. Some other studies on the effect of seeing and night visibility resulted in several publications appearing under the authorship of the writer and associates.

During the war, activities were limited to studies of optical conditions for driving as related to highway safety. Some training of ambulance drivers was done and convoy driving at night was given considerable attention through practice. Night sight was not found to be improved by wearing red glasses.

POSTWAR READJUSTMENT PERIOD

Developments of the Driving Research Laboratory were somewhat hindered in the postwar period by the enormous increase in student enrollment and the demand for teaching. Attention was given to the problem of attitudes during 1947, 1948, and 1949. During 1948 the writer spent a year in California in an administrative position and the activities of the laboratory were more or less suspended. Some studies on driving vision were done during ths period. In 1949 work was resumed and a number of studies were made relating to night visibility and the effects of tinted glass on performance. The results may be summarized briefly as follows:

Tinted glasses or windshields for night driving were not found to be beneficial in any instance. In fact they tended to reduce visual efficiency. Certain wave band filters have a pseudopsychological effect on seeing at night and lead to overoptimism on the part of the driver. The effects of colored filters are more or less relative. Certain individuals with exceptionally good vision are probably not bothered seriously by the addition of a slight amount of tinting. Other individuals with a submarginal vision may be reduced to the level of unsafe seeing by the same filter. Therefore, it may be concluded that if tinted glasses are to be used for night driving they should be worn only by prescription. Certain shades of yellow seem to create false notions of security and this observation has been confirmed by Richards of the American Optical Company's Research Laboratory. Only vision specialists who have studied the individual and know his visual condition would be able to judge whether a person might wear night driving glasses with some beneficial effects. It is a professional problem. It has been shown that with the usual type of tinting which reduces transmission, the effects of visibility are reduced proportional to the reduction of transmission of light. With polaroid or some other types of filter devices in which transmission is differentially changed so that glare is reduced more than visibility, the results would be different. Such application predisposes headlights of much greater intensity than are found on our present day automobiles in the United States or even abroad.

The researches during the postwar period include a study of attitudes. Various observations indicate that mental dispositions and habits are very essential factors in safe driving. One may have good attitudes and yet not show up well at the wheel, or vice versa. That is, he may have a reasonably good attitude and not a good driving record. However, the correlation between good attitudes and good driving records is thought to be positive. Siebrecht, the writer, and others have developed tests of attitudes which so far have shown quite satisfactory reliabilities. Studies made on these tests suggest that attitudes may be changed considerably with systematic training of drivers. Again, these inventories are somewhat subject to extraneous influence. Even the directions given examinees may affect results. Therefore the validity has been somewhat questioned, although some of the highest correlations with accidents of drivers have been obtained with measures of attitudes. Attitudes are inextricably related to emotional behavior and personality. If one is so inclined he can compensate for most of his deficiencies; it is perhaps one of the results of proper attitudes.

In summary, it may be said that during the postwar adjustment period the chief contributions of the Driving Research

Laboratory were in the field of attitude measurements, night visibility and related problems.

EXPANSION PERIOD OF THE DRIVING RESEARCH LABORATORY

In late 1948 the writer returned from California and during the next year a reorganization of the entire program was made. It was transferred back from the Engineering Experiment Station to the Industrial Science Research Institute. The author, as director of the Driving Research Laboratory, was given authority to expand and attempt to secure funds for a more comprehensive program. Although the State of Iowa has a 35 million dollar loss each year from automobile accidents alone, only a token sum has been budgeted for research on the driver education program or for other research on the human element of highway safety. Part time was allotted to a limited staff for doing this type of work but the teaching load was heavy and no outside funds could be used for teaching nor could a developmental program be initiated.

In 1950 a grant of money was obtained from the Allstate Insurance Company of Chicago for a five-year study of the young driver. About the same time smaller grants of money were obtained for specific researches at the Driving Research Laboratory from the Minnesota Mining and Manufacturing Company, the Outdoor Advertising Association, and the American Automobile Association. With these expansion efforts the Driving Laboratory was moved and housed in a new location. A fellowship program was inaugurated and several advanced students were brought in for special projects leading to the master's degree. This project was not entirely satisfactory as the requirements for a degree quite often preclude following through the segment of a project of an articulated program. However, considerable headway was made and one doctorate was conferred.

The first effort was that of analyzing ages of drivers to determine the nature and structure of the driving population in certain other respects. No authoritative data were available on the number of women in the driving population, nor as to the amount of driving being done at each age level and by the sexes at different hours of the day. Unless such correction figures are available accident records cannot be properly interpreted.

Thus during the period of 1950-53 three major studies were pursued and a number of minor studies of related nature were carried out in this area. These had to do mostly with three things — visibility at night, the effects of alleged distracting influences, and the factors of age and sex as they relate to driving and accident involvement. Certain of these researches have been published. Other papers on the various studies are in channels of publication or have been presented at scientific meetings.

SUMMARY

It suffices to say in summary that accident statistics throughout the United States are being collected voluminously, but are being analyzed inadequately. Numerous states and colleges are now working to improve the situation. The records contain invaluable information if subjected to the proper statistical analysis and information from the results obtained disseminated and put into actual practice in accident prevention. Much improvement has been noted during the last two years. There is also a need for individual accident analysis from which we may proceed by proper statistical techniques to identify certain relationships and to set up principles of highway safety, safety education and accident prevention.

The Driving Research Laboratory has had a steady growth since its inception up to 1956, and specific periods of development are identified. The contributions fall into the following categories:

Preliminary study and research on methodologies which were correlated with safe driving performance or accident records. Correlations found were never very high, indicating considerable variance was not being measured.

Development and standardization of measuring techniques and formulation of hypotheses for experimental investigation.

Field studies were designed to evaluate and introduce such techniques to the transportation industry and in driver improvement.

Evaluation of criteria to be used was made in road studies and a criterion scale developed (7).

Laboratory studies of specific driving problems dealing with composite performance, reaction time, distance judgment, vision, emotional and personality characteristics, attitudes, driving night visibility and similar factors.

The influence in developing interest in driving research at other colleges and universities is noteworthy. At present there are more than a score of schools with an active organization of some type.

Analyses of the incidence of accidents by various age groups of population in relation to sex, driving habits, methods of learning to drive, personality traits, attitudes, physical and psychophysical characteristics, and other phenomenon of performance have been followed out by several states.

The next steps have to do with further studies of driving behavior as they relate to fatigue, environmental factors and the control of conditions which lead to accidents.

REFERENCES

1. Johnson, H. M., The detection and treatment of accident-prone drivers. The Psycho. Bull., 1946, 6, 489-532.

2. Lauer, A. R. and Allgaier, Earl, A preliminary analysis of the psychophysical correlates of automotive manipulation. Amer. Jour. of Optometry, 1941, 18, No. 3, 49-53.

3. Lauer, A. R., Certain structural components of letters for improving the efficiency of the *Stop* sign. Proc. Highway Research Board, 1947, 362-379.

4. Lauer, A. R., Comparison of group paper-and-pencil tests with certain psychophysical tests for measuring driving aptitude of Army personnel. The Jour. of Applied Psychology, 39, No. 5, 1955.

5. Uhlaner, Julius E., Structural and spatial factors of letters as they affect the legibility. Unpublished masters thesis at Iowa State College, 1941.

6. Weiss, A. P. and Lauer, A. R., The psychological principles of automobile driving. Bull. 11, The Ohio State University, 1931, pp. 165.

7. Suhr, V. W., Lauer, A. R. and Allgaier, Earl, Development of a criterion for driving performance. Highway Research Board Bull. 172, 1958, 1-8.

CONTENTS

LIST OF ILLUSTRATIONS

THE PSYCHOLOGY

OF DRIVING

CHAPTER I

HOW DRIVING RESEARCH STARTED
AND ITS BASIS

INTRODUCTION

The work had a beginning in 1928 at the Ohio State University. Prior to that time considerable work in industrial psychology had been done and some studies of accidents among street car motormen had been made. Only a few studies of motorists had been attempted. During this time techniques were developed and background studies were made which are described in the following chapters. A part of this work has been published in short articles.

At that time the National Research Council had set up a project at Ohio State University to study some phases of driving. Since a grant had been received from the American Optometric Association a part of the study was devoted to visual limitations of drivers. The object was to study possible methods of examining applicants for a driver's license. The scope was broadened to include numerous phases of driving ability which are described in the monograph (3). Numerous experimenters took part and studies ranged from reaction time to sociological characteristics of the automobile driver. It developed into a cooperative project and a number of studies were started which stimulated other investigations.

Several objectives were set up in this set of researches which were more or less exploratory in nature. One problem was that there was no criterion available against which to test driving ability, vision and other traits that might be evaluated. Accident records are often sketchy and incomplete. Ordinary ratings of drivers tend to be subjective and unreliable.

To meet this problem a form of eye, foot, and hand coordination apparatus was developed against which to weigh efficiency in various fields. This apparatus consisted essentially of a steering wheel controlling a pointer which moved laterally across a space of about two feet which was located in front of the driver. The movement was made in simple harmonic motion. The steering wheel was attached to a second pointer which could be manually coordinated by the steering wheel to meet the first one at a point on the scaled background board over which the pointer moved. When both came to a marked place on the board at the same time and the driver depressed his foot simultaneously, a "stop" was accomplished. Thus the task involved the coordination of the eye, foot, and hand which would react at a given time and point simultaneously. One pointer was moving freely in a regular pattern, the other was controlled, so that at the precise moment the two came together the foot reaction accomplished the "stop" which was desired. Various auxiliary measurements were taken such as the movements made by the operator sitting on the seat. A seat contact was wired so that movements in either direction gave contacts which were recorded by an electric counter.

Reaction time was not considered in the design of this apparatus. It was not a split-second movement, but required the proper response at the proper time for accomplishing a given result. Thus an objective account of efficiency in coordination could be obtained. The amount-limit method was used to measure the operator's efficiency. By amount-limit is meant that a given task was set for the operator to accomplish in whatever time he needed. For example, the amount might be 10 stops by reaction of the foot at the proper time. The subject was asked to keep driving until he had accomplished the 10 stops and the time required used as a score.

A WEIGHING-IN INSTRUMENT

With this apparatus it was assumed that the effects of poor vision, nervousness, loss of sleep, bad attitudes, intelligence and other factors which would influence performance might be evaluated. It was the central piece of apparatus around which others were assembled in a type of driving clinic.

Two years were spent in these exploratory studies. The reader is referred to the bulletin (3) for details of these various studies. It suffices to say that during the last year the study was continued under a National Research Council fellowship in psychology. To make the project broader, as described in the introduction, it was called *psychology of the highway*. Studies were made during the second year with drivers from large department stores, the Bell Telephone Company, the Hill Cab Company, the Municipál Traffic Court and others. Later the equipment was taken to Dayton, Ohio, and set up in the offices of the Dayton Power and Light Company where field sudies were made. This phase was partly sponsored by the Chrysler Corporation whose engineers were carrying on studies in vehicle dependability at that time. Their interest stemmed from the fact that if a vehicle became involved in an accident it was difficult to tell subsequently whether a part gave way because of being defective or because damage had been done in the accident. They were interested in reducing the number of accidents to a minimum among their experimental fleet vehicles.

The next year the writer accepted a position at Iowa State University (Iowa State College at that time) and the project was transferred. Work was continued in the Department of Psychology with emphasis on the human element in driving. A new phase of the work was begun at this institution which will be described later. Mobile units were constructed and standardized for field use. Outdoor fields were devised and used in the evaluation of driving.

THE DRIVOMETER

One development at this institution should be particularly noted. As already described, the eye, foot, and hand coordination apparatus at the Ohio State University was used for weighing-in drivers or determining their all-around efficiency. Since the original apparatus seemed to give promise for this purpose it was thought that a more realistic device could be developed which would have greater face validity, that is, that it would seem more like a driving experience to the subject being tested. A device called the drivometer was built.

The first model of the drivometer was a simple cabinet containing a moving roadway about two feet wide and seven feet long which was operated by controls and transmission of a standard automobile. The steering wheel and seat were mounted some 10 or 11 feet back of the moving belt and the device could be driven in low, second, or high gear at the will of the operator. The controls were like an automobile. The accelerator operated a shifting brush motor which made it possible to control speed. (See Fig. 1, The Drivometer, for the second version of this apparatus.)

The task of the driver was to steer the wheel to keep a miniature car directly over a winding roadway painted on the moving belt. At a certain point in the trip, directions appeared which were to be observed by the driver. Thus the task involved seeing, judgment and coordination for making a successful score. Time for the trip was recorded.

ENGLISH APPARATUS

Experimenters in England had worked with a rotating drum in which the subject traced the road with a stylus. Some work in Germany had been done with two belts running at right angles to one another on which targets were placed and to which the operator was asked to make proper reactions. A method of scoring was developed whereby coincident locations of two cars or two objects could be indicated as a scoring task.

The drivometer incorporated most of these principles, but in a more realistic fashion. The following scores were used for evaluating a driver. The *first* had to do with how well the subject kept the miniature car on the highway and on the right side or in the right lane. This was recorded by a series of contacts which were coupled in series with an electric counter. The *second* score had to do with how long the operator took to make the trip or given number of revolutions of the belt. About seven revolutions were necessary to complete the cycle.

At the same time the driver was attempting to keep the minia-ture car on the small roadway, shift, and accomplish other aspects of the performance, he was to observe signs and instructions which were presented from a rotating drum. It was necessary to read these correctly in order to make the proper responses to them. The locations were indicated by painted patches representing signs on the moving belt. For example, at *1* the driver might be required to stop and shift gears; at *4* he might be required to back from one sign to another. In other words, the apparatus was so designed as to present a complex task to the driver simulating actual road work. Each revolution of the belt presented a new situation. A red and green light was one of the stimuli presented. Each time the red light appeared the operator was to stop.

A method of recording the amount of time elapsing after each presentation of the red light was developed. Thus at the end of the performance one had a score on the driver consisting of the *number of contacts made on the trip, trip time,* and *errors made in the observation of signs.*

STANDARDIZATION OF THE PROCEDURE

After any piece of apparatus is developed it takes a certain amount of time and effort to standardize the equipment. By standardization is meant the development of a suitable set of directions, the administration of the measurement to a sufficient number of people to get some information on norms of perform-ance, and the correlation of the scores with performance of various types. Norms mean the standard of achievement or basis of com-parison between persons. There are several ways of doing this. We will describe one often used. It is based on the bell shaped curve divided into the following groups: The highest 5%, A, or the superior group; the next 10%, B, or the group just below A; the next 20%, C+, the group just above the middle; the next 30%, C, is the middle group (these are indicated as C because they stand in the center of the distribution) ; the next 20%, C—, is the group just below the middle; The 10% below C— is indi-cated as D (these are presumably inferior in their performance) ; the lowest 5% are marked as E's. We should hasten to say that the low end of the scale is not always the poorest score. In the case of errors, poorest is the highest score. This method was worked out in consultation with a well-known statistician. It is not entirely new as school grades are calculated much the same way in a number of different areas and at different levels.

Ordinarily the method used for grading in the schools is the highest group of 5%, A's; next 20%, B's; the middle 50%, C's; the next 20%, D's; and the lowest 5%, E's. The difficulty with this latter system is that so many fall in the middle of the distribution and it is difficult to distinguish between differences in performance above and below the middle of the group.

Still other ways are available for comparing individuals on a test by ratings. One that is commonly used is the so-called percentile system. Here each examinee is marked as he would appear in relation to 100 other persons ranked from low to high, or the reverse. The highest is usually marked as 100th percentile and the lowest is the 1st percentile. Thus a percentile rating refers to where one stands in relation to 100 other persons of the population from which he is taken on the same measurement.

The way to standardize any test or performance rating is to administer it to a large number of groups and then to plot them according to the appropriate plan for the system being used. Most elementary statistical texts explain how to construct a percentile or other graph.

NEED FOR FIELD STUDIES

Being located at a college the first group that was used for this performance consisted of college students who are always interested in devices for trying out their skill. Records were kept on the various devices used in depicting performance. Driving experience, knowledge of driving performance, accidents and other criteria were explored. After 300 or 400 students had taken the tests in various ways, and different aspects of their performance were studied, a need was felt to try the equipment on a nonacademic population.

Consequently, a booth was set up at the Iowa State Fair under the auspices of the National Research Council. It was during the depression and space was relatively easy to obtain at that time. In this way several hundred individuals of all ages were taken through the test in order to further standardize the equipment and to study the methods of procedure, etc. These data yielded certain valuable results with respect to age, sex and certain other characteristics of driving that are of general interest. Even groups of professional racing drivers were studied.

However, the population was still a nonprofessional group and it was necessary to get into commercial fleets where experienced drivers could be studied. In order to do this, a so-called driving clinic was developed under a cooperative arrangement with utilities companies and studies made on various properties in Tennessee, Kentucky, Virginia, West Virginia, Pennsylvania and other states. Previously it had been taken to smaller utilities companies (1) and the Chrysler Corporation of Detroit where studies of drivers were made of those who would participate in the stunt driving at the World's Fair in Chicago. A typical record is shown of one of the stunt drivers that was studied in this trip. (see Fig. 3, Profile Graph, for a test driver's record)

It should be pointed out that one of the best ways of indicating performance on a number of traits is by the use of the profile graph as shown in Figure 3. Such graph is merely a list of characteristics which are laid off on a sheet with a scale to indicate the high and low performance. This works out well with the system used of A, B, C+, C, C−, D and E as individuals could be given numerical scores—7,6,5,4,3,2,1. When a composite was desired, or it was desired to equate the scores to a common scale, it was possible to use numerical values for this purpose. In order to secure sufficient measurements to make a profile graph it was necessary to standardize each measurement separately.

DRIVING CLINIC

The driving clinic was organized to include a number of characteristics which were found in the various studies noted to have some relation to driving. These have been obtained through the use of rating scales and by actual measurements.

The driving clinic plan had a number of stations for checking each driver. These were built around the drivometer as a central unit for the general evaluation. Each clinic station gave some specific information or measurement desired of the driver. A typical driving clinic would have a station for securing specific bits of information. At this station the age, number of years the driver had driven, miles he had driven, number of cars he had driven, and certain things of this type were requested.

Each of the following stations was set up to measure or evaluate one or more of the characteristics cited in the profile graph of driving ability. Each of these measures had been standardized and weighted, based on the norms that had been established from students, from lay drivers, and from commercial drivers in general, as well as from expert test drivers. At the end of each set of tests the driver's record was discussed with him. This is an essential part of the program.

It might be well to review the profile graph of the test driver shown on the sample illustration. We will only discuss it in general terms. It will be noted that the heavy zigzag lies mostly to the right of the C, or middle value. At only four points does the line pass to the left of the middle line or lower level of ability. One of these is that of attitude towards risk; another is attitude towards law and driving speed; and the last one, recklessness. These are understandable since the driver's job was to drive cars over the roads in Michigan and test them out for speed and dependability. These drivers were instructed to drive fast, take risks, sometimes even to break the law if necessary. It goes without saying that they were reckless and their driving speed was rather fast. Consequently, time for completing the test would be important because they were trying to make a good score in this particular manner. It was not generally known, but there was intention of making this a selection hurdle for the drivers that were to drive at the World's Fair in Chicago. Consequently, each was rather careful to make a good showing on the tests.

The driving clinic was instrumented by a number of different small tests which have been erroneously labeled as psychophysical tests. They actually are not psychophysical as the term is usually understood. Perhaps the best name would be psychometric test if one were to give them a single name. These include tests of blood pressure, strength as measured by a hand dynamometer, activity measured by tapping speed, the chronoscope which measured reaction time, the so-called neurostability or emotions test, a color vision test, a field of vision test, a test for measuring acuity of vision, distance judgment, eye dominance, astigmatism, glare and the alignment of the eyes or the phorias. At that time a hearing test was also included and a form of recklessness test given. The two last tests did not prove to be useful or practical. Hearing does not seem to influence driving and recklessness seems specific.

WHAT THE TESTS INDICATE

Perhaps a word of explanation might be made of the application of these various tests which were used at the several stations in the clinic so that as the driver passed through he might be given an evaluation on each. The blood pressure test needs no further explanation. A self-recording instrument was used to keep the data uniform from one examiner to another.

Strength of grip is measured by a hand dynamometer which is squeezed by the subject after being instructed to do his best. It is calibrated in kilograms, which is about 2.2 pounds, and the standards have been developed for the various ratings indicated on the profile graph—E, D, C—, C, C+, B and A. Separate standards are now used for men and women since men do 40-50 per cent better on this measure. The range for men runs mostly from about 40 up to 80 kilograms. Women range from 20 up to 45 kilograms. Very few get above this mark. Thus it is possible to assess the relative strength of the individual by referring to the proper norms.

Strength is important in driving in two respects. It is not a problem of gripping or turning the steering wheel which, even in mechanical steering type vehicles, is not too difficult. For power steering, of course, it is not a matter of strength at all. The problem of strength is useful mostly in the ability to stay with the task for a longer period. A strong person can usually keep working at a task longer without becoming fatigued.

A second advantage of strength enters in when changing tires or handling a car in emergencies. There are times when a certain amount of strength is necessary to swerve or hold a car steady and the person with more strength seems to have an advantage.

Activity as measured by what is known as the tapping test as a measure of dexterity. It seems to give quite a little information about a driver. In this test a timing device is used to get approximately a 10-second sample of the person's maximum activity rate. He is instructed to move as rapidly as possible by operating a telegraph key up and down so as to make contact on each cycle. The range for men and women is about the same on this test and it varies from 50 or less up to slightly over 100 in the 10 seconds. It is only slightly improved by training; a year to practice will not increase one's tapping rate perhaps over 10%. In other words it is a fairly valid index of inherited activity. An active driver has an advantage in several ways. A certain amount of activity is essential for skill of any kind. When driving in traffic the active person is more likely to be able to maneuver his car with dexterity.

This is not the same as reaction time in any sense. In fact it has a very low relationship to reaction time. The following analogy may be used to explain the difference between the two. Reaction is the time it takes to get started into motion. The activiy test is the ability to move once you are in motion. As may be seen these are different factors of skill and are not necessarily closely related. A freight train makes sudden jerks to get started, but moves only moderately fast once it gets under way compared with a streamliner which starts smoothly but moves fast when once under way.

On the profile chart three phases — manipulation; observational capacity, which is a measure of a person's ability to note signs, etc.; and time for the test, which is a time score for completing the simulated driving test — are taken. Manipulation is obtained by noting the degree to which a person kept the miniature car on the small roadway, the percentage of contacts he is able to make.

COLOR VISION

Color vision is measured by one form of color-blind test. The most commonly used is the Ishihara which is available at any wholesale optical company and is widely known. It is simple, having plates with different colored dots upon them. Certain of the colored dots make a number which can be read if a person has normal color vision. Certain other plates cannot be read if a person has normal color vision, but can be read if the examinee is color-blind. Thus by noting which plates are read and which plates are missed you determine the degree of color-blindness and something about its nature. Most persons who are color-blind are only color weak for red and green. About 1 man out of 10 and 1 woman out of 100 have this difficulty.

For those who are not familiar with the Ishihara Color Vision test, 13 plates were used having 17 digits. By taking the number of digits missed one can estimate the degree of color-blindness. One who has normal color vision will read the numbers in all 13 plates or 17 digits. Others will perhaps be able to read the numbers in only 2, 3 or 4 cards. For those who wish to get more detailed information on the use of tests and their interpretations, see *Learning to Drive Safely* by Lauer (2).

SIDE VISION

The field of vision is usually measured by some type of semi-circular quadrant or instrument which is held before the eyes. By use of a pencil, or other small target and moving it around to the side with a properly devised apparatus a good estimate can be made of the individual's field of vision. According to standards set up by medical groups on accident prevention, one should have nearly 180 degrees of vision. Anyone limited or reduced by as much as 20 degrees on each side is considered handicapped. Licenses are denied to persons with a 140 degree field by some organizations and states. There are persons who see very little at all to the side. In fact they have what is known as "tunnel" vision. The vision is restricted as it would be if one were looking through binoculars. This condition is rarely found in the extreme form but does exist.

The importance of a rough check on the field of vision is to catch those persons with "tunnel" vision who are to be dealt with according to the policy of the examining group. It is also used to call attention to the importance of observing to the side. To do a good job of driving one must keep the eyes moving and be aware of everything in the field of view ahead. The eyes do not fixate the center line of the road when driving.

It should be noted that the point of keenest vision is the center of the eye in a small area called the fovea. In this tiny spot we may have 20/20 vision or better, if normal, but visual acuity drops off very rapidly as you move out to the side. One sees large objects and movement at the sides, or in the periphery, but very little detail. This is one reason why the eyes must be kept moving over the area in front of the car. The driver will observe certain hazards, which would not be detected if the eyes were kept stationary, by scanning the field of view directly ahead.

It is also true that the moving eyes do not see. It is only when they fixate that sight takes place. Thus the eyes must be moving over the field of view constantly as they move by jerks, resting a moment here and there in order to become aware of all that is going on in the environment. Speed is sensed by reference to objects passed at the side. Without roadside stimuli one tends to drive too fast. When following a moving target the eyes lose about 40% of their seeing ability. This is known as dynamic visual acuity as opposed to static visual acuity. Individuals differ in this respect.

VISUAL ACUITY

We have only mentioned keenness of vision or acuity. A place is provided on the form for measuring the vision of the right eye, the left eye, and both eyes. Visual acuity, or keenness, is usually thought of either as a fraction which was developed by Snellen, or a percentage figure. The Snellen notation is written either 20/20, 20/80, 20/60, 20/40, etc. The denominator tells the distance at which the letters, or objects in case of characters, are presented and should be seen; whereas the numerator tells the distance that they are seen. In other words, 20/20 vision means that one sees a block or square letter approximately ⅜ of an inch in dimensions at a distance of 20 feet. It may be read at 40 feet. One method used for notation is merely to divide the numerator by the denominator. Thus 20/40 might be interpreted as 50% vision.

There is another vision percentage plan used which is known as the AMA system and varies considerably since it is worked out on a different scale. A person with 50% in this system has considerably better vision than that indicated by 50% with the first system suggested. Persons working with vision should know about these two systems of marking using a percentage basis. Otherwise considerable confusion is likely to result.

EYE DOMINANCE

Number 27, Figure 3, on the Profile of Driving Ability has to do with eye dominance. By eye dominance is meant the tendency to use one eye more than the other. It is the same principle as using the right hand more easily than the left hand. Persons are right- and left-eyed in the same way that they are right- and left-handed. It does not follow the same order, however. One may be right-handed and left-eyed, or left-handed and right-eyed. No relationship has been found to exist between the two.

At first eye dominance would seem to be a minor factor in driving, but it is very important. Contrary to common sense it is not particularly closely related to the strength of the two eyes. Only in case there is wide difference between the acuteness of vision of the two eyes is there likely to be dominance shown by the stronger eye. The weak eye may be the dominant eye.

The importance to driving efficiency is that the average person does not realize that he is dominant eyed. A simple test can be made to discover this condition. With the Parson's test, using a sort of a cone, one fixates an object with both eyes open. By alignment the examiner can easily detect which eye is seeing the object. The Reed-Van Osdal test is simply a square board with a ⅜ inch hole. The subject sights some object at a distance and the examiner checks which eye is being used with a card. See Appendix of *Learning to Drive Safely* (2).

Some persons always use the right eye. Only by a special process of maneuvering can it be possible for them to see an object with the left eye. Both eyes are usually about the same in strength. In driving, if right-eyed, one could be caught at the side by a car passing from the left. One may look around and not notice the car at all. On the other hand, a driver may be caught from the right by being left-eyed.

Not long ago when following a commercial truck which stopped at a signalized railroad crossing for blinking lights an incident occurred. A slow-moving electric train was coming down the track. The driver saw the signal, stopped and waited, apparently looked, and then drove directly in front of the locomotive. We have first-hand evidence that he was careful in the sense that he stopped and looked. Being markedly left-eyed he would not have noticed the locomotive with the right eye by a simple glance to the right. It would have been necessary to get his head out of the window and look directly up the track to be sure that there was no train coming.

Thus eye dominance is an important factor in safe driving, and to call a person's attention to the fact of eye dominance and that there are differences between people will help one assess his own condition.

Very frequently the eyes differ in strength. At one time it was thought the difference in vision between the two eyes would be an important factor. This factor was indicated on the Profile of Driving Ability (Fig. 3). More recently we find that the difference between the two eyes is not so important, except when the difference is great the person is likely to suppress or not use the poorer eye. Thus one becomes more or less one-eyed so far as seeing is concerned. A person with one eye is considerably handicapped and some states require an outside rear-vision mirror on the car. Most persons tend to use one eye mostly even though both are good.

A very simple test of eye dominance is for a person to use both hands, taking his ring and holding it between the thumb and first finger with the two hands extended in front of him. With both eyes open find some object at a distance and fixate, getting it in the center of the ring. When this is accomplished close one eye, then the other, and note which one is being used or sees the object. If one knows his own condition he can usually allow for a deficiency by turning the head and giving special attention to situations where the functioning of one eye would be disturbing.

The condition of eye dominance is probably a habit acquired in youth. If there is a wide difference in eyes it is more likely that one will use the stronger eye rather than the weaker one, although this does not necessarily follow. One must check himself to be sure which eye is dominant and then modify his behavior accordingly. In other words, he must learn to be more careful to offset the tendency to see with only one eye. This is a condition which affects practically everyone. Most people never have learned about it in any other type of experience. This is the main reason for using the test, to make the person aware of his tendency in this particular direction. Many marksmen shoot with both eyes open.

STEREOPSIS

Stereopsis is a term that is not ordinarily understood by the layman. It is the ability to note the third dimension or depth in a picture such as used in the old stereoscope that our grandmothers used for parlor entertainment. Sometimes stereopsis is used synonymously with depth perception. The two are not at all the same. We have listed stereopsis here since it was supposed to have relation to distance judgment. Actually we find this is a mistake at least in most respects. Some persons have excellent stereopsis but are not particularly good at distance judgment. Certain other persons who have no stereopsis at all, such as those with one eye, may have very good judgment of distance. The reason for this is that stereopsis is dependent upon only one or two factors such as the differences or disperagement of the two images. Distance judgment is dependent upon several factors, the most important perhaps of which are size of the retinal image, clearness of the atmosphere, comparison with other objects, comparative interposition of other objects which obscure a part of the view, color, and four or five others which are involved. Thus the presence of stereopsis in no way guarantees good distance judgment. Conversely, one may have good distance judgment and no stereopsis at all.

Relative to this point, one of the requirements for securing stereopsis on an instrument designed to check this ability is that the person use both eyes. Anyone can try this by using an old stereoscope and covering one eye. The third dimension immediately disappears. A certain amount of imagination may tend to leave the impression that the third dimension is there, but a slight amount of checking will convince anyone that cutting off one eye will eliminate stereopsis. We have found one-eyed persons who have very good distance judgment due to the fact that they have learned to rely on other cues which are of more help to them. They may have also used only one eye for many years.

ASTIGMATISM

Astigmatism is a condition of vision which is sometimes inherited or may be due to some damage to the eye. It reduces acuity and tends to blur the images. Also it may induce headaches on long drives. The image does not focus evenly due to irregularity of the lens or cornea of the eye.

GLARE TOLERANCE

Quite a number of persons, particularly older ones, are bothered by glare. Glare may be either the direct rays of light or reflected light which interferes with vision. Some persons are very sensitive to this effect. There are some involved ways of measuring the effects of glare which require time, but any simple straightforward method which measures the effects of seeing by light shining into the eyes will give a fairly good index of glare tolerance.

PHORIA

There are several sets of muscles which control the direction of the eyes when a person is looking. If these are not equal in strength a condition known as heterophoria may develop. With this condition the person may see double. If the tendency for the two eyes to be off alignment is more than 3 or 4 degrees, one is very likely to see double in low illumination. In extreme cases, known as strabismus, a person actually has the use of only one eye. The eye turning is noticeable in such cases as crosseyedness. These persons rarely, if ever, see double images.

HEARING

Hearing was formerly thought to have something to do with driving. Various studies over the country seem to indicate that persons with poor hearing probably drive better than those with good hearing for the simple reason that they compensate for their weakness and watch more carefully. At least their records are better. Over half the states require a hearing aid for a license as shown by an American Optical Company survey in 1958. (if deaf)

RECKLESSNESS

There is some doubt whether the concept of recklessness is a unitary trait. It probably is specific to driving or to some one thing a person does. Conversely, since it is not general it may be neglected for the general purpose of evaluating drivers. Perhaps it may some day be measurable for such classification purposes.

DISTANCE JUDGMENT

Distance Judgment is measured by having a person place pegs or small cars in some kind of alignment, preferably at a distance of 15 or 20 feet away. It cannot be measured successfully at short distances. Several different organizations build apparatus for measuring distance judgment. Probably the most commonly known is the American Automobile Association of Washington, D. C.

It has been found that commercial drivers have considerably better distance judgment than lay drivers. This would indicate that the function of judging distance is developed quite a lot by practice. An experienced driver is very likely to estimate space and distance more accurately than one who is inexperienced. Driver education instructors should devote considerable attention to this function. It is likely that systematic practice in this particular ability would help many persons to become more accurate in judgment of distance. No one so far has developed a system of training which has been used in this respect. One purpose of the test for distance judgment is to call the driver's attention to the fact that he may differ from others in this ability. Thus he will be led to become more observant and to develop the ability to estimate distances more accurately. In fact, this is the primary purpose of a driving clinic in general. It would be proper to say that the tests are of most value when used in this way.

CAN GOOD LAY DRIVERS BE SELECTED?

Driving performance is so complex that it is impossible to select good drivers with any high degree of accuracy. All one can do is to refine his estimate of the person being examined and the driving traits as are shown on the profile of driving ability. Everyone will have certain weak points for one reason or another and usually some strong points. His attention should be called to both but he should not be made over-optimistic about his skill. Some who are highly trained or are particularly adaptable to a certain type of performance will show a consistent tendency to be above or below average. The driver whose record is shown in Figure 3 is above average. We would, therefore, say that he is a very good risk as a driver and if one were selecting persons for a special driving job it would be better to pick this one rather than one whose record is shown to rate consistently to the left of the center line. In any testing procedure of this kind mistakes can be made and we have always recommended the use of a driving clinic as a sort of auxiliary checkup on the driver, rather than as a foolproof method of selecting drivers.

SUMMARY

The development of the Driving Laboratory, first as a driving clinic, has been expanded until it covers a wide range of trait measurements thought to be related to driving. There are many variations on this form of clinic and various organizations have developed equipment for measuring certain assumed qualifications of drivers. As stated, the value of these so-called tests, or evaluation instruments, is that the results are not so important in and of themselves, but they call the driver's attention to many things related to safe driving which he would not ordinarily notice. They have a place in traffic accident prevention by making the driver more critical of his own potentialities and capability as a driver. He also becomes a better judge of driver capabilities and thus may be able to develop more skill as a defensive driver. Defensive driving can reduce accidents. The point system in Iowa has been very successful and it tends to emphasize this protective type of vehicle operation.

REFERENCES

1. Allgaier, Earl and Lauer, A. R. A preliminary study of the psychological correlates of automobile manipulation. Amer. J. of Optometry, **18**, No. 2, 49-57.
2. Lauer, A. R., Learning to Drive Safely. Burgess Publishing Co., Minneapolis, 1949, pp. 136-137.
3. Weiss, A. P. and Lauer, A. R., Psychological Principles of Automobile Driving. Bull. #11, The Ohio State University Press, pp. 165.

CHAPTER II

PSYCHOLOGICAL FACTORS OF
TRAFFIC CONTROL

THE PSYCHOLOGY OF PUBLIC RELATIONS

Perhaps no one is in greater need of establishing good public relations than the traffic engineer and the highway engineer. The ramifications of these relationships range from placating the landowner through whose property a new right-of-way is being planned, to satisfying the many and various highway users concerning the nature and placement of signs, markers, lane markings and the like. Thus it is very necessary for those in charge of developing, maintaining and regulating traffic on the highway to be adept at public relations. This can be achieved, in part, by a sensible application of the principles of psychology.

Good public relations are predicated on two fundamental premises: (1) that the persons dealt with receive fair consideration in matters concerning them; and (2) that such individuals be educated to realize that the recommendations made are for their benefit. The procedure or technique of accomplishing these two results is primarily an emotional one. People rarely use reason to settle matters pertaining to emotional things such as beliefs and desires. Hence in public relations one must constantly be alert to that which motivates those with whom he is working. Such small details as tone of voice or facial expression may be the key to success or failure. Above all one must keep himself under control.

Of course a great deal of what may be called public relations ability lies in one's personality and personal make-up. These in turn go back to certain of his inherited traits and frequently to habits acquired during early training. A public relations man must be like a bridge or poker player. He must use the cards he holds in his hand and play them to the very best advantage. Sometimes men or women who by ordinary standards would not be expected to possess public relations ability are very adept in this respect. Others who should do a good job of public relations fail utterly. It should help in dealing with people to make a systematic study of the principles of psychology. While the academic psychologist may look askance on the sources suggested here, nevertheless they should help the average man in public work to understand others better and to improve his own technique in public relations.

Morgan and Webb in their book (5) have dealt with problems of human relations. Overstreet has also made a valuable contribution in his volume (6). Any law enforcement officer who is interested in public relations might well look into these two books.

HOW HIGHWAY AND TRAFFIC ENGINEERS MAY USE PSYCHOLOGY

Highway and traffic engineers, as well as enforcement officers, have numerous problems that involve public relations. Only a few illustrations may be given here. One, for example, might concern the placing of a stop-light. Someone in a community, for one reason or another, may decide a stop-light is needed at an intersection. The problem may not appear serious to the traffic engineer from the standpoint of density of traffic. He may abruptly state that there is no need for the light and assume an obstinate point of view with respect to his stand. This approach is likely to engender antagonism and arouse the interest of others. In this case it may be best to appoint a professional committee to investigate the situation and present the facts. Usually when the facts are presented the person making the request realizes that if a traffic signal is placed at this intersection, one might have to be placed at practically every other intersection in the city. If the tax load resulting from widespread installations is given, the matter usually quiets down immediately.

Also, on the other hand, a careful study of a situation may indicate that the public is right. Napoleon once said that he liked to have experts develop plans for a campaign and let laymen criticize the plans. In such instances a reversal of the engineer's opinion, in view of known facts, will never cost him prestige. Fairness and open-mindedness are the cornerstones of getting along with people. Encouraging a representative local group to study a situation and make recommendations on the basis of needs, costs, and the like, generally is the best solution.

One basic principle is to avoid raising an issue, if possible. In one case highway engineers were very much embarrassed by the problem of removing trees along the right-of-way through a small mid-western city. Apparently the situation was muffed by lack of astuteness in the initial stages and instead of letting it settle down before making any overt moves, an order was given to take the trees out irrespective of the objection of citizens. A bulldozer was put on the ground and started to operate. One woman, very violent in her protest, flung herself before a tree and defied the operator to move. Much time was lost and ill feeling generated for no reason at all because of a slip-up in the public relations procedure. Finally the trees remained and the engineers lost face. It is important to keep issues such as this from arising if at all possible.

A great many problems arise over the location of right-of-ways. In the earlier days of improved highways many of the smaller cities wanted the new roads to pass through or near the business district. At present there is a tendency to take the opposite view. They do not want the highways because of traffic problems.

By the right kind of publicity and with proper discussion of matters in an unemotional way, most such situations can be handled without engendering a great deal of sentiment either way. It is primarily a matter of using the right psychology in dealing with the situation.

HOW THE ENFORCEMENT OFFICER MAY USE PSYCHOLOGY

A few years ago it was customary for enforcement officers to

be very "hard-boiled." The tougher they were, the more successful their work was thought to be. The public had to be pushed
around to develop respect for authority. Under certain conditions
of mob violence this view may still be correct. In traffic situations, however, such an approach by enforcement personnel does
not yield the best results in the long run. If an officer is bullied
by a driver, undoubtedly there is a tendency to get a little tough.
However, the average driver is not a criminal; he is not even
averse to good driving habits. Perhaps he is just negligent, or
because of lowered attention or preoccupation he runs through
a red light or exceeds the speed limit. Hence the enforcement
officer's duty is to remind him of the law and to correct his
erroneous ideas or habits in a courteous way. Enforcement is as
much a matter of teaching as it is of policing. Education is recognized as the best long-range technique for reducing accidents.
Therefore, the traffic officer should consider himself a teacher
most of the time and should study the methods of teachers. For
the most part the techniques of teaching are quite different from
those used by police officers in handling the outlaw group of the
population.

In any case, public relations is a very important aspect of traffic-
law enforcement. Because of administrative policy most state
highway patrols have long stressed the need for courtesy toward
the driver on the part of officers. In fact this has become so deeply
ingrained that only rarely is the principle violated. The relationship between the public and the highway patrol in general is
exceptionally congenial. In Iowa, for example, it is customary
for the patrol to be invited to various types of meetings —
Parent-Teacher Associations, public school groups, civic organizations, service clubs, etc. — to give talks and advice on various
phases of highway safety. This is an excellent way to develop
good public relations. Some of the other techniques effective in
securing results may be obtained from a study of the sources
recommended above.

PUBLIC RELATIONS AND THE LAYMAN

People differ considerably in their attitudes. One person is very cooperative and anxious to conform to all the rules of society; another is a "toughy" who is anxious to violate every rule of the road. This is particularly true of a certain group of delinquent youths who have given the teen-ager a bad name. Such games as "chicken," "spider" and similar misuses of motor vehicles and traffic facilities must not be tolerated. It may be safely said that the layman, as an individual, usually responds to people pretty much as they approach him. Therefore, if treated reasonably and given proper consideration as a driver, at least 95% of all drivers will try to cooperate with the enforcement body. Herein lies the secret of the effect of public relations. When the lay driver feels that the enforcement officers are trying to help him, and not trap him, he behaves much better and tries to cooperate, and tends to avoid conditions that result in accidents or in violations of a traffic regulation.

If properly handled even the "tough guy" may soften up and show remarkable cooperation. Those who do not, however, should be dealt with in such a manner as to discourage the misuse of the privilege to drive an automobile.

TYPES OF PSYCHOLOGICAL HAZARDS

Psychological hazards may be differentiated from physical hazards in that they are the result of a certain mental state, or attitude of the driver. They often lead to an unnecessary exposure or willingness to accept responsibility while at the wheel. From our studies and observations it would seem that psychological hazards, in general, may be classified with respect to the conditions which lead up to taking unnecessary risk, namely: (1) ignorance of the situation, and (2) inattention to danger. Some persons actually drive up to 80 miles an hour without realizing that they are exceeding a safe speed. They are inattentive to danger.

One class of drivers is that in which some motive is so strong that the desire to keep within the law is forgotten or overlooked. For instance, there seem to be persons who are so impetuous that they drive recklessly for no good reason at all except that they are bored by the slow moving state of affairs. Another type may be identified as the malicious nondescripts who take pride in violating all the rules and canons of society. They vary from the irresponsible speed maniac to the malicious type of individual who drives to see how many laws he can violate.

MENTAL STATE OF THE DRIVER

The mental state of the driver has a great deal to do with his willingness and ability to drive safely. If he is excited or strongly moved to get somewhere because of an emergency, he may exceed the speed limit or fail to notice a STOP sign. If worried and under mental tension because of events transpiring immediately around him, he may be in such a state of mind as to neglect the common courtesies of the road, such as, giving hand signals, staying on the right side of the road, slowing up for the car ahead or otherwise using ordinary care in driving. Again there are other mental conditions which may be better designated as the lack of a "state of mind." Reference is made to the person who is sleepy or otherwise has his mental efficiency lowered through the monotony of highway travel. A man's conduct must be judged in terms of his mental state at a given time.

Unfortunately most accident reports contain little, if anything, relating to the driver's state of mind. Probably this is due in part to the inability to set down objective statements which identify the condition. Again it may be due to the fact that one often tends to disguise his true feelings.

Most mental conditions may be measured best indirectly. Thus indirect consideration of such conditions which may create momentary traffic hazards should be carefully studied by persons qualified to interpret them. This is where the psychological approach fits admirably into accident investigation. It is hoped that in time every city will have an accident squad that will include someone trained to make proper evaluation of the driver's mental state just prior to and at the time of the accident. This would include a routine physical check-up to ascertain whether the person had been drinking, whether he is a diabetic and perhaps suffering from an overdose of insulin, whether he is an epileptic and had a momentary seizure, or whether he is suffering from some other induced condition of a psycho-physiological nature.

An adequately trained psychologist should be on hand to investigate the pattern of behavior just before, during, and after the accident. The consistency with which the various alleged causes are given might be better evaluated. He should also solicit the advice of the medical man on matters pertaining to psychosomatic symptoms and syndromes.

AGE AND ACCIDENTS

Age is an important factor in accident involvement and the relationship is different for men than for women. In general, age is less important in considering the driving records and behavior of women than it is of men. Psychologists have not thoroughly differentiated between the masculine and feminine patterns of behavior between the ages of 15 and 30.

It is a sad commentary on the chivalry and mentality of American manhood that the driving record becomes gradually worse from the time of learning to drive for a period of about six years. It is particularly significant since women's records are improving constantly during this period. The figures were taken from the 1948-49 records of the State of Iowa. There is no reason to believe they are exceptional in any way since most of the men had been out of the Army for three or four years and there was no immediate pressure of the draft or other reasons which might abnormally affect mental processes of the individual during that time.

It would be folly to assume that the curve represents the common run-of-the-mill type of behavior characteristic of the male driving population. Actually it is not. A sizeable percentage of individuals of this age manifest such a bad showing that it spoils the good record of all others. In other words, the curve seems to be changed from its normal form, not by the combined effect of every individual being slightly accident prone, but apparently it is due to a few individuals who are involved in accidents far out of proportion to that which chance would indicate for the age group.

If these curves are studied closely it will be noted that beyond the age of 30 the sexes remain more or less equal except for a slight rise around 35 in the case of women. This may be due partly to the fact that they have family worries or that children are often riding in the car. Certain physiological changes may also be a factor. It should be noted that the upturn in the suscepti- bility to accidents for women is accelerated after 55. The curve runs on evenly for men until 60 or 65. Such findings are not to be interpreted as being fixed and unchangeable. It is very likely that 10 years hence a similar study will yield somewhat different results due to various environmental, economic and social changes. Now, women as a group, may have learned to drive later in life and therefore those who are now 55 or 60 have not had the experi- ence in driving and traffic that men have had. It will be necessary to wait and see exactly how this effect varies with different periods of driving, and with various types of traffic conditions existing over a given period.

HOW INTELLIGENCE AFFECTS DRIVING

The role of intelligence and judgment in sane driving is very important but the relationships are not all linear. In certain tests used to evaluate driving it seems that judgment particularly is an important factor in the development of good driving habits. Intelligence, as such, above a certain level is less important and may be given as a secondary cause of any apparent association with accident involvement. One investigator, for instance, has been quoted as saying "morons make the best drivers." It seems certain qualifications need to be given this statement. Our own studies have not confirmed his findings. A moron is a person with an IQ between the limits of 50 and 70. In other words, he is one who is 50 to 70% as intelligent as the average. Our studies have indicated that the safest drivers are persons from slightly below average to slightly above average, particularly among com- mercial drivers.

These findings have been confirmed to some extent by the experience of some commercial companies. It has been found that C+ drivers, those slightly above average, seem to be the most successful. In their selection they do not choose persons with extremely high intelligence for driving jobs, except for a few who are chosen to be given supervisory jobs later. The applicants are very carefully selected and only persons with a certain type of disposition or temperament are hired at this intelligence level. After a time they are taken into confidence and given a chance of qualifying themselves for supervisory and administrative leadership within the organization.

Judgment, however, while based somewhat upon the intelligence and somewhat dependent upon mental alertness, is a very important factor in driving. Unlike intelligence, it can be highly developed by training. Any person with reasonably good intelligence may develop his specific judgment to a high degree. This may be shown in almost any area where highly trained technicians are used. Because of their training, experience and knowledge concerning certain conditions and phenomena, some individuals become outstanding experts or judges in the field. Note the case of the tea tasters and the wine tasters. They must exercise their judgment as to the value of tea and wines or other drinks and beverages. There is reason to believe that no high correlation between intelligence and judgment exists. Persons above the average in the distribution of mental ability may learn faster but may not persist in mastery of a simpler function.

This is also true of traffic efficiency. Intelligence is an innate ability but judgment is acquired largely through experience. Above a certain minimum level it appears that judgment is much more important than general intellectual ability insofar as highway safety is concerned. However, the general notion that morons are the safest drivers does not fit into the general scheme of scientific facts relating to driving.

HAZARDS DUE TO INADEQUATE ROAD MARKING

This may at first appear to be a non-psychological category. However, there are conditions in which certain mental states are created by inadequate road markings. There are several factors to be considered here. In the first place, there is the condition of inadequate markings which creates an uneasiness in the mind of the driver due to a misunderstanding of signs. Forbes (1) has shown that right-turn signs tend to facilitate the movement of traffic even on such a well-regulated thoroughfare as the Los Angeles-Pasadena Freeway. Therefore it follows that where traffic flow is much less well-organized properly designed signs are of even greater importance. In some midwestern states insufficient attention has been given to route marking, especially through the cities. In one midwestern city of approximately 100,000 it was extremely difficult for a stranger to pass through without becoming lost and driving several extra blocks before locating the highway again. Such confusion and delay is entirely unnecessary and can be remedied by proper route markings.

At present some highway departments use rather large signs with letters reflectorized and up to 15 inches in height. In Canada and in certain states, pictographic or illustrative markers are used to indicate side roads, main roads, turns, crossroads, etc. These seem to be very effective in keeping the motorist at ease and properly informed as to the route he is following.

In some instances signs are not properly maintained nor placed most effectively. An example is given of two railway signs. One of these is very well maintained and set back at a reasonable distance to warn the motorist of the railroad, and the possibility of a train crossing the road. The other sign is very inadequately maintained, the paint is dull, the letters are rather illegible, and it is placed on the right-of-way, practically next to the tracks. Such inadequate markings as these tend to confuse drivers and to engender disrespect and poor attitudes toward signs in general. Although the uniform code has specifications that remedy such conditions, some states have not taken advantage of the standards for effective signs and markers set up by leading authorities on traffic. When proper psychological principles are applied to the placement, legibility and visibility of road signs and markers, safety is increased.

PSYCHOLOGICAL HAZARDS REDUCED BY DRIVER EDUCATION

The effects of driver education on subsequent accidents and violations have been studied to some extent but it is hardly correct to say that all factors were controlled in some of the studies.

Therefore, we can only reason that training in general does reduce personal hazards of driving as has been shown in industry and in other fields. To what extent training may reduce mental hazards depends on a number of factors.

Several organizations are now studying this problem and some rather specific answers may be available within the next two or three years. Various factors in driver evaluation must be very carefully controlled or erroneous conclusions may be drawn.

Studies by the American Automobile Association and others have shown that the accident rate of trained men is about half that of the untrained men. In some of these studies there were so few accidents among women that their records could not be used. It would take a very large sampling of drivers to furnish a sufficient number of accidents to properly evaluate women's records. However, it is conceivable that there are selective factors operating when making comparisons between men and women drivers. Men who are interested enough to seek driver instruction, or teen-agers whose parents were interested enough to have them trained, may constitute a different psycho-socio-economic group than those who learned to drive by themselves. The results as they stand indicate that training does reduce the possibility of an accident to about one-third or one-half of that expected when the driver is not trained. In a few instances the inferences are that the reduction may be even greater.

Again, the type of instruction may greatly influence this effect. In 14 years of driver education in Iowa, during which time we have trained several thousand drivers, it is quite evident that the effect of training is proportional to the type of instruction given. Teachers who are well trained and adept in this field undoubtedly do a great deal more for the learner than those who are inadequately prepared.

Instructors of driver education must exert their utmost to create the proper attitudes in their trainees. If the sole objective of the course is only to coach the driver so that he may be able to pass the state driver's license examination, it is doubtful whether the accident record will be affected. However, if the objectives are long-range and intended to cultivate good attitudes, as well as to develop an appreciation for the fine points in automobile driving, the results are much better.

OTHER PSYCHOLOGICAL HAZARDS

There are other types of psychological hazards of the highway. These may range from momentary anger through the various emotional states to such abnormal conditions as epilepsy, narcolepsy, amnesia, and the various degrees of insanity. We should, of course, include the mental hazards created by the use of drugs and narcotics of various types. Alcohol is perhaps the most common narcotic used and studies made by the medical profession and psychologists have shown that judgment, one of the most important factors of driving is only 40% as accurate after drinking seven and one-half ounces of gin. Many of the early types of coordination tests of drunkenness are not valid. Holcomb (2) shows that judgment is affected before the muscular system shows evidence of intoxication.

SUMMARY

Traffic engineers need a good program of public relations. It is essential that they cultivate proper attitudes and good relationship with other individuals and groups by fair dealing, and constantly working toward an appreciation of traffic engineering problems.

The art of handling people requires careful study. There is a certain amount of strategy involved. Many critical situations could be avoided by proper handling and careful consideration of others.

Hazards of traffic may be divided into physical and psychological traffic situations. There are several types of psychological hazards.

Men and women differ in temperament and personality, and should be handled differently. Likewise they have different driving habits.

Road markings could be improved. If easy to see and read, they promote good public relations. If not, the reversal is likely to be true.

Training of drivers reduces many psychological hazards.

REFERENCES

1. Forbes, T. W., Effect of "Keep Right" signs on the Arroyo-Seco Parkway. Inst. of Traffic and Trans. Eng., 1951, University of California, Research Report No. 13.
2. Holcomb, R. L., Alcohol in relation to traffic accidents. J.A.M.A., 1938, 3, 1076-1085.
3. Lauer, A. R., The motorist and outdoor advertising. Outdoor Advertising News, 1954, 45, No. 9, 23-20.
4. Lauer, A. R., Certain structural components of letters for improving efficiency of highway stop signs. Highway Research Board Proc., 1947, 27, 360-371.
5. Morgan, J. J. B. and Webb, E. T., Strategy in Handling People. 1930, Chicago, Bolton and Pierce.
6. Overstreet, H. A., Influencing Human Behavior. 1925 New York, Norton.

CHAPTER III

PSYCHOLOGICAL FACTORS OF
TRAFFIC SAFETY

WHAT IS PSYCHOLOGY?

Psychology is usually described as the science of behavior. As a laboratory science it is only about 75 years old, but during this period it has developed a definite body of facts, methods and experimental techniques which are different from the other sciences. The basic ideas are the same in all branches and systems of psychology, although the terminologies and interpretations may vary.

One of the basic ideas is that for every stimulus there is a response. Likewise, for every response there must have been a stimulus. The symbolic representation of this idea is variously written, usually in one of the following simpler forms:

$$S - R \tag{1}$$
$$\text{or}$$
$$S - O - R \tag{2}$$

Legend: S = stimulus
R = response
O = organism

Some psychologists leave out the O, or organism, while others insist it is very important and should be included.

In a traffic situation, a pedestrian (S) runs across the path of an auto. The driver (O) will react differently if he is an experienced driver than if he is inexperienced. The brake action necessary to stop the car is the response (R) and will vary with (O) or observer. Some psychologists insist that since O's differ it must be considered a vital part of the sequence, stimulus, organism and response. Others prefer merely the S-R aspect and omit the O.

In conventional psychology the basic unit of behavior is the reflex arc, the simplest form of response. Psychologists may differ in their interests, methodology and subject matter of study. They have certain common concepts, however, which are used to explain the actions or behavior of people. It is fairly certain one will deal with some of the following fundamental aspects of behavior in any practical situation.

1. There are the sensory processes such as vision, hearing, smell, taste, touch, muscle sense, equilibrium, pain, warmth, coldness and the environment. We shall not use technical terms in order to keep the discussion understandable to one not versed in psychology.

2. Next we should describe perception or interpretation of stimuli presented. It is difficult to make a division between sensation, as such, and perception except for academic purposes. Hence the common usage of the term sensory-perception is often used. It means interpretation of what we see, hear, smell, etc.

3. Imagery and imagination apply to the retention of past experience and the process of acting upon it. These two constitute a process of mental change which may never quite take place entirely. It was described by the eminent psychologist, Wm. James, as the "stream of thought" (4). Without this capacity of the mind to change, yet preserve continuity, very little could be accomplished by man. It is thought to be one of the differences between animal and human minds. Without it learning would be very difficult.

4. Closely allied with imagery is that of association and memory which make learning more efficient. These two functions help us keep our temporal orientation. They act to record and relate past experience to present day experience. This is an advantage to man under normal conditions experienced in everyday life. A driver must not only sense what is going on around him, he must interpret it properly, anticipate situations that might arise in traffic and use the knowledge and skill he has gained to meet new situations. In addition he must plan future situations and make right decisions with respect to them. The next several

aspects of man's mind in action help attend to these.

5. Volition or the "will to do things." This implies a certain degree of choice and preference, plus some emotional drive. It is usually considered a set of habits which have been built up over a period of time. It seems closely related to personality traits which seem to affect driving. The tendency for some young drivers to rush about seems to come largely from a strong self-determination and aggressiveness.

6. Judgment is the ability to make desirable choices quickly and accurately. To make reasonable and long-range rational decisions is important in behavior sequences which lead to the best accepted results. It has been found to be related to driving success. Some of the best driving tests developed are built around judgment.

7. The learning process is the culmination of these separate processes and is considered to be about the same as modification of behavior. Learning is always high on the list of psychological studies in which experiments are in progress. Certain phases of learning need to be studied in relation to driving and the acquisition of special skills. What is needed to be learned, how long does it take, and similar questions remain to be answered.

8. Emotions have to do with the acceptance of experience as being agreeable or disagreeable. With it is associated the fears, hopes, aspirations, likes, dislikes, etc., which are better known to the laymen as attitudes, sets, and various other aspects of personality. They seem a promising approach to the psychology of accident analysis and prevention since they are a powerful influence in determining behavior.

9. Thought and the thinking processes including intelligence, special aptitudes, complex habits, etc., form an important group of phenomena which have received some experimental attention. They have not been studied in relation to driving practices although most authorities will agree that man is a creature of habit. Perhaps the best way to describe a driver is to list his driving habits.

Such things as unnecessary passing, quick starts and stops, running stop signs, speeding and such are known to be dangerous in traffic. Many good habits could also be cited.

10. Various elements of behavior such as reaction time, strength, motility, coordination, endurance and similar descriptive terms constitute a highly specialized group of phenomena which have been individually studied. They relate to skill in driving only when the more complex forms of behavior to which they belong are considered. Also, there seems to be a happy medium for most of these elements. Too much or too little are sometimes undesirable. Average traits seem best.

11. There are individual patterns of overall behavior commonly referred to as personality. It has normal as well as abnormal manifestations. Very little has been done on the relationship of personality to safe living habits although lay writers often discuss it at length.

This list of eleven areas is intended only as a layman's inventory of psychological factors which need further study to determine how they are related to traffic accidents. It is an incomplete list of the psychologist's stock-in-trade. For the present purpose it may suffice to show some areas of psychological investigation in the field of human behavior on which study is needed to establish their relation to driving behavior.

Whether the studies being made are with men, women, children, primates or lower animals; whether they deal with efficiency, preferences, sanity, attitudes or aptitudes; whether they are done under controlled laboratory conditions, in the school room, in highway traffic or in the jungle, the objectives are the same. All studies may be described as attempts to understand, control and possibly to predict future behavior from cues or incomplete information at hand. In traffic behavior studies, a fundamental objective is a smooth flow of vehicles with a minimum of interference by damage and injury or loss of life through contact. If we knew which types of behavior give best results, much progress could be made in accident reduction.

HOW EXPERIMENTS ARE CARRIED OUT

As already suggested, psychology is considered a laboratory science. The nature of laboratory studies will vary with the interests of the persons doing experiments. It may be restricted to a few animal cages, feeding facilities, pencil-and-paper studies in the case of humans, a well equipped industrial laboratory or other types of equipment. In other instances it may consist of various measures of vision, hearing, taste, touch, etc. The laboratory may contain mostly puzzle boxes, dark rooms, sound-proof rooms, chronoscopes, and electronic equipment for producing, controlling and measuring the ability to fly or to drive, or similar devices measuring human capacities.

A department of psychology is judged largely by the quantity, quality and activity of its laboratory. Even the most ambitious of the so-called clinical programs will have some equipment such as a set of Rorschach ink blots, TAT* pictures, three-dimensional forms or similar devices for use in exploring projective techniques and methods.

There may be psychologists who do not use a laboratory, but no reputable department of psychology would carry on and fail to support a program of laboratory research. It is better if this program be related to real life activities outside the laboratory which often gives it the name of applied psychology.

Even though field studies in the realm of traffic are encouraged and are basically essential, the economy and efficiency of the laboratory makes it important. Frequently field observations need to be checked under controlled conditions for verification and correction. Likewise certain laboratory findings suggest field studies for the ultimate testing of ideas brought out.

Thus the field and laboratory are mutually dependent and no scientific work of merit can be carried on without some facilities for each type of approach.

NEED FOR PSYCHOLOGICAL STUDIES
IN TRAFFIC SAFETY

So far the general field of research on the human element in traffic has only been touched. While one may find 300 to 400 references in the literature most of the studies were not experi-

---

*Thematic Apperception Test.

ments set up primarily to be of psychological nature. Of those
that would qualify as psychological experiments perhaps half are
mostly of exploratory nature and designed to reveal problems
rather than to solve them. Experimentation in this area is expensive and until recently little money has been available for research
on psychology of the highway. Even now only a trickle of funds
has gone into the channel.

Of the eleven categories listed practically all the work done on
driving has been on sensation, elements of behavior and some on
perception in relation to sign reading. Only a few attempts to
investigate learning, emotions or personality have been made
while practically nothing of note has been done in the other
areas. This is largely because those who formulated the problems
for study have often not been psychologists. It is easy to press
for research on the more talked about areas.

Many studies have been done from the engineering standpoint
rather than as psychological experiments. This is no criticism of
liaison studies which are valuable but such findings do not always
give psychological information needed. In one study of headlight
illumination, it was found important to establish the effect of a
given level of illumination from opposing headlights at various
angles of declination from the line of vision, requiring laboratory
measurement of acuity of the paramacular field. The results
showed that the effect of opposing light drops off markedly as
the angle with the line of vision is increased. The basic constants
can very well be applied directly to highway construction and
design so far as headlights are concerned. This study was conceived as a psychological experiment.

It would be a stupendous task to enumerate all the problems
which need experimental investigation as they relate to psychology
and traffic situations in general. Frequently problems are un-
covered accidentally and sometimes solutions are obtained by
chance. A list of typical problems beginning with sensation will
be given with some implications. The order of presentation does
not indicate the order of importance. The list is merely suggestive.

1. To what extent can one be trained to detect dangers in

traffic more quickly by recognition training?

2. What effect do temperature and temperature changes (inside the vehicle and in general) have on driving behavior?

3. What are the effects of odors — gases and others — in transportation efficiency?

4. What are the optimal noise levels for efficient driving? Quietness sometimes induces drowsiness.

5. Muscle strain and driving. What are the effects of power controls?

6. Investigations might be made of the various eleven senses which have received scant, if any, notice.

Perception is an important factor in driving. The interpretive aspects of driving performance are very important. There are literally hundreds of problems in this area having to do with traffic hazards, signals, etc. Only a few have been investigated.

1. Reflectorized markers at night — effectiveness, shape of letters, advantages, etc., need further study.

2. Optimal marking systems. Spacing around signs for greatest effectiveness needs study. The use of different colors for route markers may have some advantages.

3. Placement of roadside stimuli to minimize hypnotic or sleep inducing effects. The temporal spacing at different speeds needs study.

4. Speed of perception of traffic hazards. Accident situations are known to occur only infrequently in traffic. Why?

5. Speed of travel and distance perception. Individual differences, effect of training, etc., on perception of speed by the driver seems important in driving.

6. Road hazards in the nature of illusory conditions. Their characteristics and methods of counteracting. Hypnogogic images and their effect have only been cited.

7. Aids to assist the driver such as special mirrors, devices to keep the driver alert, meters, tachometers and others. The use of effective prosthetic devices.

It had been shown that one can avoid mishaps by planning in advance and devising methods of averting accidents. While this area is harder to undertake, it is quite certain that preoccupation seems to be a frequent contributory cause of accidents. Investigations should be made to determine:

1. What various things a driver thinks about while moving along the road.

2. The relation between imagery types (assuming types), and accidents — visual, auditory, kinaesthetic, etc.

3. How imagination may be directed to the past, to the present, or to the future. Does a fast driver have characteristic tendencies of this sort? Does he consider himself a "conquering hero," etc.?

4. How often a driver imagines the results of an accident he may have? Would this be indicative in any way?

5. Whether he is ambitious or the reverse? Is this related to accidents and reckless driving?

6. The effects of compulsive idealism and personality traits on driving behavior.

DRIVING AND THE SENSORY PROCESSES

Only a few problems will be listed under each heading and these will not be the ones that are probably most often thought of as being related to driving. They will be typical problems and the implications in each case will be pointed out.

One of the frequent situations met in traffic is emergency conditions in which one must react quickly to situations that he sees. To what extent can one be trained to detect dangers in traffic more readily by instruction? During World War II the Air Force instigated recognition training for pilots. It was found this helped them enormously. It would seem reasonable that training drivers to react properly to emergency situations would greatly increase their efficiency. This could be done by flash cards or by slides projected on the wall. The latter would be the better since it would be larger and there would be no problem of time of presentation.

Such an experiment would not be set up as a testing situation, but rather as a training project. Certain standards could be established which would be set as goals for the subjects in training.

Another problem which would be of interest to motor vehicle designers, as well as the driving public, would be the effects of noise on driving. Quietness sometimes introduces drowsiness. Perhaps a certain amount of noise in a car is desirable to keep the driver up to par in efficiency. Some work has been done in California on the noise of trucks, but so far as we know nothing has been done on the noise levels of passenger vehicles. Also the sound level of car radios might be studied. Extremely loud noises would probably be undesirable. Likewise, a very monotonous type of low level noise might tend to induce sleep.

Muscle strain and driving efficiency undoubtedly are somewhat related to each other. With the advent of power steering, power brakes and other automatic controls, the task of driving becomes quite easy. Cars might be made to drive themselves within a given lane on the road. They use radar safety guards. Closely related to the kinaesthetic sense is the tactual sense. The type of cushions on the car, the feel of the wheel, and such factors, seem important in keeping the driver up to a high level of efficiency.

Temperature changes might well affect driving. So far as we are aware no one has ever presented data which indicates that accidents occur more frequently in cold weather than in warm weather, apart from the volume of traffic, twilight hours, and other factors which undoubtedly enter in. The temperature inside the car may have something to do with the driver's efficiency. Some heaters are much more effective than others and the temperature can be raised to a fairly high level. Some automobile bodies are much tighter than others and better control of temperature is possible. Studies could be devised to determine how a temperature level, or changes in temperature effect driver efficiency.

The role of the sense of smell in driving is well known. The driver can tell if his radiator is hot, if his fan belt is slipping, if he has a short in the wiring, sometimes possibly if the tires are low, by the sense of smell. These things are axiomatic and probably need no experimental investigation.

Smells are being introduced into movies on an experimental basis. They have been referred to as "smellies." Certain odors or perfumes might well affect the driver if studied. It has been said that the sense of smell is the most powerful of social stimuli. It could well be that a fragrance of some type introduced into the car might change the driver's tendency to speed or the reverse. At least this is a problem area that has not been touched at all in studies of driving.

There are many other sensory studies that might be made of driving situations. Pain has not been frequently mentioned but has been alluded to occasionally. Tight fitting shoes, tooth ache, headache, or certain other conditions inducing pain undoubtedly act as distractions and may be very important in driving. Given a fatiguing or cramped position due to improperly designed seats may well affect the driver's performance.

While some of these factors may at first sound farfetched, a well-known traffic engineer of the Ford Motor Company has recently pointed out that the senses are channels through which we receive information about our environment. Since there are 11 senses in all it would seem that this area would warrant some investigation. Undoubtedly vision is the most important sense and someone has made the statement that about 90% of our cues in driving come from vision. This sounds like a reasonable statement, but we need to know something about the other 10% of critical information that reaches the driver when moving rapidly along the roadway.

HOW PERCEPTION AFFECTS DRIVING

In the laymen's language, perception means the interpretation of stimuli coming to the sense organs. It is very closely related to sensation and really cannot be completely divorced from it. There are hundreds of problems in this area which have to do with the proper reaction to traffic hazards, signals, and so on. A few of them have been investigated and we shall mention certain of these with possibilities for further research.

Perhaps one of the first we might mention is that relating to what a driver sees as he moves along the highway. Some discussion has been made of dynamic visual acuity and static visual acuity. These have been shortened to DVA* and SVA*. Actually they involve more than a simple matter of sensation. They are problems dealing with perception. When one speaks of acuity he naturally thinks of going back into the field of sensation. Reading or interpreting letters is a matter of perception and whether one can read letters as rapidly when he is moving as when he is standing still has not definitely been stated. It is to be expected that it would be a disadvantage for one to be moving and that seeing would be more difficult while moving.

This brings us to another set of problems which are of interest to those designing the new interstate highway systems. What are the best marking systems? Are capital letters better for signs than lower case letters? The space around legends is known to be important from the study of license plates which we have discussed in another chapter.

Reflectorized signs are much more effective at night, but the design of letters for reflectorization is only generally understood. The reflectorized section appears to spread out into the surroundings of the letters. It is quite certain that reflectorized letters should have a narrower stroke. In other words, they should have a narrower stroke than ordinary painted letters used in daylight.

The shape of the letters has not been subject to great concern except that round letters are now recognized as having an advantage over square-shaped letters. The more background space that can be obtain on the sign, apparently the more effective the legend will be. Of course this is limited to the size of the sign and other factors.

A very important consideration is that of the placement of roadside signs or other stimuli to minimize hypnotic or sleep producing effects. Just how should such visual stimuli be placed along the road or grouped for most effective use is not definitely known. Too many signs or markers placed in a short space of roadway probably renders them less effective. Only some general indicators would serve in estimating the importance of this problem. It is known that one can get more out of a single stimulus presented separately. If more items than four to six are presented, the person observing them does not see the separate objects but

---

*DVA—dynamic visual acuity or seeing while moving, as contrasted with SVA— or static visual acuity, seeing while standing still.

tends to group them together and notices the group. From the standpoint of keeping the driver alert, successive groups of markers or signs would be desirable, but to make each one effective it would probably be better not to group them.

Closely allied to this problem is that of the speed with which traffic hazards may be perceived. Accident situations are known to occur only infrequently in traffic. It has been estimated by independent writers that one meets an accident situation about once in every 3,000 hours. The driver undoubtedly gets very little practice in dealing with actual traffic hazards. Experiments might be set up to determine the effect of a practice of interpreting traffic hazards. This might be a phase of the study which we have labeled as recognition training under sensation.

Some studies have been made on the speed of travel and perceptual efficiency. An incidental study once made has been interpreted to indicate that the field of vision tends to narrow down with speed. The results presented were not too clear in establishing this, and the person who did the experiment confided to us that he was not so sure that the conclusions drawn were valid.

There is also the problem of individual differences in the effect of speed on driver efficiency. It is a very relevant problem at the present time when reports show that about one-third of the accidents are running-off-the-road type.

The level of alertness seems to have something to do with the driver's ability to perceive signs, curves and hazards at a higher rate of speed. Some road hazards are in the nature of illusions. An illusion is a perception which is made incorrectly. This may be due either to an objective condition which refers to the nature of the stimulus, or to a subjective condition which refers to what the person is thinking of at the time. Some experimenters have reported commercial drivers seeing what is known as hypnogogic images. Hypnogogic image is a kind of image one has when he is just about to go to sleep. It is sort of a half dream and half realistic perception. While these are undoubtedly infrequent, they do happen when drivers are on the road for several hours.

Frequently an illusion may lead a driver to make sudden swerves or be misled by something he sees. In one state recently over 18% of the collisions for the year were rear-end collisions. It would seem that drivers in general must be frequently misled by the distance at which they are following and the speeds at which the vehicles ahead are traveling.

These types of psychological problems might well serve as a basis of experimentation. Since road hazards are met rather infrequently and since there are illusory effects associated with them, more information is needed about it.

Finally, under the perception, we might consider such auxiliary devices which aid the person to see, hear and determine his surroundings, as the flyer uses when flying blind. While many of such devices have been suggested they are only in the conceptual stage. In reality we have special mirrors such as rear vision mirrors, side vision mirrors, speedometers, and certain devices on the speedometer, for example, tachographs which make a recording of the person's driving habits and others. Among these various devices there are undoubtedly a number of items which might be formulated for experimental study. Is a side vision mirror used by the average driver? Does frosting over the glass on the windows make the use of such devices ineffective?

IMAGINATION IN DRIVING

Persons have imagination in varying degrees. It has been shown that one can avoid certain mishaps by planning in advance and devising methods of averting accidents. Preoccupation seems to be a frequent contributor as a cause of accidents. Perhaps if one could do a thing second-nature, which he does not do ordinarily, he would avoid many accidents. This would seem to be borne out by the fact that experienced drivers have fewer accidents than those who do not have experience. If something could be devised which would give inexperienced drivers a chance to plan in advance and invent ways of compensating, many accidents could be avoided.

There are a number of problems that might be mentioned in this connection but we shall only set down a few and the reader can use his experience to think of others.

First, it might be of value to know what a driver thinks about while moving along the road. If some pattern of thought could be established for the person at the wheel, perhaps he could be brought to give more attention to the job at hand. Does he think about where he is going, does he think about his work, does he think about what he did yesterday, or does he think about something entirely remote from the task at hand?

Some psychologists believe that persons have different imagery types such as visual imagery, auditory imagery, kinaesthetic imagery, etc. While this is not entirely accepted it is an old concept that might be worth investigating. When one is thinking, does he tend to visualize what he is thinking about, does he hear what he is thinking about, or does he have muscle sensations of what he is thinking about? These things could conceivably have something to do with the driver's set at a given time when an accident situation arises. From offhand observation it would seem that drivers tend to drive the way they think. If they think quickly they will move more rapidly. The thought habits of a driver might well be investigated to determine if there is any pattern of thinking which leads to certain traffic practices.

We see drivers dash about and for the most part it seems they are younger men. The other exception seems to be young mothers taking their children to school. Whether they are thinking about their work or in a hurry to get back to tend the smaller children is not certain, but it might be well to investigate why mothers would take unnecessary chances when taking their children to school, knowing there are pedestrians on the street and that by excessive speed they are creating a considerable hazard. A number of observers have mentioned this fact and it would be interesting to make speed checks to see whether it is a fact or just offhand observation.

As mentioned in a previous paragraph, it might be interesting to note whether the driver thinks in terms of the past, present or future. There are certain mental habits such as "the conquering hero" tendency which might affect driving. If such types are identified, does the particular thinking habits of the individual lead him to perform in a characteristic manner.

No one has studied how often a driver imagines the type of accident he may have, or if he fails to do this, does a driver ever think about the results of the accident he might have. This is an approach that has not often been mentioned but it does seem to be worth consideration. If he would think occasionally of the possibilities of careless driving and the results that might occur he might drive differently. Would this in any way be indicative and is it feasible to investigate? Clinical psychologists often consider seriously the imagination patterns of a person as an indicator of his behavior. Perhaps we have missed something in overlooking this type of approach to the problem of highway safety. It is definitely a psychological problem and might possibly be worked into some kind of an experimental setup.

Another problem related to the anticipation of a driver is whether he is ambitious or not. Some early observations have indicated that certain young drivers who were quite ambitious tended to get into trouble. They are not purposely careless, but are bored more or less by the routine of driving which is to them merely a stepping stone to something they want to do. Psychologists sometimes refer to one's ambition as attaining his level of aspiration. Does this level have anything to do with accidents and with driving habits? We are merely suggesting this to those who may be inclined to study such aspects of driving behavior.

The final item we will mention under this heading has to do with compulsive behavior. Some may prefer to call it impulsive behavior. Young male drivers are more or less on the spot with respect to the accident situation. It has been stated reliably that teen-age drivers account for twice as many accidents as one would expect from their number, not counting the mileage driven, which, for this group, is in the neighborhood of 5,000 miles per year or about half of the average driving rate for males. Perhaps some study should be developed to investigate this hypothesis. Can an instrument measuring impulsion be developed and will it indicate or tell anything about the individual's behavior? By compulsion or impulsion we mean the tendency to move fast and get there right now, or in other words, to lack patience. This is perhaps about the best we could describe the so-called compulsive behavior of young male drivers. This characteristic is often noted among young children who want something right now. They want an ice cream cone out in the desert and they want it right now. Around a college one observes a certain percentage of drivers who move around in their cars as though they would like to be where they are going practically when they start. Perhaps the strongest argument against drag strips is that it tends to emphasize this characteristic of drivers, which in general is held to be undesirable by insurance companies and driving authorities.

MEMORY AND DRIVING

Memory or retention is that characteristic of the individual which leads him to retain things that happened in the past for reproduction in the future. There are all degrees of memory, and persons vary greatly. Some persons remember certain experiences and profit by them. Others have experiences and seem not to profit. Studies of accident repeaters show that one may have one or two accidents and then improve his record. On the other hand he may have three, four or five and never seem to remember how the accident happened. We examined one· driver in an eastern state who had 129 accidents. How he happened to survive this ordeal and how he could be driving after having survived is beyond our knowledge. This case actually is known to have existed. Maybe the man couldn't remember how he got into these accidents. At least some study should be made of the relation of memory to accident situations.

In general, memory is supposed to be more or less specific. One remembers things that are liked and which he specialized in studying. Some persons have a good memory for names and faces, but a poor memory for appointments.

Besides the normal process of memory and its relation to driving, there are several peculiarities of memory that might well be studied. Drivers are known to have lapses of memory. One driver might start out on a trip and find himself well towards his destination without having the knowledge of having passed through any of the towns he knew he must have gone through. In other words, the lapse of memory might very well result in disorientation and inability to cope with situations which come up. At least if he was entirely unaware of what he was doing, he would have to depend upon second nature or automatic reactions to keep him out of trouble. The first question is, whether this is common to drivers who travel a great deal? The second question is, do those who have such a characteristic get into trouble more often than those who do not? This is a problem that might bear investigation. At least any driver can study his own way of responding to such situations and his own habits of thinking. Some have a complete lapse of memory while others might have a semi-lapse of memory. This might be temporarily due to preoccupation or thinking about other things. Certainly the problem of driving necessitates complete attention at all times. Alertness at the wheel is of the utmost importance. Lapses of attention are to be considered seriously.

Another peculiarity of memory is that known as perseveration. It is thought to be associated with certain types of accidents. In Boston drivers who had driven one type of street car during the week without trouble had many accidents when they changed to another type on Sunday. Apparently what they had been doing during the week did not fit the situation on Sunday. A driver may travel along and have some idea persist in running through his mind. A common example is that of a person having a tune run through his head. While this would probably not be a distraction it is possible that perseveration might be a factor important to safe driving. There is no measuring rod available for the tendency to perseverate. This might be worth investigating in relation to motor vehicle driving.

Finally, memory and learning are closely associated. Do slow learners have more accidents than fast learners? Do persons who learn the proper ways of driving easily tend to put them in practice better? Many other problems of memory and learning might be mentioned, but these are examples.

First and foremost, we would like more information on whether memory and learning ability are related to driving. It is a pure psychological problem and could probably be undertaken only by psychologists.

PROBLEMS OF WILL IN RELATION TO DRIVING

What the average person on the street speaks of as "will" is known to psychologists generally as volition. There are certain problems associated with volition of a common place nature which might well be studied from the standpoint of psychology.

A strong-willed or stubborn person may have a tendency to get into accidents. Frequently I have heard women complain of men who would drive through a narrow passage at a high rate of speed apparently strongly motivated to get somewhere in a hurry. It seems that men have more of a tendency in this respect than women and, from the everyday point of view, probably are more stubborn than women. There are notable exceptions in both cases, but perhaps the strongest willed persons are found among men. The tendency to get there in a hurry is associated with accidents. Many persons involved in accidents ascribe their trouble to being in a hurry. The urge to succeed is somewhat related to volitional characteristics. One study seemed to indicate a tendency for executives to get into more trouble when driving than would be expected. This area has not been considered separately. It has been hinted at from the standpoint of personality, but personality is such a gross category that it might include any number of characteristics which would be hard to isolate for individual study.

Most persons who are experienced with young people would accept the statement that youngsters tend to be more willful. It would be fair to say that there is a higher percentage of them that are willful. Some study as to the degree of willfulness or the tendency to do things in a hurry and to drive accordingly would be very revealing.

Strong motivation in a person may very well be a desirable characteristic, but on the other hand if carried too far it can be an undesirable characteristic. This problem is clearly in the field of psychology and it seems to relate to success in driving.

JUDGMENT OF TRAFFIC SITUATIONS

Judgment is thought to be more or less of specific nature. A good judge of livestock may not be a good judge of housing in cities. A good judge of architecture might not be the person to choose to decide the merits of entrants in a beauty contest. Judgment is the ability to size up a situation and arrive at a reasonable conclusion. Time may also be considered an element here. Some persons can arrive at a conclusion very quickly and have a high percentage of right choices. Others seem to have trouble in arriving at a conclusion and take considerable time to make a decision but it may or may not be right after it is made.

Some of the problems of driving judgment center around the following: What are the essentials of good driving judgment? How does driver education affect driving judgment? Does mechanical judgment safeguard against accidents? Can one judge speed accurately and is this of importance in driving? How does distance judgment relate to driving?

Considering some of these problems separately, it would be well to know what the nature of important judgments made in traffic are. A study of judgment situations which involve traffic should give considerable information. A test developed for the Army showed that judgment was a very important prognosticator of driving success. In other words, it was one of the tests that seemed to stand up better against the criterion of a driver's record. The approach made here mostly was to present pictures of situations of passing in traffic and various things of this type in a multiple choice type of question. Those who could pick out the most safe situations in the shortest time were rated as being the better drivers by their supervisors and associates.

Another angle to the problem of judgment in driving is the effect of driver education. Is enough attention given to judgment in the training? Do persons who have had driver education as a group show better judgment than those who have not? These are some of the problems that might very well lend themselves to special study.

Many persons believe mechanical judgment is important as a safeguard against accidents. It would seem that mechanics do have fewer accidents than one would expect. Perhaps the best way to study this problem would be to compare the results of persons who have had mechanical training and are apt, with those who have not. This has possibilities and could be done with relative ease. Perhaps it would be more fruitful than an attempt to measure mechanical judgment and set this up as a criterion.

One specific type of judgment which could be mentioned is that of the judgment of speed. There is only a moderate correlation between the judgment of speed and judgment of distance, although they both involve some form of estimates with respect to space. Judgment of distance has been analyzed quite in detail by psychologists. It is generally spoken of as depth perception and there are seven or eight different factors which are involved, such as size of the retinal image, angle at which the two eyes view the object, distinctness of the image, haze in the atmosphere, position of other objects, and comparative size.

So far as actual situations are concerned, the color of the car and background seem to have quite a lot to do with estimation of distance. Unless there is considerable contrast between the object and the background, some have raised the question as to whether the height of cars is important in distance judgment. This would probably not be important except in cases of the car coming over a hill where sight distance would be cut somewhat by a lower vehicle. There are certain other factors or influences which might be studied in connection with distance judgment.

Speed is another problem, although it can perhaps be analyzed. Experiments have shown that the estimations of speed at lower velocities tend to be underestimated, while those at higher velocities tend to be overestimated. In other words, persons driving at a lower speed actually move faster than they think they are going. Those driving at higher speeds are actually going slower than they think. This was found from a study involving several kinds of estimations, both by drivers in the car and by pedestrians. It is against expectations, as we had supposed that there might be a tendency for persons driving fast to underestimate their speed which would be an excuse for some fast driving. This does not seem to be the case. Persons on the average, driving at higher speeds, are quite aware of the fact and if questioned at any time would probably estimate their speed as faster than what they are actually driving.

LEARNING AS A PHASE OF DRIVING

Probably no topic has received more attention by psychologists in various lines of experimental work than learning. There are very definitely established laws and principles which are known to hold for the different types of learning. Such things as the transfer effect from one type of learning to another, interference effects, the rate and extent of learning, and a number of things of this type, are of much importance in driving. Their application to motor vehicle problems, however, has not been studied to any great extent. Although not studied specifically in this connotation, effects of different modes of operation of different vehicles should be studied. There are differences in the rate of pickup among cars, the action of the brakes, type of shifting, and the movements of the various devices for control of the car. The term perseveration has already been mentioned in an earlier section. This persistence in doing a thing in a certain way undoubtedly affects the persons ability to change from one type of car to another if the manipulation is considerably different. Since several types of motion are necessary in order to maneuver the average car, it is a human engineering problem to determine the most effective method for handling controls.

No one has shown so far the effect of knowledge of road laws. One study showed that men do slightly better. It is natural to assume that a grounding in road laws and safe driving practices would increase traffic safety. This should be true, but it is one of those things that has not been subjected to an experimental attack. According to Army findings it is an advantage to have greater driver know-how. This turned out to be one of their better tests but the criterion was not accidents.

We should also like to know more about the effect of driving experience. Out of nearly 60,000 accidents in Minnesota, less than 1% in one study had less than one year of driving. What types of experience are necessary to make a driver safe? Effects of drag races and drag strips and certain other pastimes in driving would be of interest. Stock car racing has only been studied slightly. From a report of stock car racing in which motion pictures were used, no great effect was noted between those who attended races regularly and those who did not.

Another phase of driving related to learning is that of knowledge of characteristics of the road being used. Some bus runs of certain companies use shorter trips for their schedules. One driver takes the bus for a certain number of miles and it is turned over to another driver. This keeps the driver on a given stretch of road so that he may be aware of traffic hazards of whatever nature might be experienced. It might be well to ascertain whether lay drivers have more trouble on long drives or on short drives. This has not been thoroughly investigated. Of course some controls would need to be used since perhaps the majority of mileage is made by drivers on short runs.

The above and many other things relating to phases of learning and of traffic problems would make good subjects for investigation. Many persons may purport to have the answer but the only valid ones can be obtained by an experimental approach.

DRIVING AND THE EMOTIONS

The emotions are usually considered very important to handling emergencies in traffic driving. Everyone is familiar with the term "emotions," but we may say they are generally considered as two or three patterns. One is the aggressive emotions, another is the retracting type of emotions, and a third is a more or less quiet type of emotion — the person reacts in neither direction. We refer here to the types of activity the person expresses.

One study at the University of California had to do with the urgency of the traffic situation and the degree of emotion expressed. A fair degree of correspondence was obtained between the person's reaction and seriousness of the hazard or situation encountered.

Writers on driving generally recommend that one try to control his emotions in driving. Of course this is good general advice,

THE PSYCHOLOGY OF DRIVING

as it is wise to control one's emotions under any circumstance. Very little has been done to show the relation of emotionality to certain types of accidents. When the car goes out of control, has the driver lost his nerve or did he just goof?

Also the problem of alcohol enters into the emotionality of a driver. Alcohol tends to accentuate the emotions and to cause one to go to extreme in various types of reaction. He may show undue fear and pull off the road, or he may be unduly aggressive and try to drive the other person off the road. The New York Police Department report that there is a higher percentage of avoidance reaction in drunken driving than one would expect. The driver tries to get out of the way of other traffic and runs into someone or into some object. It was not stated whether this was the drinking driver or the drunken driver.

The problem of personality and temperament as they relate to driving is also worth investigation. Personality is quite highly colored by emotional patterns. Emotion is a temporary state usually and would not lend itself to testing perhaps unless the testing were done on the spot. Probably an approach to the temperament side would be more feasible. Everyone recognizes there are persons having a slow, even temperament and those with a hot, fiery temperament. If some classification of temperament could be made of accident involved persons it would be interesting to note what relationships exist between these and driving situations.

Thus the relationship of emotional patterns and traffic behavior would be worth investigating. As stated, perhaps the temperament side would be the better approach.

TRAFFIC BEHAVIOR AS RELATED TO THOUGHT AND THINKING

Thought and thinking processes are known to be related to intelligence. An intelligent person usually thinks clearly and perhaps more quickly than one less intelligent. This area has received some attention by psychologists in a general sense, but much more could be done. It would probably have to be approached in a more general way if any results were to be obtained with relation to traffic.

One approach would be to consider the problem from the standpoint of competent and incompetent persons. It is generally believed that the harum-scarum type of person is less stable and more likely to become involved in accidents. This is so strongly entrenched in people's thinking that some insurance companies will not take a young driver who attaches squirrel tails, large dice, baby shoes, or other such paraphernalia to his car. The theory is that it is indicative of his general competency and stability and therefore a bad omen.

Several years ago there was a radio program on the Sunday driver. From the records and from observations over the years it would appear that the Sunday driver is a different type than those driving during the week. Either he has a different mental makeup, having spent a week in manual labor, behind a desk with instruments, or is not fully cognizant of the hazards surrounding him. No study has been made to determine the relation of thinking habits to accident involvement.

So far as intelligence is concerned, one writer has made the statement that a moron is the safest driver. Early studies we have made indicate this not to be true. It would seem that safeness at the wheel would increase with intelligence up to average, then would drop some until about 20% above average. There is some evidence it would rise again beyond this point. In other words, a person with low intelligence is not a safe driver; a person with somewhat above average is easily bored; and the best all-around driver would be one having about average intelligence or one having considerably above average intelligence. More experimental work should be done on this problem.

It is in these more complex forms of behavior probably that any classification of accident risks will be obtained more accurately.

MOTOR PHENOMENON AND SKILL

A great many studies of reaction time and various aspects of devices for measuring skill have been used in connection with driving. Even the sampling of driving obtained by the average driver's licensing bureau is little more than an indication of the dexterity with which a driver handles an automobile. His chances of meeting a crucial driving situation are quite remote in a short test. This is probably fortunate as examiners tell us of some hair raising escapes which they have had over several years of testing drivers for an examination. One examiner was involved in a collision with a truck load of potatoes which overturned at an intersection causing considerable trouble. It is miraculous that so few serious accidents occur during a driving examination, although examiners report many narrow escapes. Probably in time all examinations will be conducted with dual-control cars which would be very advantageous.

The areas of endurance, fatigue and similar problems related to motor phenomenon should be followed further. We have found that a rest pause every hour or hour and a half will increase efficiency of drivers around 10%. The presence of signs along the highway and various other stimuli of interest tend to keep the driver awake and offset fatigue. This is shown by the large number of accidents in the open country in the west and the relatively low rate of accidents in many eastern states where stimuli are numerous.

Perception and motor action are quite closely related. The onset of fatigue in relation to certain adjustment in the seat and other parts of the car are not fully understood. This is a phase of human engineering that needs a great deal of attention. Small European cars seem to induce more fatigue than the ordinary run of American cars. This is perhaps due to the fact that they require considerably more gear shifting, etc. and have less room in them. Some American manufacturers are emphasizing space and roominess. Some attention should be given to the frequency of accidents of smaller cars. It is alleged that they are more dangerous because of weight.

In one study made it was found that drivers of newer cars were more likely to get into accidents than some with cars four or five years old. Of course there are many factors such as increased speed which might account for more accidents. We have no way of knowing how much is due to speed, as such, which is undoubtedly easier to develop in the newer cars.

Gross coordination is undoubtedly an advantage to a driver. In other words, a dexterous person can usually get along better at the wheel than one who is rather clumsy. Army tests of gross coordination proved to be one of the best indicators of driving. It seems that delicate skills are not closely related to driving. We refer here to finer types of reaction such as those involved in handwriting, sewing, and fine instrument work.

HOW PERSONALITY AFFECTS DRIVING

It might be well to say a word about personality before discussing its relation to driving. Many think of personality as the general overall appearance of a person. Psychologists define personality as the sum total of all of one's characteristics. They tend to emphasize personality traits or behavior patterns more than appearance.

The traits covered by personality tests are not always universally accepted. What one investigator may accept as the traits of personality may not fit into another's rationale. We shall only mention two or three such as have been identified by Cattell (3) at the University of Illinois. Practical concernedness as opposed to bohemianism show a significant difference when drivers are grouped according to the way supervisors had grouped them for efficiency. Other factors which seemed to be associated with better driving were emotional stability, what he calls a positive indicator, and a quiet and trustfulness, or stability, in the absence of nervous tension. The latter difference was not markedly significant. This may be because the test itself did not measure the characteristic well.

Other investigators have mentioned emotional balance, even temperament and conservativeness. A number of studies have seemed to indicate that a conservative driver tends to have better success than an unstable type of driver, or the driver who is more or less radical.

Clinical psychologists have a number of techniques for measuring personality. One of the common devices is known as projective techniques. A person is allowed to observe a picture or other device and he then gives his reaction to it. From the kind of response he gives a pattern of personality is built up. Not too much has been done in this field in relation to driving.

A limited study of Navy medical personnel showed that persons having accidents, when compared with those accident free, had less respect for law and did not take their responsibilities too seriously. In other words, the persons not having accidents were more trustworthy and took their responsibilities more seriously. They had a more tranquil home life and were in general more conservative and had a better approach in dealing with other people. These findings seem to agree with those most widely accepted with respect to personality traits.

Studies have shown that accident-free individuals have better religious attitudes, fewer internal conflicts or conflicts with their environment, and are not frustrated. This might be expected since they would probably be more conscientious and conservative and would pay better attention to the job while driving. The investigators of this study, however, of 264 airmen in Colorado are careful in their conclusions. Their findings would fit in with the general picture that other investigators have been able to piece together.

Some insurance executives are very much interested in the approach to the problem of identifying risks. Although not in any highly developed form, the results seem to be indicative of the pattern that might well aid in identifying problem cases. Delinquency is often associated with accident involvement directly and indirectly.

Particularly is the matter of delinquency of interest in considering youthful drivers. The trouble makers in school and in communities are considered a poor risk by underwriters. Ages of those in the accident involvement group correspond very closely to the ages of delinquency. This again would fit in very well with the picture given above that those traits identified with accident involvement are the opposite more or less from those of the accident free.

One trait which has not been studied widely but which is generally found important is conservatism. Practically all experimental and other approaches of related nature have suggested such a factor as desirable in safe driving.

Conservatism usually is associated with carefulness at the wheel. The careful driver is more likely to be courteous and to drive with consideration for other drivers.

SUMMARY

In this chapter we have tried to call attention to the nature of psychology in rather simple terms and to give some orientation as to the way psychology is related to driving. It is not intended as a technical approach but more as an introduction to the problems of psychology as they relate to driving.

Most of these are problems suggested from findings of earlier studies. The intention is to stimulate thinking about the causes of bad driving and accident involvement. Further reading of standard psychological literature will help the student of driving problems.

REFERENCES

1. Dashiell, J. F., Fundamentals of General Psychology. Boston, Houghton Mifflin, 1937.
2. Guthrie, Edw. R. and Edwards, Allen J., Psychology. 1949, pp. 303.
3. Cattell, R. B., The 16 P.F. Test. IPAT, Champaign, Ill., 1949.
4. James, Wm., The Principles of Psychology. Henry Holt and Co., 1890.
5. Ruch, F. L., Psychology and Life. Chicago, Scott, Foresman, 1941.
6. Warren, H. C., Dictionary of Psychology. San Francisco, Calif., Houghton Mifflin Co.

CHAPTER IV

IMPROVING CONDITIONS FOR SAFE DRIVING

THE HAZARDS OF CITY BORDERS

The problem of making our highways safer is a much discussed subject and various opinions have been voiced which often have little or no scientific foundation. It is axiomatic that properly surfaced, banked and designed highways, which are wide enough to take care of present day traffic, are of the utmost importance. That traffic markers and signs must be large enough to be legible at sufficient distances seems a truism. Many erroneous opinions have been expressed regarding certain other aspects of the highway, especially those relating to roadside stimulation. Studies have been made in which it was shown that there are more roadside sources of stimulation just outside city limits. Also it is known that there are more accidents in these areas.

It would be a fallacy to assume that because there are more accidents in any given location that any one factor of the environment should be solely responsible for them. In other words, a correlation does not imply cause and effect, but is merely a matter of association. Two sources of error in reasoning need be noted in such instances. One is that because they are found in the similar location one is the cause of the other. The other is the old fallacy of why white sheep eat more than black sheep. The simple answer of the shepherd was that there were more white sheep. Since there is more traffic close to cities, there are more accidents.

The transition from urban to rural driving is extremely difficult to control. In the first place enforcement officers are deployed about a city much as one would expect according to population density. Therefore, these border areas are probably policed less intensely per mile of street or highway. In the second place it is difficult for a driver to adjust his speed and general attention when passing from a lesser populated area driving at higher speeds to a more densely populated area, or vice versa. In passing from the urban area into the country one is also likely to drop his vigilance.

There is also a tendency to continue at a higher speed after reaching city limits, thus exceeding the safe speed limits. Conversely, when traveling out of town the driver may be in a hurry and pick up speed before he should.

HOW DRIVING EFFICIENCY IS AFFECTED BY DISTRACTION

The problem we wish to discuss here is confined not only to urban areas but also has to do with the interurban or rural areas. It is commonly believed that anything which distracts a person is detrimental to his performance at a skill such as driving (1). In the first place many things which at first appear as distractors are actually beneficial to efficiency. It has been shown in certain psychological experiments that a limited amount of distraction is an asset to performance. When one wishes to solve a problem connected with his business or profession he rarely ever seats himself comfortably in an arm chair before the fireplace and adjusts the light to just the proper degree of intensity. If he so places himself, the chances are he will soon be asleep and nothing is accomplished on his problem.

It is not uncommon for drivers to fall asleep while driving on a long stretch of monotonous highway (3). It is rare indeed that an accident is attributed to sleep while driving within a city and especially in the more thickly settled areas. Practically all such accidents occur in the country or in the borders of cities. It is also true that throughout the country, locations that have the best accident records are in areas which have numerous types of distraction along the roadways.

Experiments have shown that a certain amount of distraction is an advantage to performance (2). This has been tried in a number of instances and similar results obtained. That distractions are not necessarily a disturbance is borne out by the fact that in most factories considerable noise exists and some recent experiments have shown that the presence of reasonable noise is not in any way detrimental to performance. In fact it sometimes speeds up production, acting as a stimulant when not too intense.

Another facet of the study is that distractions not only improved certain functions and kinds of performance but also tended to keep the person awake and aware of his surroundings. This is particularly true of driving and many instances have been cited which indicate that lack of stimulation induces what is called "highway hypnosis" and resultant accidents. This condition particularly has been noted along some turnpikes where there has been much effort given to the problem of limiting roadside stimulation in the way of business places, roadside resistance and signs. Insurance companies report that their losses from rear-end collisions are very heavy on such roads. Some drivers unconsciously follow another vehicle off the highway and run into a truck or bus which is pulling into a station. This indicates that there is some psychological condition existing which is not conducive to safety at the wheel. A certain minimum of external stimulation, visual or otherwise, is needed. In order to understand the underlying principles involved, it is necessary to consider some of the phases of vision and certain functions of the visual mechanism.

ASPECTS AND FUNCTIONS OF VISION AND SEEING

It must be remembered that the eye is a very versatile mechanism and can adapt itself to most of the ordinary conditions of everyday experience. For example, one can see to some extent in dim starlight where the illumination is less than a thousandth of a foot-candle. The eye can also adjust to conditions of broad daylight in which illumination sometimes runs up to as high as ten thousand foot candles. Further, the eye is so designed that the point of keenest vision in the fovea rapidly decreases through the macular area into the paramacular field and then into the periphery. This is due to a different distribution of rods and cones which respond to low illumination and high illumination respectively. While detail is seen best in the central point of the fovea, movement is sensed best at the periphery. It is said that the Indians would lie on their backs and observe movement in the bushes out of the corner of their eyes. Color is also sensed best near the center of the fovea, but this function drops off considerably as you move outward to the periphery.

It is also necessary to consider the movements of the eyes in relation to driving. The eye does not see when it is moving. Therefore glances to the side with the head stationary induces temporary lapses of blindness which are not ordinarily important to the function of driving since they are of the order of approximately $\frac{1}{10}$ second. There is no reason why the eye need be kept in a stationary position to look down the highway. Eye movement cues are equally essential for driving a vehicle safely. Thus the whole visual field is important in driving an automobile and there is no reason to assume that movement of the eyes in any direction is detrimental to efficient seeing, since movement cues are not lacking even if the eyes are off the immediate line of vision for an instant. The important fact to remember is that the eyes keep roving about the environment to pick up objects of stimulation as will tend to keep up interest in the task and to keep the driver alert. When such stimuli, regardless of their nature, are absent the tendency to go to sleep may well be induced. New wraparound windshields tend to broaden the field of view.

VISUAL FUNCTIONS NECESSARY FOR SAFETY IN DRIVING

It must be conceded therefore that several functions of vision are needed for safe driving. One is the ability to see detail or acute vision for reading signs and other details along the highway, quickly and accurately. Also, movement in the periphery is very important in giving certain cues as to the nature of the objects in the field of vision, such as moving animals, vehicles, and so on.

It must be remembered that movement is relative. It is this changing relationship of the environment of the driver that provides the proper stimulation for orientation on the highway. If the eyes are fixed on any given point and continue to be fixed, unnecessary fatigue develops and even the condition of sleep and mild "hypnotic effects" are induced. Fixation of the eyes artificially and for prolonged periods is one of the prime requisites for inducing hypnosis. Anyone who has observed hypnotic seances will have noted this technique which is used in various forms. Furthermore, there must be relaxation of the eyes and any tendency to retain a fixed position will greatly interfere with normal functioning of vision (2).

Whatever conditions may be imposed it is impossible to keep the eyes of a normal person stationary for any great length of time. A driver is bound to be observant of objects around him such as distant mountain tops, clouds, persons and animals on the landscape, field erosion, crops, etc. Most of these objects and conditions are likely to be far removed from the highway, as much as a mile or so to the right or left where it is necessary to turn the head noticeably in order to get any view at all. Therefore it is conceivable that any object which would confine the observation of the driver to a given area within a 10 to 15 degree angle to the side of direct vision might actually be beneficial rather than detrimental. This, of course, presupposes that the period of fixation of the eyes is not long. In reading and other studies it is noted that the eye fixates for only a fraction of a second. Whole paragraphs can be read in a fraction of a second. In tachistoscopic studies periods as low as $\frac{1}{100}$ second are given in which certain persons are able to grasp whole paragraphs. Any supposition that reading a line or so would take a great length of time is erroneous. Eye fixations are quick and of short duration. If a driver goes down the highway he usually glances off at a reasonable angle without moving his eyes appreciably. A glance at any object such as a house, a sign, an animal or marker requires only momentary fixation in order to pick up newer objects of interest. This normal function of the eyes is to be expected and cannot be forestalled.

GENERAL SUMMARY AND CONCLUSIONS

In this brief review of the problem of visual efficiency in driving we have only touched on a few of the aspects which go into visual efficiency at the wheel. It suffices to say in summarizing that the function of external stimuli in driving performance is extremely important. In fact, it is the stimuli within the car that usually causes trouble. Most of the external stimuli that are alleged to cause accidents are imaginary. It is the absence of cues rather than too many that result in accidents. Complaints are usually in the nature of alibis for one's behavior in general.

In other words, the eyes function to give two types of basic data or experience of visual nature. First is that of fine detail which is necessary in reading signs, markers or to pick up detailed cues necessary in recognition of persons, landscapes or other objects along the way. For one to ride along and say that he saw cattle in the field is one thing. For him to note that there were sixteen Jerseys, one Holstein and perhaps one Hereford, is another. To do this he must make detailed observation and have keen foveal vision. In driving through a new country, if one is to get anything out of his trip at all, he must observe certain details. For safety he must be able to read signs quickly and accurately.

Now it so happens that the external stimuli have other functions. One is the matter of orientation for the details which a driver gets principally through foveal vision. External conditions and sources of stimulation such as trees, moving objects, fences, railings, signs along the highway and other objects tend to keep his interest in the problem of driving, which is monotonous to say the least, and to thus heighten his general level of alertness throughout a longer period. The surroundings provide the framework for making things more meaningful in relation to details which may be observed.

Therefore it is necessary to provide certain objects of artificial nature in the field of vision to maintain the level of efficiency in driving at its highest point. Man, from his earliest remembrances, is constantly dividing his attention between specific points in his seeing and of the general surroundings. A child is kept interested by having toys to look at while in his cradle. It is known that a generalized stimulation of color and objects about the room will tend to keep the child in a happy state and to improve his general intellectual development. It would be a highly artificial situation in which the field of vision would be restricted and varied stimuli arbitrarily withdrawn. This is shown quite well in the condition of restricted field of vision such as found in the condition of tunnel vision. Such persons actually do not see at the side and thus get into trouble because they are unable to properly orient themselves with respect to surroundings which they are unable to integrate with experience from the direct line of vision which constitutes their total experience.

Therefore, it must be argued from all known facts that any attempt to strip the roadside of non-moving objects which produce illusory or relative movement with relation to a moving car would be detrimental to driving. On the other hand they are more likely to be beneficial to driving performance so long as they are incidental. This would, of course, preclude the presence of objects which restrict or obstruct the field of vision, either within or without the car. In other words, the eyes should be allowed to function in the normal way such as they have done since infancy in order to produce the most desirable results of a driver at the wheel. Thus we would conclude by saying that pleasing stimulation in the visual fields is beneficial to the driver and improves his performance at the wheel. Likewise, inadequate stimulation may lead to boredom and result in lack of alertness which is detrimental to driving.

Highways should not be denuded of objects upon which the eyes may be fixed from time to time if they are to be safe. Many accidents occur at night when traffic is not dense and drivers have little to look at or see. One fundamental principle of the Smith System (2) is that the driver always gets the big picture. Many persons confuse their own personal feelings with the facts regarding driving safety.

REFERENCES

1. Courts, F. A., Relations between experimentally induced muscular tension and memorization. J. Exper. Psych., 1939, 25, 235-236.
2. Ford Motor Company, The Smith System (16 mm) sound film. Detroit.

3. Lauer, A. R. and McMonagle, J. Carl, Do road signs affect accidents? Traffic Quarterly, July 1955, 328-329.
4. Morgan, J. J. B., The overcoming of distraction and other resistances. Archives of Psychology, 1916, No. 35.

CHAPTER V

WHAT WE KNOW ABOUT THE AUTOMOBILE DRIVER

HOW SCIENCE OF DRIVING DEVELOPED

Since the year 1500 science has progressed at an accelerated pace. Almost every known type of problem has been experimentally attacked and methods have been developed for unraveling the riddle of various particular phenomenon of interest. The scope of scientific research extends from the investigation of the nucleus of the atom to the classification of facts known about distant stellar space. This relentless quest has probed into the secrets of living organisms and has run the gamut from explorations of the submicroscopic, nonfilterable virus, to the courtship and living habits of the Stone Age man of New Guinea. Homo sapiens has only recently come around to exposing himself to the searchlight of scientific investigation in many respects. Particularly, the automobile driver has only been submitted to a sketchy investigation.

According to one author, traffic safety is composed of three elements—the road, the car, and the driver, but since accident reduction is very much a human problem, the driver is the most crucial factor.

Delay in applying the principles of science to man is exemplified by the fact that biology and the life sciences are much newer than the sciences of nonliving matter. We shall not use the term *natural sciences* since one science is as natural as another. Only during the last 150 years have the biological sciences rested on a firm theoretical and experimental basis. Until the cell theory was enunciated by Schleiden (5) and Schwann (6), biology had no scientific basis.

Only a little over 100 years ago Wöhler, the chemist, wrote to a friend with regard to organic chemistry: "Organic chemistry just now is enough to drive one mad. It gives me the impression of a primeval tropical forest full of the most remarkable things in a monstrous and bottomless thicket with no way of escaping to which one may well dread to enter."

Physics developed a little earlier but still relatively late. Physical sciences under the impetus of Galileo's contributions had about 300 years lead on the biological sciences. Psychology has had less than 100 years in which to establish itself as an experimental science. It usually is considered to start with Wundt in 1879. Applied psychology is much newer and certain areas of psychology are very new. Genetics is only slightly older, or younger, depending upon whether one chooses to count from the time of Mendel or of De Vries.

We might want to consider the wide range of phases of interest in human behavior. Titles ranging from the hearing mechanisms of the porpoise to the intelligence of the cockroach have been subjects for doctoral dissertations. Binet, principal originator of many present day intelligence tests, studied a wide range of behavior areas. His doctoral thesis was on some phase of the digestive system of micro-organisms while he indulged in explorations in psychic research and other occult phenomena during his later years. Thorndike once remarked, after the passing of Binet, "We will now have a thousand fewer pages of French to translate each year."

A NEGLECTED PHENOMENON

Although persons have been driving automobiles since 1895, there being four in the country at that time, very little scientific attention was given the automobile driver until in the 1920's. A few studies at that time were directed toward the matter of accident involvement. We shall not take the time to review all the studies of the driver at this time. This particular variety of homo sapiens we wish to discuss briefly. There are now at least 72 million throughout the United States and we know some things about them at the present time. There are many other facts which should be known and these are being gradually eked out. There are numerous parameters which have not been explored at all. We can cover only a few of the outstanding characteristics of the automobile driver at the present time.

Unlike most mammals the sexes are unequally divided. There are about twice as many males as there are females. The reason for this lies in the fact that the male is the more aggressive and has a tendency to take the initiative in furnishing a means of transportation. The ratio is changing, however, and there may come a time when the sexes will be more nearly equal. Not only is the female in the minority, but since the male possesses most of the means of locomotion as a group, she drives only about 10% as far each year. She travels usually at a lower speed, except on occasions when some impulse causes her to exceed the speed limit. She is most active between 10 and 11 A.M., from 2 to 3 P.M. and during the early evening hours. She is rarely found on the highway after midnight in charge of a motor vehicle. Although often slandered by the male as being indecisive and hesitant in her driving, she has a record for safe mobility that is enviable. Particularly her record for obeying the traffic ordinances is much above that of the male. Very few female drivers we have investigated had more than three accidents. Males may run up to eight or ten accidents quite frequently. In Connecticut we found one driver with 19 accidents and one in California who had over 100 accidents and still retained his license. How this could happen no one has given a satisfactory explanation.

The female driver drives only about 1500 miles a year during her first five years of driving. This mileage gradually builds up until it reaches a peak around 50 when she drives in the neighborhood of 4500 miles a year. From there on her driving record gradually decreases until around 80 when she does very little driving.

CHARACTERISTICS OF THE MALE DRIVER

The average male driver is in the neighborhood of 35 years of age. He drives a car between four and five years old with approximately 40,000 miles on the speedometer. The average male driver has driven about 20 years and travels slightly over 10,000 miles a year in his automobile. We should say this is the mode. This mileage is reached between the ages of 25 and 30. The mileage of male drivers builds up from around 4,000 at 16 to something over 13,000 at 27, then gradually goes down until the age of 40 when it levels off until about 55, after which there is a second drop down to about age 70. Mileage then levels off again until about 75 or 80. Beyond 80 the curve rapidly approaches the base line of zero travel. About 4,000 miles are driven in darkness and around 700 to 1,000 miles between midnight and 6 A.M. The average male drives his car around 8,000 miles during the year in daylight.

This individual is just short of having completed a high school education but the trend is upwards. Ultimately about six males out of ten are caught and booked for violating traffic ordinances when records are examined. There is no way of determining the number that are not caught. One in ten has a serious accident annually in his various migrations. One in eight has a major reportable accident or violation of traffic law and ordinance recorded against him annually. He learns slowly and often after getting a license to drive tends to become progressively worse in his mobile habits for the first six years compared with his own record. When mileage is taken out of the equation he is found to have a worse record during his earliest years of driving and progresses slowly toward a better record up until around the age of 30.

THE FEMALE OF THE SPECIES

The female of the species is somewhat younger, the median being only about 30 years of age. We have described some of her characteristics previously, but she drives a slightly later car and has fewer miles on the speedometer. She averages around 15 years of driving experience. Considerably less ambitious she travels only around 3,500 to 4,000 miles, about 3,000 of which are in daylight, 700 after dark and something over 100 between midnight and 6 A.M. She averages at least one year more of schooling than the male, for the most part having finished high school and attended college for two or three quarters. Only about 1 out of 200 of her sex is caught violating the motor code each year, 1 out of 33 has an accident and 1 out of 30 has an accident or violation recorded against her record in the state files annually. It is to be noted that these ratios are not constant and may vary with the length of time that the person has driven. Therefore they would vary from one year to another and would probably be increasing in frequency with the higher mileages driven.

Accident reporting depends upon the emphasis placed upon it by the state laws. For example, one state went from 6% of the total number of accidents reported to 28% of the total previously reported in one year. Reported accidents had been averaging about 6% per year of the total number on the records, but during that year jumped to 28% with the inauguration of a financial responsibility law. Such a law requires that all accidents be reported under penalty of having the car attached or removed from the road. Some of the records reported here are based on experiences prior to 1948 since the study covered a longer period of time and they might well change if considered since 1948.

SIGNIFICANCE OF SEX DIFFERENCES

When most of the differences in driving habits and characteristics noted between sexes were subjected to evaluation they are found to be fairly substantial and hence the two sexes must be considered as groups of individuals for comparative purposes.

When mileage is equated some very interesting trends in the efficiency of mobility is shown. Whereas the male apparently excells in skillful manipulation from the age of 15 and above, so far as his official record is concerned in data collected over several years, his involvement in accidents is higher when mileage is controlled, up to and about the age of 32. His sister, on the other hand, improves gradually up to the age of 32-33 when there is a slight upsurge in accident susceptibility during the early 30's. The reasons for this are only speculative, perhaps worries over children, interference of small fellow passengers or certain psychosomatic changes characteristic of this period of life. The trend then turns upward until about the age of 55 when there is a greater number of accidents shown than before. One reason for this upward swing prior to 55 is the increased number of miles that females drive. The high point of their driving is shown to be slightly over 50. For the male, from 30 on the record remains fairly consistent up until about the age of 65 when there is another upward swing which increases gradually when corrected for mileage.

Fig. 4. Distance Judgment. One form of distance judgment apparatus is shown. The subject sees the cars in the mirror at about 8 feet effective distance. He looks into the end and sets the cars with the round knobs.

When an overall comparison is made between male and female drivers on a mileage basis the latter have a considerable advantage from the standpoint of the frequency of accidents. The ratio throughout the age range is about 2½ to 1 on a mileage basis with men having the poorer record.

That the male driver has a poor record is fairly evident from data of insurance companies. One statement attributed to the National Bureau of Casualty Underwriters reads "cars owned or principally operated by unmarried young men under age 25 are classified as the most hazardous class of private passenger car risks. The rates for these cars are increased and the increases range from the limits of the basic policy ($5,000, $10,000, $5,000) by $16 to $54 according to the territory."

On the other hand, a number of insurance companies now give special rates to families with only young girls driving the car. They find there is no reason for increasing the premium for those who have only young girls driving a car in addition to the parents. One writer has summarized the characteristics of young male drivers as follows (bad risks):

"1. He is resentful of authority and doesn't like to take orders from anyone, at home, at school, or on the job.
2. He is a poor sport and won't follow the rules of the game.
3. He tends to be an exhibitionist and decorates his car with squirrel tails or various other devices.
4. He is irresponsible, undependable and tends to change jobs frequently.
5. He is likely to be on the delinquent side, at least there is a close parallel between the ages at which youths get into trouble generally and when they get into traffic difficulties.
6. At the wheel he is given to speeding, tailgating and unnecessary passing.
7. He is overly confident about his driving — thinks he has more skill than he actually has."

We might paraphrase it with the description of the female driver point by point (desirable traits).

1. She is generally respectful of authority and if she violates it is usually due to some lack of information or lack of knowledge about the regulations.
2. She follows the rules of the game and is a good sport generally.
3. So far as automobiles are concerned she is not an exhibitionist. While she may like colored cars she does not go in for a lot of the frills that men quite often like.
4. She tends to lack confidence and is sometimes annoying in the type of work she does.
5. She is likely to be on the stable side; less likely to be de-

linquent in general, and less likely to get into traffic trouble.

6. At the wheel she is more conservative; follows at a greater distance and is·more careful in passing.

7. She tends to lack confidence and is sometimes annoying because of her tendency to wait to be sure if the traffic is cleared.

These differences are likely due mostly to personality traits. Personality is thought to have considerable to do with driving habits. All the studies that have been carried out in this area by various investigators tend to link personality with driving habits.

It is not to be inferred that all younger male drivers are bad. From studies we have made it would appear that not over 10 to 20% can be classified as bad risks. The other 80% at the troublesome age are safe drivers. In all of our studies only three women have been found who were really bad drivers. In one case an alcoholic was having considerable trouble. In another a young coed was rather malicious when "picked up" by officers. The third was a young lady working for a motor vehicle department who had several accidents that seemed to stem from a bad disposition. She had been in trouble several times.

YOUNG MALE DRIVERS MOST AFFECTED

One particularly noticeable feature when considering data on male drivers is the erratic behavior of certain groups between the ages of 17 and 27. This might be termed a "d'Artagnan complex." An estimated 10 to 20% of the male population seem to be afflicted with this disturbance. The characteristic symptoms are a daredevil nature and a tendency to dash about without respect for persons, conditions, or objects. The victims appear to suffer from delusions of clairvoyance and space distortion. They think they can see around corners, through vertical curves, shrubbery, rain, sleet, fog, or even blank walls. One is reminded of the horse that ran into trees and was described as having good vision but of not caring where he went. The extensiveness of this mode of behavior warrants serious consideration. A military uniform, or the presence of the opposite sex, seems to enhance the symptoms particularly during week-end periods.

OTHER SYMPTOMS

There are other symptoms which should be taken into consideration. Some of these symptoms are excessive spurts of locomotion, sudden and disastrous decelerations or stops, unprecedented swerves, zig-zag motions laterally from the line of travel and a phobia for remaining with the moving group. They apparently have to forge ahead and pass even if the destination is only 200 feet beyond the point of passing.

ABOUT PASSING

There are as many ideas about passing perhaps as there are automobile drivers, but a recent release of the National Safety Council showed that 47% of accidents were traceable to excessive speed. Anyone who drives at an excessive speed is bound to have a high passing index. Therefore on the merits of the case it must be argued that anyone with a high passing index is to be categorized as a poor risk as a driver. Every time one passes he must get on the wrong side of the road; he must face oncoming vehicles; and he must take chances in getting out and back into his lane of traffic. Some passing is necessary but there are drivers who abuse the privilege and pass when it is not necessary. Therefore we must categorically argue that anyone with a high passing index should be rated down as a driver. Of course if account could be taken of the condition under which he passes he may be rated down much further. This view is predicated on the assumption that a certain number of passes are necessary but an undue proportion of passes tends to rate the driver down since they indicate taking unnecessary risks.

FURTHER SYMPTOMS

Returning to the symptoms of the complex described, gyrations of locomotion of various types, and sudden reversal of direction are not uncommon. The victim seems beset by indecisions and contradictory impulses. We are now speaking of the young male driver in the particularly hazardous group. The law of gravity seems particularly irritating to the victim and he has no esthetic or logical appreciation of momentum. The principles of Newton are utterly disregarded.

Another symptom is following near the bumper of the vehicle ahead. Space judgment seems to be particularly erratic and sporadic stops to reduce the number of contacts made, is frequently observed. An abnormal perception of space, plus a strong bullying tendency, often result in many occasions for concern by fellow motorists moving in the same or opposite directions.

At night this tendency is particularly lethal. Not infrequently accident reports are made which indicate the presence of poor space judgment at night. In fact in some instances it appears that there is an absolute lack of space judgment. Either this condition is present or the attention is interrupted and turned in some other direction than the line of travel. Some types of accidents are very difficult to explain.

Since the victim is supposedly most affected at the time his physical capacities should be the highest, perhaps the condition might be termed "automotive amentia." According to the best psychological theory amentia is congenital and incurable. From the appearance of the data on this phenomenon, or disease, it would appear that this specific malady of the young male automobile driver is a type of amentia which remains incipient until about the age of 16, then waxes briskly until the age of 24 or 25 when it wanes gradually until in most cases it subsides or disappears at around the age of 32. A few cases persist, like infantilism, and the symptoms never completely disappear. This incurable segment of the driving population often eliminate themselves by heedless driving or represent the accident prone.

NIGHT DRIVING

A common symptom of this highly lethal malady of a certain segment of the young male driving population is an extreme tendency towards nocturnal migrations at high speed. The victim may travel up to 80 to 100 miles an hour between 1 and 4 A.M. for no apparent reason. Most of his brothers on the road travel at a moderate rate of speed and arrive without mishaps. The average road speed during this time of day, in one study, was 53 miles an hour compared with the mean of 47 miles for other hours of the day. At the present it would be higher, more perhaps average 55 miles an hour in daytime and 60 miles at night for this group who drive at excessive speeds. The percentage of lower age groups who drive reasonably is higher. Only a small group apparently drive at excessive speeds at night or otherwise.

Under certain conditions the influence of proximity to the opposite sex seems to amplify the general symptoms under consideration. Hyper-agility during the late nocturnal period, however, cannot be explained on this basis since it is shown that the female is rarely along at these hours. If anything, the presence of the female might be expected to reduce the rate of speed in the later hours of the night. In other words, the young male does not tend to show off or to hurry home with his female companion, but is more likely to take his time. It is after he leaves her at her domicile and rushes to get home before the daylight catches him that excessive speeds are found. As already stated, this is not the general run of the male population but a certain small segment that gets into very much trouble as shown by the records.

LIVING HABITS

It is said that most young mammals spend the greatest part of their industry on three aspects of their own welfare: food getting, shelter, procreation and care of the young. Locomotion is usually dependent upon morphological considerations and requires little attention on the part of the parent or offspring. Excessive speeds of normal locomotion in and of themselves rarely lead to difficulties.

The particular group of individuals under consideration differs considerably from the rule in this respect. A large proportion of the young male driver's efforts above 16, and much of it before, is spent in improving his means of locomotion or getting about from one place to another. Note the interest in bicycles, motor scooters, hot rod activities, as well as drag races and the more mature desire for possession of an automobile. The automobile has now gone to college it seems. One fraternity at our school recently reported 34 automobiles and 32 men at the house. Many schools have banned the presence of automobiles to some classes, particularly the freshmen. It is likely this would be a good thing and would be supported by the parents if a general vote were taken.

ECONOMICS INVOLVED

To further emphasize this category of differential characteristics on a comparative basis, the automobile driver invests about as much of his annual industry in means of locomotion as he does for protection from the elements, and approximately half as much as he spends for food for his entire family. This can readily be calculated, assuming the mileage to be 12,000 miles a year. The cost of driving an automobile at present prices is estimated to be something over 10¢ a mile by an outstanding automotive economist associated with the industry. This would be $1200 a year. The estimate is most likely to be conservative. One hundred dollars a month would about pay his rent, while $200 would probably pay the rent and buy most of the necessities for the average family. Many families now possess two cars which would throw the comparison out of balance to some extent.

Another characteristic of what might be called motor mania in general is the craving for a new vehicle annually. The individual is usually satisfied to stay in the same home or shelter for several years, in fact usually prefers it for sentimental reasons, even though many times outmoded and inadequate. At the same time his means of transportation must be the most modern and shiny model available. It must be powered for speeds nearly three times that required for safe locomotion, must carry numerous expensive gadgets and be given the finest mechanical care, even if the family wardrobe is shabby, the life insurance cut or dropped, and dental or medical care suspended.

The automobile, although highly beneficial to mankind in many respects as an auxiliary aid to his industry, besides the pleasure of getting about, has a tendency to be detrimental to the driver himself and his nonmechanized fellow creatures. Hazards of man's industrial, recreational and locomotive activities stand high in the cause of premature death and injury. Each year there are nearly 40,000 motor vehicle deaths alone and a total of 95,000 accidental deaths of all kinds. There were injuries to 9,500,000 in the same year. Usually it is estimated that around

400,000 are permanently injured and rendered partially dependent upon the national economy. The economic loss from all accidents is estimated to be $11,200,000,000 in the *Accident Facts,* 1957 edition. It is stated a conservative estimate of motor vehicle accidents is around 7½ billion dollars. This would amortize the national debt within 20 to 30 years. One average state finds its losses run 30 to 40 million dollars a year from automobile mismaps alone. This estimate is based on conservative figures.

TRENDS

An interesting commentary on this situation is that although the rate per hundred million vehicle miles is going down, the actual number of vehicles is going up. The cost also is going up. This is due to increased traffic, the increased number of drivers, and the increased number of miles driven. While motor vehicle fatalities are reasonably low compared with other major causes of death in the United States, one writer has observed that most of the diseases are more noticeable at the older ages. The highest fatality rates for motor vehicle fatalities are between the ages of 15 to 24. Diseases and other causes strike various ages which deserves special attention. Accidents take a toll at the healthiest ages.

As stated, the most serious part of the problem is the high mortality rate among the healthy young. Man has largely offset the inroads of children's diseases by application of scientific methods and medical treatment, but accidents from automobiles and otherwise, stand highest in the causes of death to young people. A careful review of the following paragraph may clarify this statement.

Considering all causes of death to persons under the age of 1, accidents rank seventeenth; between 1 and 4 accidents rank first; between 5 and 14 accidents rank first; between 15 and 24 accidents rank first; and between 24 and 44 accidents rank first. Although dropping to some extent in rank as age increases, accidents still stand third as the cause of death to males and females at the adult level. Below the age of 35 accidents stand as first cause of all deaths in the United States.

POSSIBILITIES OF CHANGING THE DRIVER'S
CHARACTERISTICS

To what extent can we change a driver's characteristics? It seems we are changing them gradually and perhaps the two most potent influences in changing his characteristics are enforcement and education. No one deliberately wants to get into trouble but he either doesn't think or doesn't think quickly enough. If he had planned his route in advance and had thought through many of the hazards he is likely to face, it is probable that his characteristics would tend to change in time. In fact the situation is not as futile as it is made to appear. Some progress has been made. The chances of a fatal accident per mile travel, as stated, today is about one-third of that expected three decades ago even though the average road speed has increased about 20 to 30 miles an hour and traffic is much more congested. This improvement is perhaps due primarily to four factors: (1) better trained drivers, (2) better roads, (3) better cars, and (4) better laws, regulations and enforcement. The proper weighing of these four is difficult to establish. All need to be improved.

ABOUT HIGHER HORSEPOWER

In the first place it must be admitted by anyone that a great deal of the horsepower advertised is on paper. It actually is calculated but is never used, nor is it fully available for speed. In the second place automobiles have greater pickup today and are more powerful. They will move faster but some of the alleged horsepower is purely a matter of calculation. Some of the power goes into such things as air conditioning, is lost by imperfect adjustment, and for other reasons is not available. Most everyone now, including automobile manufacturers, will agree that horsepower has about reached its peak. Economy is being emphasized.

There are several other matters which would generally help reduce accidents. Every driver education course in the country should emphasize the proper use of power. It is not essentially needed for passing or for driving at high speeds. It can be employed for economy in the use of the motor. Each driver should know his rate of speed and the range at which he can drive safely. One driver may drive faster than another, and we should not want to say how much faster, but there is a difference. Apparently from the frequency of accidents reported as running off the road there is a breaking point for every person and if he exceeds such limit there is danger of losing control of his car. We would say that the possibilities of changing a driver's characteristics are apparently strong if he is taken early enough. The evidence seems to indicate that the classroom course in driver education should be given at an earlier age when attitudes can be developed and sane thinking along the line of proper observance of speed and of safety rules taught successfully.

ATTITUDES VERSUS SKILLS

Most authorities in the field now would say that attitudes so far as safe driving on the highway is concerned are more important, beyond a certain point, than skills. In other words, skill is necessary to negotiate a car in traffic with some degree of accuracy. However, the most serious accidents occurring in heavy traffic result more frequently from poor attitudes on the part of drivers than from the lack of skill. At least lack of skill is shown by drivers largely because of their poor attitudes toward others and toward traffic flow.

ATTITUDES CAN BE CULTIVATED

It has been shown in a number of studies that attitudes are susceptible to training. If a systematic attempt is made to improve attitudes while improving skill there is a definite shift in the desirable direction. Thus it is indicated that training to improve attitudes toward traffic might be more fruitful than training for skill. Skill in and of itself is somewhat dependent upon natural aptitude. Of course the same might be said of attitudes. Many years ago. Dr. Stack (7) of New York University said that attitudes can be caught rather than taught.

CLASSIFICATION OF UNDESIRABLE DRIVING HABITS

Much more could be done to improve driving habits of all

types that would help make our highways safer. Habits of driving, good or bad, fall under three general categories of classification:

(a) Those relating to skill at the wheel. Improvement in this respect can usually be accomplished by better training of drivers. By skill at the wheel we not only mean driving the car but actually handling the wheel. A great many accidents today are reported as running off the road. In experimental studies we have found that the proper handling of the wheel is one of the important phases of good driving. When a number of criteria are grouped, factors having to do with handling the wheel are shown to have very much to do with safe driving.

(b) Those habits relating to a more nearly complete knowledge of driving, conditions and habits of defensive driving, as well as demonstration of ability to apply one's knowledge of traffic and driving are most helpful in successful driving. This involves a wide acquaintance with ordinances and practices in driving as well as some knowledge of the automobile. Good training and experience are important factors to obtain this objective.

It would require a much better preparation of each driver before he receives a license. By preparation we mean actual study of the motor code in such a way as to acquire certain mastery of the details of items which have to do with driving. In no other area do we license persons to practice and then police the licensees into correct performance on the job. Isn't the cart before the horse? The driver's examination should be made much more rigid and should require more study of the fundamentals of safe driving. It would be assumed that considerable study be made of phases of driving before the license examination is taken. This is in line with the new plan in Michigan where each licensee under 18 must have a course in driving before he will be permitted to take the examination for a license. The plan is being considered favorably by the Iowa legislature. This is an ideal situation, providing the proper training facilities are available for those who wish to take advantage of them.

(c) Another set of desirable habits are those relating to attitudes and courtesy on the highway. Most accidents could be prevented by careful observation on the part of the driver, and practice of common courtesies as are observed by pedestrians when meeting or passing on the sidewalk. Safe driving is courteous driving. One columnist recently has said that the schools cannot teach safe driving but they can teach driving. Perhaps he had a good thought in this statement. His point was that the parents should have already taught the child the principles of courtesy as they apply to the driving situation. Unfortunately it does not appear that they are being properly taught or there is much undesirable transfer from other walks of life.

We cannot say that it is entirely the young drivers either. There are a certain number of older drivers who get into trouble just as readily as the younger drivers. Most accidents could be prevented by careful observation on the part of the driver and practices of common courtesies as are observed by pedestrians when meeting and passing on the sidewalk. Less than 5% of the drivers are classified as accident-prone. While the term is not universally accepted, the fact still remains that a very small percentage have most of the accidents. Apparently they have acquired habits which operate in such a way as to get them into trouble most of the time. Again, about 25% of the population have accidents only occasionally and may be classified as accident susceptible. This segment of the population has more than the average number of accidents but actually accidents occur rarely in their experience. It seems from an analysis of their driving habits and their general outlook on life that they are persons who do not intend to get into trouble but at times become confused and slip below the average level of performance. One writer observes that the bewildered driver is a hazard to all others in his vicinity. Occasionally persons get caught in a train of circumstances that tend to bewilder them. The causes of bewilderment are varied and numerous. Persons who are in this category should be taught to be extremely careful all the time and exercise an unusual amount of precaution.

About 70% of all drivers rarely have accidents. The average is about one every ten years. This is reasonable evidence that the other 30% could avoid most accidents which occur by more caution and thus reduce the toll from traffic by a large amount. There are several fallacies of thought that will need be corrected before automobile driving and highway travel can be brought to a maximum point of safety. Authorities in the field now consider it theoretically possible to achieve, under present conditions, a reduction of about 30,000, or about 75%, of fatalities. This would mean about 10,000 motor vehicle deaths each year rather than 40,000. Some common false theories regarding accidents need to be corrected. We shall enumerate ten of these falacies.

1. Accidents happen according to the law of averages. This is not scientifically sound or experimentally true when individuals are concerned.

2. That one is powerless to avoid an accident if his number is up. Acceptance of this tenet would render most of man's efforts at self preservation as useless. This reminds us of the naive individual who was afraid of flying. According to his argument believing in numbers is all right, but suppose the pilot's number comes up while we are up there.

3. That one's past record and success guarantees immunity from accidents. A large proportion of fatalities occur after the first year of driving experience. Minnesota at one time made a study and found that only about 1% of accidents occurred during the first year of driving.

4. That accidents will only happen to the other fellow is a common fallacy. It can't happen to me is a very dangerous attitude. This self-induced personal philosophy is highly dangerous if followed consistently.

5. That good roads and safe cars will eliminate accidents. Over 90% of all accidents are attributed to the driver. New cars with all the modern safety devices and superhighways often show a high association with motor vehicle fatalities on a mileage basis which would not seem warranted. While they reduce most of the physical hazards as recognized by engineers, superhighways, freeways and turnpikes still have about one-fourth to one-third the accident rate as the regular highways which retain most all the hazards.

6. That drivers can be trained too young. There is more evi-

dence to support the opposite point of view. In most all other fields early training is an advantage. While there is a reason why children cannot be taught the actual over-the-road driving, they may learn elements of skill, attitudes and safe practices on laboratory devices which are now available for teaching purposes.

7. That normal roadside developments, business, objects of interest and signs along the road increase accidents. All the evidence is on the other side of the argument. Such devices seem to aid in providing necessary conveniences to motorists and also help to keep the driver alert.

8. An eighth fallacy which might be suggested is that all accidents are caused by one group of drivers, one type of conditions, or one set of circumstances. The one-remedy theory has long been discredited. That excessive speed, or any other factor, is the sole cause of accidents is misleading. It is true that some violations are more serious than others, but they all enter into the picture and must be handled or considered if we are going to reduce accidents.

9. The fallacy that all persons can be policed into safe driving habits is widely prevalent. No state or commonwealth could afford enough patrolmen to eliminate reckless driving entirely. Each driver on the highway must be his own policing officer or agency. Until such time as each person becomes responsible for policing himself, accidents will continue to happen. Unfortunately one driver policing himself and the other not sometimes may lead to trouble even though the good driver is highly defensive in his maneuvering. Proper training before licensing would greatly aid in reaching this objective.

10. Another false premise is that accidents are the price of progress. Nothing is further from the truth. New industries of all types have better safety records on the average than the older industries. Lumbering and mining are some of the oldest industries known to man, yet today they are among the most dangerous. Accidents with rare exceptions begin and are consummated in the mind. External conditions and circumstances are only contributory influences which merely set off the accident-protential situation.

GENERAL SUMMARY AND CONCLUSION

In this discussion an attempt has been made to summarize the data on characteristics of the automobile driver and driving problems in such a way as to bring out some known facts. Further, an attempt has been made to suggest the basic principles of accident prevention which would lead to an alleviation of this scourge to society. It is literally much worse and devastating than war. It continues every day, every hour of the day, throughout the length and breadth of the country. There is no moratorium on accidents.

If this chapter has seemed informal at times it has been in the interest of brevity and economy of time. A scientific approach to the problem of driving will eventually provide a body of working knowledge that should greatly reduce motor vehicle accidents in general. It is going to take a concentrated effort of all the sciences to accomplish this result. It is also going to be necessary for us to correct some of the fallacies of thinking which were enumerated in the previous section.

The following readings may be of interest to stimulate further thinking along the line of accident reduction.

REFERENCES

1. Hafstad, Lawrence R., Research as Applied to Traffic Engineering. Given before the 27th Annual Meeting of the Institute for Traffic Engineering, Detroit, 1957.
2. Lauer, A. R., Travaux du Driving Research Laboratory. Le Travail Humain, 1953, XVII Annee, Nox. 1-2, 41-52, Paris.
3. Pledge, H. T., Science Since 1500. Philosophical Library, 1947, pp. 329.
4. Russell, Bertrand, Dictionary of Mind, Matter and Morals. Philosophical Library, New York, 1952, pp. 290.
5. Schleiden, Matthias J., Principles of Scientific Botany. pp. 1842-43.
6. Schwann, Theodor, Microscopic Investigations on the Accordance in the Structure and Growth of Plants and Annuals. Berlin, 1839. (Trans. Sydenham Society, 1847)
7. Stack, Herbert J., Personal Characteristics of Traffic Accident Repeaters. The Eno Foundation for Traffic Control, 1948.
8. Lauer, A. R., Tomorrow's Drivers. Lyon and Carnahan, 1958.

CHAPTER VI

WHAT IS THE BEST CRITERION
FOR SAFE DRIVING?

Many different groups are now looking for some kind of prognostic instrument to determine qualities of safe driving. Motor vehicle departments have the problem of reducing accidents in the general population of their constituents. High accident rate is thought to reflect somewhat on the efficiency of those in charge of the program. This includes the patrol, as well as the educational and administrative personnel in the driver's licensing program. Another interested group is the automobile insurance companies. They are having a problem of keeping losses below their premium rates. According to one source, they have made no profit on casualty insurance since 1954. In only 3 of the past 11 years have the companies been able to show a black ledger on automobile insurance underwriting.

Likewise, individuals even are getting to the point where they would like to know what their potentialities are as drivers. Therefore, the problem of selecting safe drivers is rather acute and deserves considerable attention.

Since the only approach in such case is to rely on some type of judgment, the question arises as to what the judgment shall be. One judgment is that of opinion of persons in the field. This criterion is subject to weaknesses and is not entirely satisfactory. At least it has marked limitations. The other criterion is that of experimental evidence on the problem and there is a dearth of such information available.

A number of studies have been reported on the effects of driver education (4). Each has been for a different purpose. Many investigators did not impose the proper controls for critical evaluation of results of such training. Such items as the number of men and women in the class, previous driving experience, miles traveled a year and similar variables were not considered.

The present study represents an attempt to give an overview of some of the results to evaluate the effectiveness of driver education and to summarize several facts that seem to stand out as important.

Fig. 5. A Serial Reaction Apparatus. The subject sits on the chair with his foot on the pedal and reacts to one of three lights, red, green, or orange. If red appears he is to shift his foot quickly to the other pedal. The time is measured. If green appears and the subject shifts his foot, an error is recorded. The orange light is the warning signal. (After Stalder.)

HOW THE PROBLEM IS STUDIED

Several sources of data have been reviewed. The avenues of approach and results were noted. The varied and sometimes conflicting findings seem to point out the problems encountered in attempting to evaluate the effectiveness of driver education. More questions seem to have been raised than have been answered by many studies. Research often brings to light many hidden uncertainties.

The lasting effect of driver education presents a moot problem and is certainly one to be reckoned with if a comprehensive evaluation is to be made. In other words, the effects of training wear off. The extent to which accidents are inherent in the nature of youth poses another problem. This, of course, is to be considered academic since about 80% of youthful drivers have good records. What ails the other 20%?

Included among other problems met in evaluating driving are the following:

1. Has allowance been made for "exposure," that is, the amount of driving done in terms of time and mileage as well as under more hazardous conditions such as heavier traffic, bad roads, and weather conditions, or when fatigued late at night and other factors? It is known that per mile of driving young women have much better records. It is not known whether their exposure risk is similar. One would suppose that it is not as great since they drive mostly in daytime.

2. What is the most important aspect of good driving performance? Is it skill in handling vehicles? Some research suggests that a measure of driving skills alone would be an inadequate criterion. At least one investigator (9) distinguishes between "good" driving and "safe" driving. He found that the accident repeater is frequently a highly skilled manipulator of his vehicle. Other investigators (1) have concluded that "safe driving as evaluated by freedom from accidents, and good driving as evidenced by adeptness at the wheel are not the same." It is now known that violations, as well as near-accidents, are acceptable criteria of efficiency at the wheel.

Most studies, to date, have based the criteria of good driving performance on accident and/or violation records. However, the criterion of reported accidents has been found to be quite unreliable. Correlations as low as .30 have been reported for the same drivers in two successive 3-year periods (8).

3. How does a driver education program restructure attitudes which seemingly are the core of an individual's successful performance? The magnitude of this problem is emphasized by the following statement made by the Advisory Group on Highway Safety Research for the President's Highway Safety Conference. "We believe attitude is important, but we are not sure just what it is or how to improve it" (4). Many times the term is loosely used to include habits, bad training and lack of discipline.

4. Is there selective bias in driver education? In other words, is the presence of a student in an elective driver education class an index of his safety attitude? Does he come from better regulated families? Conversely, is it possible that the potential accident repeater eliminates himself from driver education? This problem will persist until the outcome of a compulsory universal program can be evaluated. It is known that there is an association in frequency of accidents and juvenile delinquency.

5. Qualitative and quantitative differences in the instructional program are troublesome problems in any evaluation of effectiveness of training. A noted authority (2) has pointed out that "if the instructor is poorly equipped to give the course or lacks the basic interest to put it across, the instruction has failed before it even began." It is reported (3) that some states have instructors teaching driving who do not have a driver's license themselves.

6. Any study which compares the performance of men and women grouped together should be carefully scrutinized. More women than men take the course and men are subjected to greater exposure (8), at least in miles driven at perhaps more dangerous hours.

The National Education Association has recently released a critical review of driver education research (4). This was a rather comprehensive study and covers most of the research on driver education that has been done and is in progress throughout the nation. Although the findings were varied and sometimes contradictory, a few general conclusions seem warranted.

1. There is overwhelming evidence that the designing of a truly effective program for driver evaluation is no simple, cut and dried matter.

2. The need for a driver education and training program that is known to be effective and which remains effective is tremendous.

3. The significance of the deeply rooted nature of the accident repeater's personality and behavior problems have been frequently overlooked. This phase of investigation is much more subtle and elusive and is a good basic indicator of safe driving.

4. The various studies show indisputably that those who have had driver education have better driving records than those who have not had driver education. The extent to which this particular educational experience was causal, that is, the extent to which the better driving record resulted from the instruction, has not been so clearly shown.

A study on the effectiveness of driver education was reported before the American Association for the Advancement of Science at its annual meeting in New York City (8). Research begun in 1950 covers a five-year study initiated at Iowa State College in cooperation with the Allstate Insurance Company to determine what effect driver education has on the reported accident records of drivers.

Two samplings of 7,693 in 1950, and 7,335 in 1953 were drawn in a systematic fashion from the driver's license files of the State of Iowa. These persons were polled to determine whether or not they had received training in the schools and comparisons made of the driving records by ages.

Here are some of the findings. In spite of the fact that during the last ten-year period, 1947-1956, over six million youths have been enrolled in driver education courses in the U.S., the Iowa study would indicate that not over 5% of drivers on the road have received training in the high schools since the course was introduced in 1938. In recent years the ratio of trained to untrained drivers has been stepped up appreciably, although in this state in 1955 only about 16,000 high school students were being trained. It is estimated that during the current year approximately 18,000 to 20,000 are receiving training in about 400 high schools offering the course in Iowa. Total enrollment in the Iowa high schools in 1955-56 was 127,187. Only 83,380 were enrolled in schools offering an opportunity to take driver education. Thus it would appear that only a fractional part of future drivers in the United States, probably not nearly half, are receiving regular systematic instruction from extrapolation of Iowa data.

The following observations indicate reasonably well the status and effectiveness of driver education at present. We will list these as a set of inferences to be considered in assessing the effectiveness of driver education.

INFERENCES

1. The first is that only a small percentage of youthful drivers have an opportunity of getting a course in driver education, especially since it is given mostly at the high school level.

2. Another indication is that development of attitudes is much more important than the training of skills in driver education in the schools. It is reasonable to believe from the experimental studies that attitudes can be developed just as readily, if not easier, in the lower grades as at the higher levels. It is suggested that the classroom training be moved down into the elementary and junior high school.

3. Some persons who are trained as teachers do not seem to be putting the best effort of which they are capable into the work. Some are inadequately trained.

4. Analysis of some of the findings would lead us to the following conclusion. More attention should be given to vicarious experience, problems and emergency situations in the driver education program than has been done in the past. More time at the wheel may help a driver get a license but mar his safety record later.

5. It is fairly obvious and the inference tends to emerge from experimental studies (6) that teachers should be more highly selected and better trained. It is a mistaken notion that because one can drive a car he can teach driving. This is as fallacious as saying that anyone who speaks English can teach English.

6. When all aspects are considered the schools have only half-heartedly accepted the driver education program in a large majority of districts. This may be due partly to outside pressure from the public to have the course taught. Supervision of teaching is often left entirely in the hands of the instructor with little administrative direction.

7. From the data accumulated the effect of training seems to be more highly beneficial to women than to men. Training seems to cut women's accidents by about half but reduces men's accidents at the earlier age by only 25%. Among men it seems to wear off after the age of 21 to 22 for unaccountable reasons.

8. There seems to be only a weak association between trainee saturation of geographical areas and such criteria of successful driving as suspensions, revocations, accidents, and fatalities. The problem of what constitutes good driving has many facets.

REFERENCES

1. Allgaier, E. and Lauer, A. R., A preliminary analysis of the psycho-physical correlatives of automobile manipulation. American Jour. of Optometry. 18:49-57. February 1941.

2. Brody, Leon and Stack, Herbert J., editors, Highway safety and driver education. New York. Prentice-Hall. 1954.

3. Knight, Goodwin J., Address to President's Traffic Safety Conference, Western Region. San Francisco, California, May 31, 1956. Caldea Calendar. 3(No. 5) :16. May-June 1956.

4. National Education Association, A critical analysis of driver education research. Washington, D. C., The Association. 1957.

5. President's Highway Safety Conference, A highway safety research program. Report of the Advisory Group on Highway Safety Research. Washington, D. C. The Conference. April 1949, p. 2. (Original not examined. Quoted in 4.)

6. Siebrecht, Elmer B., Evaluation of driver education. Proc. Iowa Academy of Science. 62:479-484. 1955.

7. Stack, Herbert J., Driver education as I see it. Paper given before the Driver Education Section, National Safety Congress, October 1956.

8. Suhr, Virtus W. and Lauer, A. R., Some inferences from a five-year experimental study on the effectiveness of driver education. Paper

presented before Section Q, AAAS, Friday, December 28, 1956 in New York, N.Y.

9. Tillman, William Anthony, The psychiatric and social approach to the detection of accident prone drivers. Master's thesis. London: University of Western Ontario, 1948. (Original not examined. Quoted in 4.)

CHAPTER VII

THE EFFECTIVENESS OF DRIVER EDUCATION

INTRODUCTION

Comparatively speaking, driver education is a relatively new subject to the program of studies of the secondary schools of the nation. It originated at Pennsylvania State College in 1932 when Amos E. Neyhart started a course for students and teachers. The growth in this work has been phenomenal. One authority reports that in 1932 only six high schools offered the course. In 1956 there were about 10,000 schools giving driver education. In the past ten years 6,000,000 youngsters have been enrolled in driver education courses. About 50% of the nation's high schools now offer instruction in driving.

A number of plans for teaching the course have been used. Perhaps the most common is the method originated at Pennsylvania State College whereby an instructor takes four students in an automobile equipped with dual control pedals. One student is given behind-the-wheel instruction and allowed to practice while the other three observe. The class time is systematically allotted so that by the end of the period all four students will have spent the same amount of time behind the wheel.

Even the automobile manufacturers are disturbed about the traffic problem as it is likely to affect the market in a greater or lesser degree. Fancy tails and frills of the modern American automobile are boomeranging to some extent by market competition from smaller and simpler designed foreign cars. The little Volkswagen has developed a considerable market, not only because of its low cost of operation, but because of its simplicity of design and structural characteristics. Even the delivery services are rapidly taking over the small-size delivery vehicle in preference to the larger, elaborate and more expensive American makes of trucks. The market for the latter has been good up to date but there is every evidence that a change in trends may very well affect it adversely.

The experience of insurance companies is not the least of the reasons why these changes are taking place. In one instance an American car built with the body and frame integrated was placed in a special premium bracket by a company that writes casualty insurance. They had found their loss-ratio was much higher on this particular automobile due to the excessive cost of repairs in case of damage.

The problem arises as to how and what data should be secured to give information which will be most useful in selecting drivers. It is quite certain that no foolproof instrument is immediately forthcoming which may be used to differentiate good drivers and bad drivers. We are safe in saying that this is basically sound regardless of the type of instrument being considered. However, if the objective is to increase the feeling of responsibility of the individual driver while on the road, there are several approaches that may be made. We shall outline some of the techniques that have been considered and are being used for the evaluation of drivers. We shall consider each in turn and discuss the advantages and disadvantages of the technique considered.

Before considering any of the various categories below we should discuss two or three concepts which are of fundamental importance.

The first concept is that of reliability. Reliability refers to the consistency of a measure or test; the degree to which it can be repeated with the same results. In other words, if one gives a test today and gives it over a second time tomorrow, will he get the same, or very nearly the same, results? Reliability can be established fairly easily by one or more administrations of a test to a given population, correlating the two results. Unless a test is reliable there is very little reason for attempting to use it.

The second concept is that of validity which refers to whether the test measures what it is supposed to measure. For example, an item which is supposed to indicate carelessness, but which has no relation to carelessness when tested under experimental conditions, is said to have slight, if any, validity. Validities, of course, may vary but a statistical index of comparison is available for indicating the degree to which any test 'or item is valid. Of course the validity cannot be expected to be perfect and some allowance must be made. In general, the statistical index of validity may be lower than the statistical index of reliability without undue concern on the part of the experimenter or user.

Another concept is that of objectivity. Objectivity refers to the form of marking which can be scored by different examiners to obtain the same results. Or it may be that the same examiner grades the same test at different times. He should get the same results both times.

ATTITUDES

Most authorities at the present time consider attitudes as the most important factor in safe driving. The term is used rather loosely and very often a clear distinction is not made between attitudes, habits, knowledge, and certain other aspects of driving.

Attitude is actually an old term and has been used by some psychologists as synonymous with posture. It is a bent or tendency to do a certain thing under given stimulation and is largely a mental concept. In other words, if one has a mental tendency or bent which would predispose him to act in a certain way, it is assumed that certain verbalizations can be set down or selected which will be accepted by the person being tested in proportion to the degree of subjective feeling which he has toward the concept. It is further assumed that such a concept will dictate to some extent one's reactions under a given condition. Basically this is the theory underlying the measurement of all attitudes regardless of what technique may be used.

Attitude measurement has been used in vocational guidance and in certain other areas using tests with various formats. Some have used questions which would tend to bring out the individual's degree of feeling with respect to a given concept. Others have used statements or short phrases for a similar purpose.

Strong (6), in his vocational guidance test, has selected state-ments of situations to which the individual responds by marking (L) for like, (I) for indifferent, and (D) for dislike. Likert has used questions which tend to focalize the individual's attention on a certain concept that he marks as acceptable in some degree. Siebrecht (5), using the same format, has developed an attitude test which has been used to some extent for the measurement of driver's attitudes. Remmers has worked on various types of edu-cational attitude measurement using a similar type of technique. Thurstone (8), working on attitudes toward races, has used statements which are selected and marked as best suit the indi-vidual's bent or inclination. Lauer (3) and others have adapted some of the techniques of these authors, notably those of Strong, in a type of attitude test of drivers.

It suffices to say that all of these devices are subject to some manipulation or management on the part of the person taking the test to alter his record. Attempts have been made to secure an indicator of this tendency, but in the field of driving this has not been completely worked out to the satisfaction of investiga-tors. Many other tests or inventories have been developed for specific purposes, mostly through asking the person's opinion about certain aspects of the trait to be measured.

PERSONALITY TESTS

Closely allied to the whole field of attitude testing in relation to any particular aspect of behavior is that of personality. In fact, personality manifests itself largely through the attitudes of a person. In other words, one's attitudes are indicators of his per-sonality type. Therefore, there are a number of personality tests which have been only slightly explored with respect to driving. One is the Cattell (1) 16 PF Personality Test which was studied by Suhr (7). Three or four categories in this inventory seemed to give some promise of being indicators of accident susceptibility. More needs to be done in this area. Likewise, the Minnesota Multi-Phasic might be conceived as a possibility for use in driver classification. However, it is rather involved and much too long for practical use in this connection. In other words, a test must be reasonable in length and require a relatively short period for administration to be considered.

The Thurstone Temperament Schedule and the Cattell 16 PF Personality Inventory fit this need reasonably well, but have not been sufficiently explored to establish facts. A considerable amount of research needs to be done on both of these instruments before a conclusion can be reached with respect to their use for this purpose. Personality is complex and more needs to be learned regarding the relationship between personality types and actions. Perhaps Cattell has done more to relate these factors than anyone else in the field. We need to know how an individual will react under a given situation and the likelihood with which such behavior will lead to accidents, or the elimination of accidents, while driving. In other words, this is a fruitful field for research and needs to be approached from a basic point of view, rather than being studied as an applied phase. The long range gains from such studies have great possibilities, but the immediate application of the principles would need considerable research before the desired answers are known.

TRAFFIC LAWS

Motor vehicle departments and many others place most emphasis upon traffic laws. If one knows the law he passes the examination. If he does not know the law, he does not pass. It seems reasonable that this is a valid way of thinking. It might be said that if one does not know the rules regarding pedestrians and traffic he will be unable to avoid pedestrians while driving. One cannot play baseball if he does not know the rules. This is certainly true but to reverse the reasoning would not necessarily hold true. One might know all of the rules of the game and yet not be willing to follow them, or not be able to play the game. Undoubtedly umpires know the rules of the game better than most other persons, but to put them in as substitute players at a critical time would probably be disastrous. Therefore, we should not put all our eggs in one basket. We should not depend entirely upon knowledge of traffic laws or rules of driving for establishing the degree of risk which a driver will take. This is particularly unwise when the reliability and validity of the tests concerned are not satisfactory. In other words, unless the road law test has a satisfactory reliability it may reveal very little. Validity and reliability are somewhat related and a low reliability tends to indicate a low validity in tests of this type.

DRIVING INFORMATION AND KNOWLEDGE

A category which is rarely included in the driver's license examination is driver knowledge or know-how. This would involve rules of safety and traffic manipulation somewhat independent of the rules of traffic as stated in the law books. In other words, it covers certain elements of courtesy as well as knowledge of driving. It is somewhat related to attitudes as one is likely to maneuver his car as he feels regardless of the coded laws of traffic. This has been shown very well in studies of speed signs. A speed sign setting the speed limits in a given area is not followed unless it fits the driving habits of the public. Changing a sign from 45 to 35 or 25 miles an hour will not greatly reduce the speed. However, inserting a curve in a straight section of road or tangent will tend to reduce speed considerably for most drivers. This is not invariable as some do drive too fast and may miss the curve. Many one-car accidents are actually running-off-the-road types, usually at curves. Several sets of figures show this to be about one in three. Thirty years ago about the same results were obtained.

Driving knowledge, or know-how, can be fairly accurately measured and has been found in studies made for the Army to be a good indicator of one's driving ability (4). Although the criteria of accidents is relatively weak and unreliable it does show that driving knowledge is important in safe driving. A good test of driving knowledge is perhaps the most dependable test that can be developed at the present time from all points of view. It is freer from the criticisms that might be leveled at it than perhaps any one of the others cited except a well designed objective test on legal items. The latter is open to question in many ways.

The difficulty in the development of a satisfactory driving knowledge test is the format used. Items tend to be confusing and must be selected with the utmost care. Items must not indicate the possible answers, that is, be too obvious. On the other hand, the answers must not be confusing. It would perhaps be best that each question have only one answer, and the answer should be very specific and reasonable. The items must be selected with particular care and the form very carefully analyzed when compiled. This is the only way validity can be established in the selection of driving knowledge items. To one making a test, what appears at first to be an excellent item may well seem very unsatisfactory after careful scrutiny by giving the test to someone else. It takes much thought and careful selection of items to make up a good knowledge test. It usually has to be given to a group of persons and scored before certain inherent defects may be located and eliminated.

PSYCHOPHYSICAL TESTS

A type of test for drivers, which has been particularly appealing to many persons, is the so-called psychophysical tests. These include a group of tests of functions related to driving such as vision, field of vision, reaction time, strength, distance judgment, activity, and other such measurements. These tests are all quite reliable and valid in and of themselves. They do not always, however, guarantee that the performance of the person will be on a par with his capacity to perform. They are more nearly measures of basic capacity and will tell what a person *ought* to do rather than what he will do.

One weakness of the psychophysical tests overall is that they must be given to individuals, one at a time, and require too much time to be administered. The known psychophysical tests which are in common use take possibly an hour for each individual in order for him to finish each test and make an evaluation of his record. This may be justified in a training course as it demonstrates to the driver many things about himself which he does not know otherwise. It also dramatizes certain good practices in driving. However, it has been found that a good pencil-and-paper test will do a better selection job (4) at less cost in time and effort.

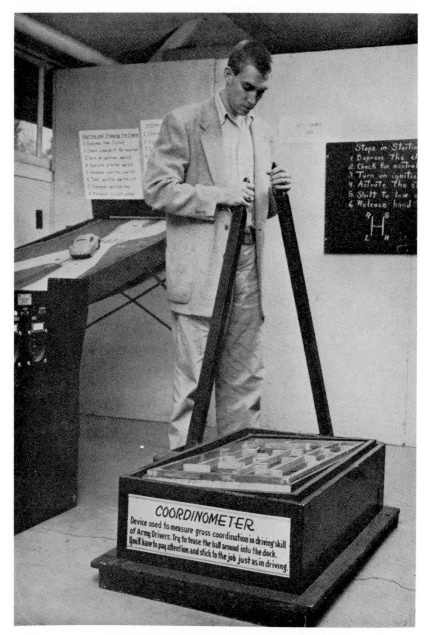

Fig. 6. Coordinometer. Gross coordination was used to classify Army driving personnel and was found to be one of the most effective.

In an employment situation where only a few drivers are taken through at a time, perhaps two or three, it can be handled very successfully and is a great asset in the selection procedure. However, for a motor vehicle department it would be practically impossible and this is one of the reasons for a proposal that the driver's licensing system be changed to delegate the evaluation of many traits to persons other than the licensing examiners. An eye physician can make a vision check very quickly and include many of the things which a license examiner never thought of checking. It would seem more practical to have each person applying for a license go to his regular eye physician and get the examination he needs to become a safe manipulator of a car as he does in the case of aviation. The Civil Aeronautics Authority designates certain individuals to make such measurements and report to them. They act merely as inspectors and review the examination given by a specialist.

By and large we have found (4) experimentally that one can give a 30- or 40-minute written group test to drivers and secure the same information regarding their abilities as drivers as with psychophysical tests which can be given to only one person. Much economy in time may be obtained in the administration of the tests in this way. Admittedly the psychophysicals will give the driver more information about himself and probably be of more value from an educational point of view. We are thinking here of the amount of information the examiner gets out of the time spent in checking up on the driver.

A COMBINATION OF FACTORS

We should indicate the possibility of combining all of these factors into one instrument of measurement. Some attempts have been made to do this with reasonable success. In our studies 40 items were selected from a battery of 162 items which had been taken from numerous categories known to have some validity. These were reduced to 40 items by a process known as cross validation after giving them to about 3,000 persons. Cross validation refers to the administration of the tests a second time, or to another group, to determine whether the test holds up the second time given. In this case it did hold up reasonably well for certain items, but when tried out in the shorter form the reliability did not seem to be as satisfactory as was desired. It might be that the short form weakened the test.

Other items have been picked which seem to be indicative of safe driving and which have been found to differentiate in some degree between good and bad drivers. These have not been tried out sufficiently in cross validation to determine whether or not they would or would not be useful. The only way to accomplish this is by an experimental procedure. This would mean that the forms as now setup should be used on a group whose records are known to determine whether the instrument as a whole will be effective or whether certain items are more useful than others in selecting accident cases.

SUMMARY

After carefully considering all of the six categories it would seem that four have possibilities for exploration on an experimental basis which should yield some rather interesting information for the driver's licensing bureaus as well as for insurance companies. We state specifically and categorically this is an experimental problem and those who would enter into it should do so with the understanding that the by-products of the study may perhaps be of more immediate value to them than the application of the specific results from the test which may be obtained. In other words, there are things which need to be known in general and which would orient future investigators and persons who wish to apply results, rather than to develop specific selection instruments which can be applied to situations for the solutions of their problems.

If any progress is to be made in this field, and if we can make any comparisons with other fields, the only way by which such information or progress can be obtained is through experimentation.

Considering the six avenues of approach suggested and the six types of instruments which might be incorporated into such study, it is the judgment of the writer that the order of approach for practical application might well be as follows. It would be most practical to develop first *a driving information or knowledge test* which would have sufficient reliability and validity for use in any particular case of driver selection. No test used currently is satisfactory for this purpose.

The second choice of instruments would be the sixth, or a *combination* of factors, which would involve considerable experimental work in order to evaluate selected factors used in the form. So far as needs are concerned we would next mention *traffic attitudes* which need a very thorough and exacting study starting from the ground up. It is undoubtedly a rich field of investigation but must be approached in a scientific manner with an aim of getting information that would be of most value to the people who wish to use the study.

Personality tests would probably rank fourth on the list in the need of further exploration and possibilities from the experimental point of view. A careful study should be made, first, with respect to the personality test itself and type used; and second, with respect to its validation. Many such tests are unwieldy and too long for ordinary administration.

The fifth approach, probably of most importance, would be the study of how knowledge of *traffic laws* predict traffic accidents. This cluster of approaches would seem to form the nucleus of several problems for research that would have far-reaching results and effects on the selection of drivers in the future. The whole problem of driver selection is in a more or less chaotic state and needs careful study and further investigation.

REFERENCES

1. Cattell, R. B., 16 PF Test, 1949, I.P.A.T., Champaign, Illinois.
2. Dennis, Wayne, Readings in General Psychology, 1949, Prentice-Hall, pp. 227-234.
3. Lauer, A. R., Iowa State College Driver Reaction Inventory, 1956, The Iowa State College Press.
4. Lauer, A. R., Comparison of group paper-and-pencil tests with certain psychophysical tests for measuring driving aptitude of Army personnel. 1955. Jour. of Applied Psychol., 39, No. 5, 318-321.

5. Siebrecht, Elmer B., Measuring Driver Attitudes. Research Contribution to Center for Safety Education. Safety Education, 1941, No. 3.

6. Strong, E. K., Vocational Interest Test. Stanford University Press.

7. Suhr, V. W., The Cattell 16 PF test as a prognosticator of accident susceptibility. Proc. Iowa Acad. of Science, 60, 558-561.

8. Thurstone, L. I. (see Dennis, pp. 405-414).

CHAPTER VIII

SELECTION AND TRAINING OF DRIVERS

In 1940, the National Education Association published their *Yearbook* covering many phases of driver education. The committee reporting changed the name from driver training to driver education. The implications were that driver education is broader in nature and emphasizes attitudes, knowledge of safe driving and similar aspects rather than merely preparing the learner for his state driver's examination.

THE NATURE OF DRIVER EDUCATION

Driver education has been greatly influenced by the methods developed by Amos E. Neyhart of Pennsylvania State University. His method is very practical and has been widely successful and highly popularized. The fact of its workableness and popularity, however, does not necessarily argue for highest efficiency. Some educators have considered the cost per pupil as high. The procedure in general is to start the driver just before the age or period at which he may wish to secure a driver's license. This seems to be the logical time to train a driver. Four students are taken as a group in a car and with varying amounts of classroom instruction are carried through at least 15 or 30 hours of behind-the-wheel practice. Schools usually give the recommended one-semester course for credit. This requires around 50 clock hours for all types of instruction.

Other schools such as Lane Technical High School in Chicago use "dummy" driving mechanisms in a large classroom or laboratory where the students react to lights mounted on a panel for learning mechanisms and proper movements for operating

111

the controls. Starts and stops are made and the lights indicate wrong movements or maneuvers. At a later stage motion pictures of driving situations are shown which the students are to follow. Finally practice is given in actual driving. In some schools the instruction is limited to classroom work. In Detroit each student is put in a car by himself as early as possible, with an instructor observing from a vantage point on the field. The relative merits of these various methods have not been thoroughly investigated.

In general, driver training consists of three phases: (1) practice behind-the-wheel, (2) reading and class discussion on certain phases of safe driving, and (3) evaluation of performance by means of various objective and subjective testing techniques.

HOW DRIVER TRAINING CAN BE IMPROVED

First and foremost is the matter of properly trained instructors which has not been emphasized sufficiently. In an attempt to get the driver education movement started in the schools, the American Automobile Association and others have offered 40 hour training courses for driving instructors (1). This has resulted in the development of a sufficient corps of teachers to take care of the demand in most instances. A successful driving instructor needs such traits as: enthusiasm, mechanical knowledge, and a desire to produce results. In some instances instructors are recruited from among poorly prepared teachers. A young man was sent in to take the course at our school who did not have a driver's license. He was expected to learn enough to get his driver's license in a two-week training period. In addition he was to learn enough to teach the youngsters whom he would have in his classes, some of whom may have driven, perhaps illegally, but enough to be quite proficient at the wheel. His lack of enthusiasm and poor personality handicapped him further. He was not accepted.

SOME LIAISON NEEDED BETWEEN SCHOOLS AND LAW ENFORCEMENT GROUPS

For several reasons this is highly desirable and necessary. One is the need for good public relations and mutual understanding of objectives. The problem of safe driving is one of teaching, and whether law enforcement personnel or teachers are involved, close cooperation between the groups is highly essential and mutually beneficial. The teacher must know the problems of the law enforcement officer in order to be able to do an effective job in teaching. The law enforcement officer, on the other hand, must keep in touch with teaching methods and be sympathetic toward driver education. Teachers should emphasize that the law enforcement officer is placed on the highway to assist the driver and to protect the public at large against poor driving habits and irresponsible persons who may not be qualified to drive. The driver-education instructor must appreciate the problem of the traffic engineer and the law enforcement officer in order to teach the essentials of good driving. It might even be a good plan to have every teacher of driving serve for three months or so on the highway patrol as a special project for which he might receive credit.

THE VALUE OF THE DRIVER'S EXAMINATION

The examination for a driver's license may be considered from several points of view. In some states the reasons cited for a driver's license are not in agreement with the fundamental purposes of the examination. It should be given solely to help make the driver safer and to increase the safety of the driving public. In some cases, however, the licensing authorities have been sidetracked by the following narrow, short range objectives: (1) to obtain a complete registry of all drivers; (2) to conform with practices in other states; (3) to make identification of the drivers easier upon arrest; and (4) to raise revenue.

Although the first three reasons are legitimate and need not be questioned, they are secondary and would result from any adequate licensing plan. The fourth reason, however, is entirely unjustified and should be legislated out of existence, especially when the money received does not benefit the driver directly and is not used for purposes of developing a driver-improvement program.

From a psychological point of view the driver's license helps to place responsibility for safe driving upon the driver himself.

He is responsible to the state and to the public for safe manipulation of a motor vehicle. Unless a driver's license accomplishes this, it's use for other purposes is hardly justified.

In order to be most effective in placing responsibility for safe operation of a motor vehicle there should be different grades of licensing. Thus, a young driver should have some form of probational or junior license for a certain time during his learning period. His privileges would be restricted in certain instances, especially if he becomes involved in an accident or some type of violation. A driver does seem to pass through various stages, such as apprentice, journeyman, and finally master driver. It is doubtful whether the driver's license will accomplish its best results until every state has some form of graded licensing system which will help tighten the responsibility placed upon the driver.

When considering applications of psychology to enforcement policy it must be predicated on a fairly sound basis if it is to be effective. To set down specific rules to follow is very difficult as conditions vary from situation to situation. We can only sketch some of the general principles or approaches which may be used to influence the behavior of persons so that a minimum of actual force will be necessary to accomplish the results desired. In any psychological approach one of the fundamental principles is that of using novelty and change in the technique. It is necessary to constantly change the approach to enforcement or the public becomes wary and the method ineffective. Drivers tend to ignore and even try to outguess enforcement agencies.

RESULTS OBTAINED THROUGH PUBLICITY

By publicity we mean informing the public of the conditions that exist and of certain types of activities that are being carried out to increase safety and accident prevention. Publicity may be secured through talks to civic groups, service clubs, schools, etc. It can be a part of the programs of safety councils, junior chambers of commerce, schools, churches, and the like. Such devices as posters, stickers on cars, accident bulletins and news releases are typical. Radio and television offer excellent facilities for publicity in the way of bringing highway hazards and enforcement objectives to the individual driver. Iowa at one time adopted the policy of displaying on each patrol car the number of persons killed to date. This one factor may be a valuable aspect of publicity.

STRATEGY AS A PSYCHOLOGICAL ASPECT OF ENFORCEMENT

"Spot enforcement" and other types of strategy have been used to help increase public safety and to make enforcement more effective. Some states have used white vehicles so that the patrol car may be noticed more readily, assuming that to be effective the patrol is kept moving about the highway. This, of course, has another side since in some instances drivers may spot the patrol car easier and perhaps try to play "cat and mouse" with the enforcement group. Which of these is most effective has not been studied experimentally to the writer's knowledge and perhaps some controlled research would be enlightening. It would seem, therefore, that patrol cars should be of two types — marked and unmarked.

The form of strategy known as "spot enforcement" is purely of a psychological nature. The patrol concentrates on certain areas and does a rather thorough job, then jumps to some other location, presumably where accidents have been most frequent. The public is uncertain as to where the law will strike next. It should be the function of the accident statistics division of the driver's licensing bureau to locate areas of the state which are having the most accidents at a given period. The patrol can then take these data and lay out their plan of attack to reduce accidents.

Some states use another type of strategy. They do not paint their patrol cars an unusual color, but have only a modest identification or seal on the doors. Then when a football game or other event resulting in a concentration of traffic is anticipated the highway patrol delegates a number of its patrolmen to drive through traffic and mingle with it, or to park at the side of the road so that their patrol cars can be noticed by every passing motorist. Since the patrol cars are in evidence, motorists are more alert to the possibilities of arrest, should they violate traffic regulations or ordinances, and hence they refrain from doing so. Other illustrations of strategy could be given, but these are sufficient to emphasize the need for strategy.

SECURING ENFORCEMENT THROUGH GOOD WILL

Perhaps no other factor in enforcement is more effective than that of public good will toward the enforcement agencies. And probably no other approach requires the application of psychology more than that of securing such good will. In England it is said that the police have the respect of the public to the extent that when a policeman is taken advantage of by a gang, the public pitches in to help the officer. Unfortunately, in America, we can hardly say that this is true. It may even be said, somewhat facetiously, that the public is more likely to take the part of the culprit rather than that of the police. This may stem from undesirable police methods used in the past. Present day highway patrols are trained in another type of school, and represent a different type of law enforcement. Needless to say, methods have changed. However, without proper respect of the public it is very difficult to secure enforcement. A reason for the regulation is necessary.

The traffic officer and safety engineer must constantly be on guard against pseudo-remedies and panaceas for accident control. Anyone having followed the field of safety for a period of time is aware of numerous cranks who have developed "cracked" notions, "fads" and gadgets guaranteed to eliminate accidents. One of the prime indicators of an amateur in safety is emphasis on a single remedy.

REGARDING VISION

It is very difficult to show a high correlation between poor vision and accidents as a whole. Perhaps if every accident were traced down, and its precise cause determined along with other existing facts and circumstances, a much higher relationship would be found. What is not generally considered is the fact that the person who has some defect is very likely to compensate for this defect and thus offset the additional hazard. At one time it was thought that a large number of accidents were due to color blindness. This idea has been thoroughly studied and found not true.

A common fallacy of the present day is that the driver's eyes must be fixed on the pavement at all times for safety. Perhaps nothing is farther from the truth. Obviously a person who is leisurely driving and turning his head to examine the landscape without reference to where he is going, is a hazard. It appears from certain observations which have been made that keeping the eyes fixed in a given position will tend to induce fatigue and drowsiness. When one is reading he becomes drowsy unless occasionally he looks off into the distance to rest his eyes. In driving the same is true. It is necessary that a driver look off to the side to some extent and at periodic intervals. From studies conducted in the Iowa State College Driving Research Laboratory, it appears that anything happening within an angle of 0 to 30 degrees to each side has little affect when it is of a casual nature. Beyond this range there is practically no effect. If some very unusual occurrence such as a burning house, an automobile rolling down an embankment, or some other such condition exists, perhaps this does tend to distract the driver and result in a hazard. However, any ordinary kind of stimulus object which is not moving, and is not likely to interfere with or run across the path of the driver, seems to aid in keeping him awake and at a higher level of efficiency, thus increasing safety.

Another aspect of the problem is that if one's eyes are fixed on the road he will not notice what is going on around him. He may not notice traffic coming from the right or from the left, nor be aware of other hazards which may move across his path. Therefore, it is safe to say that the eyes must be roving and constantly searching for stimuli which will need to be evaluated in terms of safety. To restrict normal stimulation in the field of vision, or movement of the eyes, is to impose extra hazards.

The common theory of highway designers now is that all types of interference, visual and otherwise, should be reduced to the minimum on superhighways. This has been carried out to such an extent that it is defeating its own purpose. All are agreed that right angle traffic should be eliminated on superhighways. Certainly this is an excellent principle to follow and has accomplished much to reduce accident hazards. However, the idea that the driver is perfectly safe and in no danger whatever, by virtue of eliminating cross traffic, is far from the truth. He lulls himself to sleep with a false sense of security and therefore frequently gets into trouble. It would appear that some type of exciting stimulation should be introduced along the highway periodically in order that the driver may be kept at his highest level of efficiency.

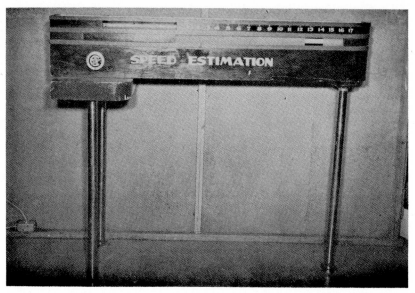

Fig. 7. Speed Estimation. In this apparatus, a small car travels across the opening and behind the numbers. The panel shown just below the numbers is lighted; when the car passes a preselected number, the light goes off. The subject is to judge the position of the car at that instant. (Courtesy, Chicago Motor Club.)

NOISE AND OTHER TYPES OF SENSORY STIMULATION AND HIGHWAY SAFETY

The place of noise in the safe operation of a motor vehicle has been widely discussed and various theories proposed. An outstanding authority in the field of safety was at one time very much opposed to car radios. There is no valid evidence, however, that a radio, per se, has ever influenced a driver so as to cause an accident. Of course, it would not be correct to say that it has never happened since many accidents do occur without a known reason. It is conceivable that under certain conditions a radio does interfere. On the other hand, it may provide the necessary stimulation that is lacking in the environment through the visual sense.

There is a question as to whether the absence of noise, as such, has any deleterious effect upon driving. It has been reported that increased quietness of commercial vehicles has been associated with an increase in accidents. No studies, however, are available that show the effects of smooth pavements and quiet running cars on the efficiency of driving. In general there may be a positive correlation between quietness of operation and accidents, but no one knows to what extent such relationship, if any, holds.

HIGHWAY HYPNOSIS

This subject has received considerable attention recently in various newspapers, periodicals and magazines. Again there is little experimental evidence to support the distraction theory. Some studies from the Iowa State College Laboratory indicate that superimposing stimuli upon a normal driving situation, up to a certain point, tends to stimulate performance, at least no loss in efficiency was noted. In other words, driving efficiency may be increased by introducing certain auxiliary stimuli into the situation.

The term "highway hypnosis" is probably somewhat overworked as a cause of accidents. It is more nearly correct to speak of lowered attention due to the lack of adequate stimulation. However, there is a possibility that fixation of the eyes on the pavement or a taillight may produce a drowsy condition which does result in the driver momentarily falling asleep. Every driver, especially in his younger days, has experienced this phenomenon. Whether it is hypnosis, lowered attention, drowsiness, or something else, the results are the same, namely an increased number of accidents on the highway due to insufficient stimulation of the driver.

PSYCHOLOGICAL VERSUS LEGAL RESPONSIBILITY

Only a few decades ago the insane were whipped for the purpose of driving evil spirits from them on the theory that they were fully responsible for their acts and that sufficient punishment would restore proper behavior. This theory is no longer held. In fact, we have even begun to recognize a criminal as not entirely responsible for his acts.

In a similar way, we are beginning to recognize that passing through stop-signs or stop-lights is not entirely a deliberate act. In one test situation during the Ford Good Driver League finals in 1940 and 1941, it was found that approximately 90% of the contestants, when put in a test situation involving a stop-light, missed the signal, even though a $5,000 scholarship was at stake. Since they were instructed to observe all signals, there is no reason to believe that they deliberately missed the lights. It is probably safe to say that a large percentage of other violations are unintentional and not willful. They happen because of poor training, bad habits, lack of understanding of traffic situations and of traffic signals themselves.

Recently, when driving in New York City, the writer was faced with the choice, as he was moving up along the West-Side Drive, of going through the Holland Tunnel, the Lincoln Tunnel, or of moving on up further to the George Washington Bridge. The two tunnels were very clearly marked, but directions to the bridge were confusing. Therefore due to inadequate route markings, the driver hesitated, slowed traffic and without a doubt riled some of the drivers behind him. Although the driver's response was somewhat inadequate in that situation, there was nothing intentional about it. Therefore it is a question whether one should be held responsible for acts that are involuntary.

These few instances help to explain to some extent what is meant by psychological responsibility as contrasted with legal responsibility. Quite obviously it is the latter that is most frequently recognized and accepted by law enforcement agencies. When psychological responsibility, however, becomes better accepted and we are able to differentiate it from legal responsibility, law enforcement practices will without doubt change considerably.

Psychology is just beginning to be considered an important factor in traffic engineering. Some have approached the problem from the standpoint of the driver. Others have done research on the effects of location of "right-turn" signs, types of letters, etc. More recently radar speed detectors have been used widely, partly for psychological effect. Following a very effective publicity drive, a radar meter used in Des Moines greatly reduced the speed on city streets. The public is full alerted to the fact that many new instruments are available and are being used. Signs indicating that a street or road is patrolled by radar speed detection methods puts the public on guard. Knowing that the equipment cannot always be observed, they become cautious and speed is slowed down enormously. In one instance on the New Jersey Turnpike a speed detector hidden from view even slowed traffic coming from the opposite direction, which is rather remarkable.

USE OF BASIC PRINCIPLES OF PSYCHOLOGY

The application of psychology is best effected when certain basic principles are understood and recognized. Certain simple principles must be kept in mind by the traffic engineer at all times. One of these is that an observer cannot perceive all the things presented in the range of vision. This has been known for decades through tachistoscopic and other studies in the field of psychology. The sooner traffic engineers recognize this fact the better road markings will be.

Another principle that must be recognized is that of the necessity of optimal stimulation. Stimuli must not be presented too rapidly nor too slowly. Neither must it be too sparse, or too concentrated. A certain in-between rate is most suitable for the average person. The principle is almost universal in its application and relates to quantity and quality, as well as to the rate of stimulus presentation.

A third principle that must be recognized is that of individual differences. Not all drivers can drive at 60 miles an hour with safety. Although some may drive 50 miles an hour with safety, at 20 miles an hour they may become unsafe drivers. It is equally true that many who drive 15 or 20 miles an hour safely are unsafe at 50. The principle of individual differences in abilities must be recognized and practiced in traffic direction and enforcement.

THE TRAINING OF TRAFFIC CONTROL PERSONNEL

The effective implementation of any program must be done through properly trained personnel. It would be unfair to expect every traffic enforcement officer to be a college graduate or to have had courses in psychology. It is, however, well within the realm of feasibility to give every traffic officer a short course in the principles of psychology and their application. It is our thought that within the next few years much more of this type of training will be given.

SUMMARY AND RECOMMENDATIONS

In this chapter we have tried to summarize some of the salient features of the psychological approach to traffic engineering. The matter of public relations has been presented as an important phase of traffic control. Certain psychological hazards also have been cited which are associated with the age, the mental state, the judgment and intelligence of the driver, to show how they may be related to accident susceptibility. Psychological hazards that stem from defective road markings and improper training of drivers were also considered, and other miscellaneous mental hazards were pointed out.

Driver education was discussed only to the extent that its function is misunderstood by some persons. Suggestions were given, however, as to how it can be improved through cooperation between the schools and law enforcement groups.

Enforcement practices were considered and it was shown that publicity can be of great help in enforcement. Considerable emphasis was given to strategy, good will, and public relations since all enforcement must be based on a willingness of those policed to follow the dictates of those doing the enforcing.

Certain faulty theories of highway and safety engineering were pointed out, such as those relating to methods of placing signs and other stimuli along the roadsides. It has been assumed that the removal of all stimulating objects from the right-of-way, including cross traffic and pedestrian travel, will reduce accidents to zero or to very near the minimum. This is not entirely true of superhighways. It must be remembered that the roadway is not usually the cause of the accident.

Perhaps sometime in the future every driver will be required to secure a special permit, record of safe performance or proficiency certificate, in addition to his license before he will be allowed to enter the superhighway's toll gates. A point system of merit rating might well be used more widely in various states. Then before a driver would be allowed to enter a superhighway he would be required to show his driver's license showing his point rating. Although some drivers would object to this, others would be willing to cooperate. Some gradation of licensing is needed.

Finally, psychological principles need to be applied in the field of traffic engineering. Traffic personnel trained in such principles have demonstrated that they do a superior job. However, much more needs to be learned about the psychological aspects of traffic engineering before spectacular advances can be made in this area.

REFERENCES

1. A.A.A., Sportsmanlike Driving, 3rd ed. 1955, pp. 478.
2. Halsey, Max, Let's Drive Right. Scott-Foresman and Co., 1958, pp. 307.
3. Lauer, A. R., Learning to Drive Safely. Burgess Publishing Co., 1949, pp. 145.
4. Lauer, A. R., Tomorrow's Drivers. Lyons and Carnahan, 1958, pp. 176.
5. Whitney, Albert W., Man and the Motor Car, 5th ed. Prentice-Hall, 1957, pp. 358.

CHAPTER IX

VISION AND DRIVING

There are at least three factors in safe driving directly dependent on good vision:

1. People or obstructions and road signs are more likely to be seen in sufficient time to avoid accidents.

2. With good vision, there is less danger of overdriving the headlights at night.

3. A person with good vision is more at ease on the highway, hence quick decisions are not hindered by inadequate sight.

STATISTICS ON VISION

The relationship between poor vision and accidents undoubtedly will always have to be accepted on laboratory findings. Accident statistics seldom trace causes far enough to uncover visual faults, chiefly because few traffic bureaus are equipped with personnel or instruments to examine the people involved.

The Driving Research Laboratory at Iowa State College has conducted research for the Motorists' Vision Committee of the American Optometric Association for many years. After examining many thousands of persons in the driving clinic they group the visual levels of drivers into seven classifications. In this system the letters "A" to "E" have been used to rate vision in classifying visual acuity, color vision, glare, depth perception, and field of vision. Under each classification, except color vision, this table will be repeated with recommendations for standards and suggestions about those who fall below the safety levels.

In Table I are the letter ratings as adapted to vision. The proportions were determined through research, in which the vision of thousands of drivers was checked. It describes the percentages found among persons usually applying for a motor vehicle license.

TABLE I

VISUAL CLASSIFICATION BY LETTER RATINGS

A	5%	of examinees having very superior vision
B	10%	of those just below those having "A" rating—about 20/20
C+	20%	of those who are slightly better than average
C	30%	of those in the middle of the distribution
C—	20%	of those who are just below average
D	10%	of those next to the "E" group
E	5%	of those having least satisfactory vision—abnormal

Table I shows that 35% of the driving public is quite definitely below average. At least 15% of this group have vision that may render them dangerous when they drive a car. A restricted operator's license can handle this group, especially when they know their visual limitations. Persons with visual deficiencies who are warned and properly corrected may drive as well as others. However, accident repeaters should be required to report for re-examination. This is not being done in some states. Progress is being made through the driver improvement program which re-examines problem cases.

RECOGNITION

While an automobile driver may recognize a car as a vehicle and a pedestrian as a person, it does not follow that he truly sees them. The amount of acuity required for such limited vision as recognition may be far below what is necessary for clear identification of cars and people. At driving speed vision drops in the vicinity of 40% from stationary vision.

Such commonplace road hazards as bridge abutments or large broken places in the pavement call for a higher level of vision than mere recognition. The same standard of vision is needed to interpret accurately the signs and signals that are an essential part of our highway system.

As a driver moves along the road or street he must interpret the various situations and conditions as they arise. In traffic, especially, action must follow quickly after the first glance for efficiency. Quickness and accuracy of perception depend on vision, as does reaction time. A person with good vision sees *more quickly and easily*. No time is lost in taking a second or reassuring look; he knows what he sees at the first glance. Drivers with lowered visual acuity or other defects take longer to decide what to do and longer to act upon their decisions than do those with good vision.

PERCEPTION

Perception is the interpretation of stimuli from any sense organ. It depends partly upon perfection of the sensory channels. Many drivers have no idea of their own visual inefficiencies. However, when tests show them what is wrong they usually are anxious to cooperate. Therefore, it should be one of the chief purposes of the license examiner to convince the driver of the need for being careful in the particular way in which he needs to use caution.

Visual efficiency contributes to driving in manifold ways, such as:

1. It makes accurate reading of markers possible.

2. It gives the driver a feeling of security and assurance which reduces fatigue.

3. It relieves actual physical and mental strain by making driving easier.

4. It lengthens the perceptual distance (not sight distance) a very important factor recognized by highway and safety engineers.

5. It tends to act, automatically, in control of the car even though the driver may be temporarily distracted.

All these factors enter into the perception or recognition of danger while in traffic.

REACTION TIME

After visual perception of any object or person there is a measurable time required for normal reactions to the visual stimuli. In other words, when a driver sees a car infringing on his own right of way, there is an unavoidable period of time required for his mind to tell his arms and feet to turn the wheel and put on the brakes, or speed up out of danger, as the case may be.

Reaction time, consequently, is tied in closely with every aspect of safe driving. In stopping a car going 20 miles an hour, the average reaction time of a driver with good vision causes him to move about 22 feet beyond the place where his eyes first saw the danger, *before* he applies the brakes. Traveling 40 miles an hour, this same driver would be 44 feet down the road before stepping on the brake, and at 60 miles an hour the reaction time lag is estimated to be at least 66 feet. The poorer the vision, the slower the visual reaction time, which emphasizes again why drivers should have good vision. The figures given are by Ford Motor Company. We are inclined to think they are underestimates. It takes the average person 1/2 to 3/4 of a second to react. A car travels nearly 1 1/2 times the miles an hour in feet per second. One can easily calculate the distances for a given m.p.h.

SPEED

The speed each driver may safely travel, within the legal limits, should be governed by his vision, provided other factors, such as road and condition of the car, are equal, because vision is one of the most important controls that govern emergency stopping. Unless the eye sees and identifies danger far enough in advance of actual contact to stop the car, a collision is often the result.

Under the very best road conditions with good handling, dry pavement, clear weather, and unobstructed vision, a car going 25 miles an hour travels about 63 feet before it can be stopped. Under the same conditions, a car traveling 50 miles an hour covers 220 feet before the wheels stop rolling. When the speed reaches 70 miles an hour, the driver finds himself 436 feet, or more, beyond the place where he first applied the brakes. These are conservative distances and often are exceeded. On gravel all stopping distances are increased 1 1/2 times the distance for dry pavement. Snow doubles the stopping distance and ice may require over five times the stopping distance necessary for dry pavement. The latter are all approximations.

When the driver is handicapped by having less than 20/40 vision, these stopping distances, both for clear and stormy weather, are greatly increased. The average traffic sign with five-inch letters can be read at about 280 feet by the driver who has 20/20 Snellen vision. The driver with 20/40 vision, which is the minimum that the American Optometric Association advises, must approach to within half the distance of the sign before he can read it. The driver with only 20/50 vision must approach to 90 feet before he can see the sign clearly. Therefore, at 60 miles an hour, a driver with 20/50 vision will be 90 feet from such a sign before he sees it clearly and, under the best road conditions, he will be about 200 feet beyond the sign before his car stops. For this reason, if no other, good visual acuity is a prime necessity for good driving.

The only safe driver is the one who can bring his car under control, after a quick identifying glance at the situation, in time to avoid trouble.

TABLE II

SAFE STOPPING DISTANCES*

(In Feet Under Different Road Conditions)

Miles per Hour	Dry Concrete	Gravel	Wet Pavement	Packed Snow	Ice or Sleet
20	42	63	70	94	210 or more
30	84	129	140	185	410 or more
40	143	223	242	322	715 or more
50	220	339	366	490	1100 or more
60	317	486	526	700	1585 or more
70	436	670	723	970	2170 or more

*Based on figures from a pamphlet on Winter Driving Hazards by the National Safety Council.

ROAD SIGNS

The effectiveness of road signs depends on their being seen and read in time by the driver. If the operator of a motor vehicle must drive beyond the stopping distances given in Table II before he can read a sign, its value is lost.

When the light on road signs is less than full daylight it becomes more difficult for even the keenest eye to read them. When the expected vision drop occurs and the driver has less than 20/20 vision he is even more handicapped.

Reduction of illumination reduces the acuity of vision. For this reason vision specialists are careful to keep the lighting on their vision testing charts constant when measuring vision; otherwise a person with normal visual acuity may be rated lower depending upon the amount of light used.

NIGHT DRIVING

Eighty-five per cent of the total fatalities in motor-vehicle driving each year occur at night, according to figures published by the National Safety Council. This figure was reached after the mileage was adjusted for equality.

Statistics (National Safety Council) show that 58% of the pedestrians killed between 6 and 7 P.M. are killed during the quarter of the year covered by the months of November, December, and January, when that hour is darker. Reduced visibility is probably one of the causes of this greatly increased accident rate for these months. Winter driving and conditions continue through February and March, but the hour between 6 and 7 P.M. is again lighter, and the accident rate usually is decreased.

The night fatal accident rate per mile of travel is about three times as high as the day rate. During the past two decades the speed of cars has greatly increased which calls for the keenest of vision. Night driving demands three important visual factors: (1) the ability to see efficiently under low illumination, (2) the ability to see against glare, and (3) rapid recovery after being blinded by the glare of oncoming headlights.

WINTER DRIVING

The special hazards of winter driving in relation to the driver's vision are found in the effect which storms or weather has on visibility. Snow and sleet are hazardous in direct relationship to their density and severity. The driver's vision in one out of every five fatal accidents has been reported to be obscured or hindered.* About two-fifths of the obscurements were on the vehicle itself, in the form of rain, snow or sleet. The driver with lowered acuity finds himself doubly handicapped by snow and sleet and should take greater caution by reducing speed and increasing alertness during such storms.

The stopping distance of a car is greatly increased by highway hazards resulting from snow, sleet, and ice. In Table II, a car traveling 30 miles an hour goes 185 feet on packed snow, and 410 or more on ice or sleet in comparison to the 84 feet required for dry pavement. While 30 miles an hour is considered a safe speed during a storm by most drivers, the hazards of driving faster multiply out of all seeming proportion, until a car doing 50 miles an hour does not stop on snow until 490 feet are covered.

The lowered visibility that storms bring usually keeps the driver from seeing an approaching hazard until he is beyond the limit of the storm stopping distances. Just as in night driving, a collision is inevitable when a driver cannot see a hazard in time to stop.

HOW WE SEE

A receptive mechanism sensitive to light enables us to see. In darkness we do not see. Even the person with perfect eyesight can see nothing in total darkness. Rays of light enter the eye and strike the retina inside the eye, setting up impulses that are transmitted to the brain. These nerve impulses are in turn interpreted as people or objects, as the person evaluates them from his previous knowledge and experience.

A very small part of the retina interprets the finer details of form and shape. This highly sensitive area is called the macula and is situated directly back of the pupil. The fovea is at the center.

The retinal area surrounding the macula interprets gross form and motion. It is spoken of as the field of vision. The lateral field of vision ordinarily is about 180 degrees with both eyes. Less than 70 degrees in either eye constitutes a serious restriction.

FACTORS IN SEEING

(1) Light

Light, therefore, is absolutely necessary for vision. How much light is needed varies with the object a person wishes to see and

---

*Authority: 1947 *Accident Facts.*

with his visual efficiency. More light is needed for reading or close work, for instance, than for walking about a room. Up to a certain point one's vision is proportional to the amount of light. On the other hand, too much light directed into the eyes may be a cause of accidents. Driving into the setting sun or bright head-lights can be and often is a factor in collision with cars and pedestrians. If the light that shines in the driver's eyes is brighter than the surrounding illumination, it dims vision in proportion to its contrast.

Under such conditions as haze, smoke, rain, and snow, light is broken up by minute particles in the atmosphere and vision is thus reduced. Research shows that this reduction in vision is proportional to the acuity of vision which the driver may possess and to its nearness to the line of sight.

(2) Fatigue

Body fatigue in general lowers the response of all sensory and motor functions, including vision. Certain visual deficiencies tend to make a person drowsy, a dangerous thing to happen to an automobile driver.

Thus, fatigue can be the cause of and, in turn, is the result of a lowered visual efficiency and so contributes its share to highway accidents. It is established practice, enforced by the Interstate Commerce Commission, for drivers of transcontinental trucks to rest and sleep at stated intervals. This is a wise precaution that pays off in eliminating accidents due to fatigue. Many private car drivers push themselves beyond a safe fatigue point in an effort to clock off a high mileage rate each day. This is an invitation to accidents.

The examiner in the license division does not have the training or equipment to make tests to uncover certain visual deficiencies that can cause fatigue. In accident cases where the cause is re-ported, "fell asleep at the wheel," the driver should be given a more thorough examination, either by the department or by referral to a vision specialist, before permitting him to drive a car again. Certain visual defects are known to induce fatigue.

(3) Age

As one grows older his responses slow down and render him

less fit to drive a car. Just when physical infirmities might over-take a person cannot be predicted. People differ too much to make any rules along this line. Research conducted by the Motorists' Vision Committee with a group of 2,500 drivers in 15 counties of Iowa showed, however, that visual efficiency drops appreciably after 55 years of age. Distance judgment seems to increase somewhat up to the age of 35 and then decrease. This is an expected trend as the function of distance judgment is a learned skill and dependent upon previous experience.

(4) Intoxicants

Only a limited amount of data is available on the effects of alcohol and other intoxicants on vision. Alcohol lowers visual efficiency in general and may cause one to see double and lose some efficiency in muscular coordination.

A study was made by the Motorists' Vision Committee of the American Optometric Association on mild intoxication caused by alcohol in the blood varying from .074% to .124%. (In the opinion of most traffic bureaus, a person may be considered to be under the influence of alcohol who has from .05 to .15% in the blood stream, while a person who has .15% is definitely intoxicated.) The results of this study showed that the sensory functions studied were reduced about 13.8%, judgment factors about 23.1%, and skills about 24.6% on the average. Acuity may be decreased 5 to 10% when a person is mildly intoxicated. Distance judgment, as well as glare resistance and recovery, may be decreased as much as 20 to 30% when enough alcohol has been consumed to show traces in the blood stream to the extent given above.

A crucial factor seems to be the psychological problem of attention or proper use of the sense organs. This seems to decrease as much as 30% with mild drinking. Naturally, it is an individual matter, and probably is affected by numerous other factors, such as personal drinking habits, and so on. It does indicate that a driver who drinks periodically should be subject to more strict adherence to the legal limits set for his visual tests.

Figures released by the National Research Council show that an average of one out of every five drivers involved in a fatal accident had been drinking. It is also shown that one out of every four pedestrians killed in motor vehicle accidents had been drinking. These figures vary from year to year but they suffice to indicate the seriousness of the problem.

(5) Smoke, Fog, and Haze

Although smoke is less of a handicap than fog or haze to an operator of a motor vehicle, it is a factor in shortening a driver's effective perpetual distance. In certain industrial cities smoke is, in itself, a contributing cause to accidents, but where it is combined with fog and haze, it becomes a real hazard. There even has been a word coined — smog — to cover the combined effect of the two. Smudge fires along a highway create hazards.

How these factors affect vision is comparable to the seeing loss induced by driving at dusk. Persons who already have a loss in visual acuity are more handicapped by smoke and fog than the driver with 20/20, or so-called normal vision.

VISION TESTS

As visual acuity relates to the automobile driver, it may be said that being able to read signs and to see people or objects accurately at the greatest possible distance is necessary. If an object is not clear at a distance we must move closer until we can "see" it (see Figs. 4 and 13). The reason it cannot be seen in the distance is because the eyes cannot define or resolve it. Hence a person with subnormal vision must get closer to everything to "see" than one with normal vision — how much closer depends on the degree and nature of visual deficiency.

A license examiner needs only to be concerned with the broader aspects of visual testing, leaving the finer differences to the vision specialist. Acuity, field of vision, distance judgment, and night vision tests are the chief types of visual checks needed to be given by the license examiner. Those failing on these tests should be referred to a vision specialist.

HISTORY OF VISION TESTS—SNELLEN

Probably the simplest method of measuring visual acuity is by the method which was originated by Snellen. He devised a chart, consisting of letters and symbols, that furnishes a means of measuring acuity. This chart at present is commonly accepted as a useful device for rating keenness of vision.

MEANING OF 20/20 VISION

In determining visual acuity a chart is placed 20 feet from the person to be examined, and on the chart are printed letters of correct size and shape as outlined by Snellen from which the subject reads. Determine the smallest line of type that the subject can read with each eye separately and with both together. The letters on the 20/20 line are approximately ⅜ of an inch high. If they can be read at 20 feet, the person is said to have 20/20 vision. If the subject can only read at 20 feet the line of letters that the "normal" eye sees at 40 feet he is said to have 20/40 vision. This same interpretation holds for the other acuity ratings, such as 20/15, 20/70, and so forth.

Distance vision is the chief requisite of the automobile driver so the driver's license examining need not be concerned with checking the near vision of applicants for a motor vehicle license.

TESTING THE DRIVER'S ACUITY

Some licensing bureaus rate their findings by projector type instruments. One is called the Clason Acuity Meter. Table III gives the equivalent for Snellen and Clason notations and their readings in letters "A" to "E." An explanation of letter ratings was given earlier in this chapter.

TABLE III

EQUIVALENT RATINGS FOR ACUITY

	Snellen	*Clason (%)*
A	20/21 to 20/20	95-100
B	20/25 to 20/22	85- 94
C+	20/26 to 20/24	75- 84
C	20/31 to 20/27	65- 74
C—	20/36 to 20/30	55- 64
D	20/50 to 20/37	40- 54
E	Below 20/50	Below 40

Vision should be measured under controlled lighting, or the results will be far from accurate. The eye does not respond to the same extent under low illumination as it does under adequate light. For this reason the vision test should be given to applicants where there is absolute control over the light that falls on the chart, as well as the general illumination of the room.

For most accurate results in testing driver's visual acuity, the general level of room illumination should not be less than 5 to 10 foot-candles. The test chart itself should have between 10 and 20 foot-candles of incidental light upon it. None of the supplementary light upon the chart should shine directly into the eyes of the person being tested. Table IV on illumination was compiled under these conditions. Metal reflectors of good quality were used, and the lamps were ordinary household white, inside frosted, American-made electric bulbs for 120 volts. All light bulbs were new. Old or dirty bulbs or corroded reflectors would necessitate a decrease in distance for equivalent illumination.

TABLE IV

Illumination

Number of Lamps	Watts	Distance from Chart (when 2 lights were used both were equally distant from chart)	Resultant Foot-candles or Light on Chart*
1	40	18"	15
2	40	23"	15
1	60	27"	15
2	60	34"	15
1	75	29"	15
2	75	42"	15
1	100	41"	15
2	100	46"	15

*Foot-candle readings were taken directly upon the Chart with a General Electric Foot-Candle Exposure Meter, Model 8DW58Y1, which may be obtained from any good photographic supply store. Four foot-candles of light is about average for a room illuminated by ordinary daylight or well illuminated by artificial light.

If the Snellen system of measuring vision· is desired, either a wall-type chart or projector-type instrument may be used. Both use the Snellen-type letters.

The Snellen wall-type has black letters printed on a white background and care must be taken to see that the white chart is clean. Any discoloration from soil will affect the accuracy of the test. Charts with a colored background should never be used.

The wall chart has light shining on it from the general illumination of the room and from any special source directed upon it. The projector type has a light inside the instrument by which letters are projected upon a screen. The letters are on a slide within the projector and are thrown on the screen by a light. For either type of chart the general illumination in the room must be controlled or kept uniform from person to person in the administration of tests.

The exposed chart on the wall has certain disadvantages — namely, that it can be memorized and that it is exposed to dust and dirt. Also, unless it is carefully placed and has a hood over and around it with special lighting, the illumination will not always be uniform. The standard of from 10 to 20 foot-candles of light on the chart must be maintained for less than the prescribed light will reduce the applicant's rating considerably.

Most projector type charts have letters that can be changed at will in size or sequence which gives less chance for memorization. They have the advantage of a constant light on the screen when the tests are given under conditions of controlled light in the room.

The applicant should stand or sit 20 feet from the chart with the eye at a level with the center of the chart. Where space does not permit placing the chart 20 feet from the applicant it is recommended that the examiner consult with the local or state chairman of the Motorists' Vision Committee of the State Optometric Association, or others, for recommendations on testing for their particular conditions. Since minimums vary in states, it is impossible to set forth here the necessary data to meet each situation.

Each eye should be tested separately. If glasses are worn, it is suggested that the test be given first with glasses and then without. The examiner should hold a card or occlusion disc in front of one eye while the other eye is being tested. This is a more satisfactory method of closing off the vision of one eye than putting a hand before it. By all means the examinee should not shut one eye. Care should be taken that the applicant does not squint as the vision may be sharpened by this means. With a card in front of the right eye, then the left, the applicant is asked to read the letters on the chart. Directions something like the following may be used: "Read aloud the smallest row of letters that you can see on the chart."

Pass all applicants who meet the visual standards required by the state. Allow only one error in each line for credit on that line. There are approximately eight letters on the 20/20 line, and fewer on each line, as the sizes of the letters increase. The rating is made on each eye separately. If there is no state recommendation for vision, it is recommended that applicants be required to have a minimum of 20/40 in each eye separately for general driving privileges without a special examination.

Refer all applicants who fall below the state's visual requirements to an optometrist, ophthalmologist, or vision specialist for further examination. Send a card along with the applicant for the doctor to fill out with his recommendations as to the visual fitness of the person to drive an automobile.

Restriction rather than rejection of the driver is a much more effective and desirable way of handling many cases. It should be the objective of the licensing division to keep more drivers on the highways and to keep them driving safely.

COLOR VISION

Experiments have been made with color filters to help those who cannot distinguish between red and green. The results are not entirely satisfactory to date. Color blindess is not a cause of many accidents.

GLARE RESISTANCE AND RECOVERY

Glare is the undesirable effect of a superfluous amount of light directed into the eyes, over and above the amount needed for clear and distinct vision. The effect depends upon the volume and location of the same. People differ in their tolerance and reaction to glare. Some drivers are so blinded by the glare of headlights that they are unable to see the road in front of them. The sun is one source of glare which bothers many persons.

Table V shows an analysis of a thousand commercial drivers' records and the distribution of scale readings on the glarometer test. This is a test for glare resistance. It seems to correlate quite well with seeing ability in glare light.

TABLE V

NORMS ON EFFECT OF GLARE

(Based on 1,014 Commercial Drivers)

Percentage of Drivers in Classification	Rating	Scale Readings on Glaremeter	Foot-candles of Light at the Eye (3 foot-candles added for extraneous light)
5	A	75-93	18.1-37.0
10	B	69-74	15.6-18.0
20	C+	62-68	11.1-15.5
30	C	56-61	9.1-11.0
20	C—	48-55	7.0- 9.0
10	D	36-47	4.4- 6.9
5	E	14-35	3.0- 4.3

While not perfect, the glarometer is successful in picking out the persons who are abnormally affected by headlights of cars. It is a simple rheostat device for controlling the light. Drivers who fall below 30 as indicated by scale readings on the glarometer, that is, those who are blinded by 3 foot-candles of light at a distance of 20 feet, are considered to have poor resistance to glare.

LOW ILLUMINATION

Low illumination in the form of fog, smoke, snow, and sleet, as well as the darkness of twilight and night, influence driving ability. Laboratory findings show that persons with reduced visual efficiency are much more handicapped under conditions of lowered visibility than are persons with efficient vision. It was also revealed that anyone who has a tendency toward color blindness has even more difficulty in distinguishing color in low illumination, or at night, than during the day. Night vision tests are not sufficiently standardized to be placed in general use at licensing bureaus.

DEPTH PERCEPTION OR DISTANCE JUDGMENT

Tests for depth perception should be incorporated into a first-class driver's visual examination, because drivers are continually being called upon to exercise their distance and space perception in estimating such distances as that between their own cars and the edge of the road, people, bicycles, or other vehicles on the highway. Distance judgment is partially dependent on stereopsis, or depth perception, and partly upon other factors such as haze, shadows, and general illumination. Collisions in darkness are sometimes caused because this ability often decreases appreciably at night and drivers cannot estimate the position of their own cars in relation to other cars or objects.

Improper passing accounts for a considerable number of our highway accidents. Space perception is especially needed in passing other cars.

A well-known test for space perception is known as the Army Peg Test or the Howard-Dohlman Rod Test. A variation of this test has the substitution of miniature automobiles for the pegs. Light is controlled and conditions are carefully standardized. Each instrument must be calibrated after it is built to be sure of accuracy since illumination, type of cars used, and other factors affect readings.

Anything that will impress the driver about his limitations with respect to his ability to judge space between his car and the highway, or the speed of approaching vehicles, will contribute to safety in driving.

The test objects must be evenly illuminated, and the angular position of the eyes must remain constant with relation to the miniature roadway. A calibration device should be built into the machine so that it can be properly aligned at regular intervals. The applicant is seated and shown how to move the test cars. He is told where they are to be set and then the following verbatim instructions are given:

"You are to move the small cars by holding the strings lightly. Set the front axles at the posts, or even with the posts, the two center cars at the center post, the right car at the right post, and the left car at the left post. Do it as quickly as you can. Begin."

Settings are made on equipment with a high-grade reflecting mirror at three positions: 10 feet, 15 feet, and 20 feet. A second reading at 15 feet may be made if 16 trials are desired. The applicant may look at the cars and pegs between trials only. For practical purposes, 4 trials at 20 feet are usually sufficient.

The score is the total error in centimeters of all cars from the proper position as measured with a small T-square, and this is converted into the rating (Table VI). The main source of error lies in the tendency of the equipment to change its characteristics due to improper alignment. As noted above, it is essential that a calibrating device be built into the instrument and used regularly to check the characteristics of the device with respect to the angle of viewing.

TABLE VI
STANDARDS FOR DISTANCE JUDGMENT OF THE ORIGINAL SMALL CAR TEST*

Rating	Error (cm.)
A	0- 39
B	40- 46
C+	47- 56
C	57- 78
C—	79- 93
D	94-131
E	132-200

*Each instrument built must be standardized under the conditions, and with the particular drivers with which it is to be used. There have been found to be some geographical differences that may be due to the need for greater skill in judging distances in some parts of the country. The results are given merely as a guide to the ranges of scores that might be expected.

The illumination should come from directly above this type of perception test so that the cars will not cast a shadow which would assist in estimating their position. Pass those rating A, B, C+, and C. Applicants rating C— or D should have a notation on their license: "Care in Passing." Those rating E should be referred to an optometrist or opthalmologist for a careful check-up. It is to be noted that some persons do about five times better than others on this test.

FIELD OF VISION

The lateral field of vision is very important in driving and the recognition of its importance is even more essential to the driver for safe motoring. While it is impossible to increase the field of vision by a simple test, we can call the attention of the applicant to the importance of good field, or good side vision. When the fields cannot be enlarged, a driver can be taught to turn his head and eyes, especially at intersections, to compensate for his restricted fields. Extreme cases of restricted or narrow field of vision are commonly described as "tunnel vision." The person so afflicted can only see straight ahead and cannot detect motion without turning his head or eyes from side to side.

License examiners can make only an abbreviated test for the field of vision, but Nuchols devised a simple test, that was improved by Lauer (2), which is easy to use. It is merely a quadrant divided, or calibrated into 220 degrees and cut out to fit the face as closely as possible. The subject is asked to fixate the finger of the examiner at the center. The test object, such as a pencil, is moved slowly back and forth along the edge of the chart until it cannot be seen. The scale gives width of the field in degrees.

TABLE VII

FIELD OF VISION INDEX

Rating	Per Cent in the Group	Percentages of Drivers above the Lower Limit	Degrees of Arc in Binocular Vision
A	5	5	Above 195
B	10	15	185-194
C+	20	35	176-184
C	30	65	169-175
C—	20	85	159-168
D	10	95	145-158
E	5	100	Below 144

There are no special conditions to be observed with this test, except that the instrument is to be held properly and a light colored pencil used for the target. The applicant must stand so a shadow will not be cast from the pencil.

The examiner should insert the index and small finger of his left hand in the two holes of the perimeter and balance it lightly on the two middle fingers extended in a relaxed manner. A little practice is necessary to do this easily and deftly. Be sure the index or fixation finger is perpendicular. Set the perimeter squarely against the face and give the following directions: "Now look straight at my index finger." With your right hand carry the target above the edge of the perimeter. Start out beyond 200 degrees and move back and forth slowly and by short movements, working toward the center. Add these directions: "When you see movement at the side, say 'Now.'" The position when the applicant says "Now" should be checked several times before recording to be certain of the limits of discrimination. Hold the target lightly against the perimeter and read as accurately as possible to the nearest degree.

Reverse hands and measure the other side, holding the perimeter the same way, but on the other side. Space is to be provided on the form for *left* and *right* entries and also a place for *total field*, which is merely the sum of the two. The subject should be watched carefully that he does not peek. The perimeter should be held level and square with the face, and the target finger must be held perpendicularly. Move the target back and forth until you are sure of the vanishing point.

Pass those with A, B, C+, and C rating (Table VII). Persons with a C– or D should have a notation on the license, "Restricted Field."

Refer anyone who has vision in two eyes and has an E rating to a vision specialist.

If a perimeter check of the field of vision shows abnormality, the driver should be allowed to drive only under a restricted license at the discretion of the examiner.

SUMMARY

Vision is a complicated phenomenon and there are many phases that should be measured. Usually the driver's license examiner only measure visual acuity, but occasionally check the field of vision. These are the basic measures expected of license examiners. Other factors involved should be considered when vision is being studied.

The great urge is to get persons through the examination. Shortage of personnel is one reason. Some states require re-examination every two years and some every four or more years. It would probably be better to give a more thorough re-examination less frequently. It hardly seems necessary to examine the eyes of all the population below age 40-45 every two years. Above that age it may be warranted. Ordinarily vision at the lower levels does not change a great deal unless through injury.

REFERENCES

1. Fletcher, Edwin C., California Journal of Secondary Education, 1939, 14, #8, 470-473.
2. Lauer, A. R. and Getman, G. N., An abbreviated clinical procedure for motor vehicle drivers. Yearbook of Optometry, 1937, 109-115.
3. Rinsland, Henry D., Constructing tests and grading. Prentice-Hall, Inc., 1937, pp. 314.
4. Silver, E. H. and Silver, Ida Phelps, Manual on Driver's Vision Test. A.O.M.V.A. and A.O.A., 1949, pp. 38.
5. Silver, E. H., Report of the Research Department of the American Optometric Assoc., Jour. Am. Optometric Assoc., 1930, 1, #6.

CHAPTER X

THE EFFECT OF A REST PAUSE

ON DRIVING EFFICIENCY

There has been some concern regarding the possibility of fatigue of drivers on the highway. Some work has been done but little experimental evidence is available. Rest pauses have been used effectively in certain industries to reduce work decrement and to increase output which has lagged because of fatigue and monotony. There is no complete agreement with respect to the length of time needed for the pause or where it should be introduced in the work period (9). Few who have studied problems of production, however, will deny its practicability and there is every reason to feel that driving efficiency decreases some after beginning driving.

Insurance companies have found that most of their accidents occur within the first three hours of driving. Some support to this has been given by commercial concerns, although a correction factor needs to be introduced here. It is probable that most persons driving, who are insured or are working with a commercial company, do not drive longer than three hours at the beginning of the day. At least those who are driving locally would not drive in such a way that they would require more than three hours at one time. We do not know whether the persons who set out for a longer trip are better prepared to withstand fatigue, or whether more accidents occur during the first few hours of driving. Furthermore, we may ask the question as to how much fatigue there is in driving?

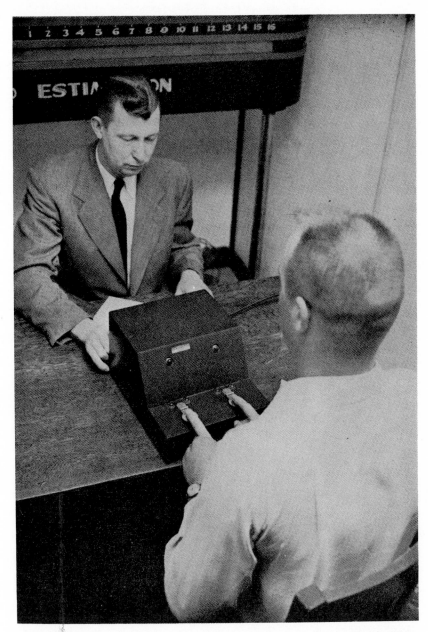

Fig. 8. Choice Reaction Time. The subject reacts to each of the light combinations given by the experimenter. The time clock is at the back for ease of reading.

IS DRIVING TIRESOME?

Early research (8) has shown that long sustained activity tends to cause a loss of efficiency of certain discriminative functions, associative processes, and motor reactions similar to those required in driving. These observations also suggest that an extended automobile drive may render an operator temporarily susceptible to accidents. The Interstate Commerce Commission has limited the period of driving of commercial operators after making an extended study. Their study was based upon various types of tests made after certain periods of driving. It was very difficult to control conditions of the experiment and only general conclusions could be made based on the data obtained.

Another problem which confronts the highway user is that of so-called highway hypnosis. Regardless of the facts about it, there is undoubtedly the matter of reduced attention which develops after driving in a monotonous situation. One study reported by Lauer and McMonagle (5) touches on some phases of this problem. It was found that a certain amount of stimulation was necessary in order to keep the driver at the highest level of alertness as determined by certain measurements of his attention and ability to guard against accidents.

As stated, the records of insurance companies indicate that a large percentage of accidents, even among commercial drivers, occur early in the driving period. Some of these men probably drive for several hours, hence the conclusions are not entirely clear. There must be a decrement in efficiency taking place earlier in the trip which needs to be studied. Application of such findings to lay drivers is not entirely unexpected as most drivers do not make trips lasting over three hours at one time. In other words, they drive shorter distances and complete the trip before the end of three hours. Therefore, it would be expected that most of their accidents would occur during the first part of a trip. In any case, it seemed worthwhile to set up an experimental situation to determine what effects, if any, the introduction of a rest pause with refreshments at regular intervals would have on the performance.

In order to investigate this problem a great deal of time was spent in studying the possibilities. Since road runs are rather expensive it seemed to be desirable to first make a laboratory study with simulated devices (11).

In cooperation with certain industrial groups a study was devised which would tend to measure the effects of rest pauses on driving performance with tea as a refreshment. The study was set up to cover a six-hour period of performance. This was preceded by a three-hour practice period to determine what trends could be noted and to accustom subjects to the device. The rationale back of the three-hour period was the report from insurance companies that most of the accidents occur during the early part of a trip. A study was set up to test the hypothesis that driving performance is subject to improvement by practice and may be affected by rest pauses with refreshments, and the basic efficiency changes could be noted in the organism.

Two groups of 28 subjects each were used in this study and were matched with respect to certain characteristics related to driving, such as age, sex and experience. The subjects were first taken through a three-hour practice phase, as stated, and later through a six-hour continuous run, half of the subjects having a rest pause with refreshments every 90 minutes and half of them running constantly without a pause. This part of the study will hereinafter be referred to as Experiment A. It was of two years duration and was the basis for a doctor's thesis by Dr. V. W. Suhr which is available in the Iowa State College Library and may be obtained through an interlibrary loan.

After completing this study it was thought that a road adaptation of the simulated laboratory procedure might be worthwhile to determine to what extent the results found in the laboratory would hold in regular road driving. Since road driving is essentially expensive and requires consideration of variables that are difficult to control, a special highway route was chosen, 50 miles in length, over which the trip would be made. It was found that it takes approximately an hour for the average driver to make the 50-mile trip. Therefore a three-hour run would require three trips over this course which could be made in about three hours. To extend the investigation further, the last subjects used were given four trips. The trends noted in the first three hours were sufficient to give a prognostic account of what would happen during this time.

This study involved a road driving situation which required about a year to complete, during which time a total of 7,500 miles were driven under fairly well-controlled conditions of traffic. Eighteen subjects were taken each on two trips, making a total of 36 trips. In this study a restricted randomization method of selecting the subjects for experimental or controlled conditions was used. Thus this part of the experiment will be described later under Experiment B. Each of the studies will be described separately and the most important results given in condensed form for each. The present review is intended to be an extended abstract of the two studies in order to give the reader some idea of the experiments conducted and the results obtained on the effect of a rest pause with refreshments.

EXPERIMENT A

Method

In order to control conditions as nearly as possible, two groups of subjects were matched with respect to age, sex and driving experience. In order to be considered for the experiment one had to have at least three years driving experience, or have driven at least 10,000 miles. This could not be checked exactly but was obtained in a preliminary interview, supplementing it by some previous knowledge of the drivers. It was considered to be reasonably accurate.

A short description of the test run simulating device will be made to orient the reader with respect to its nature. The central piece of apparatus used was the drivometer, a general view of which is shown in Figure 1. This simulator had been used in a number of studies previously and was found to be quite efficient and reliable.

A schedule of the experiment was made up some time in advance, since each driver had to spend approximately 15 hours in all to complete the various tests given. It was thought advisable to measure the functions involved with respect to efficiency before the driving period began. These are designated as the before driving tests. Following this the subject was placed on the drivometer and given the regular driving run. Each had a three-hour practice run on a previous day. During ,the experimental run certain tests were made, such as checking the driver's time to react to signs, to react to a miniature train which passed across the highway, and his reaction time to certain signals. This series of tests were designated as intransit tests. The intransit tests were given, either while the person was actually performing or at regular intervals during the performance test, both with and without the rest pause and refreshments. At the end of the simulated driving run the subject was again taken through the series of psychological and psychophysical tests to determine whether or not he had lost in efficiency. An analysis was made of these before and after tests to determine the magnitude of the changes, if any. Covariance was used. A very brief description of the tests will be given under their respective headings.

Before the subject actually began he was given a self-rating blank of subjective nature to determine his state of well-being for the day and a self-estimate of his condition for such an experiment. After this, three groups of tests were administered designed to measure: (1) general body states and conditions, (2) physical alertness and dexterity, and (3) mental alertness and dexterity.

Samples of group (1) tests would include blood pressure made by the Tycos Self-Recording Sphygmomanometer, a steadiness test made to measure the degree of muscle control or lack of tremor, and grip endurance measured by the Smedley hand dynamometer with a pneumatic plunger attached to a tambour and recorded on a Weiss-Renshaw polygraph. In addition to this, the subject's basic resistance to an electric current was made using the Stoelting deceptograph. Pulse and respiration changes are made on the same device.

In the second group of tests, including dexterity and alertness, the subject was given a serial choice reaction time test. In this he was allowed to react to a series of red, green and amber stimulus lights presented as rapidly as he could maneuver to present them and react properly. Also gross coordination was measured by the coordinometer shown in Figure 6 which had been found to be more closely related to driving than any of the psychophysical tests in a study made for the Army (2). This device consists of two levers, approximately 43½ inches long. These control a tilting maze through which a ⅞ inch steel ball bearing was guided past holes made in the alleys to get around to the goal or loading dock as it was called. Considerable interest develops around this test which requires a great deal of attention, as well as coordination, to maneuver properly. The trial, or trip, is terminated at any point where the subject loses control of the ball and lets it drop through a pocket or hole. The holes are numbered progressively so that the further the ball advances around the maze, before it falls through a hole, the higher the score. Five trials are usually made and the sum of the numbers of the holes where the ball was lost constitutes the score. Thus a high score would be good and a low score poor manipulation. The simulator, itself, is one of this type of tests but was not used *before* and *after*.

The third type of function measured in the *before* and *after* tests is that of mental dexterity and consists of a number of arithmetical and perceptual problems which involve close attention to detail and careful observation. We shall not describe all of these in detail since most everyone is familiar with this type of performance. Card sorting was a type which involved the combination of both physical maneuvering and mental alertness. A detailed description of all of the scores obtained will *not* be given in this description since they were published for the first part of the study (4) and may be obtained in complete form through the thesis which is in the Iowa State College Library (10).

It suffices to say that practically none of the measures used *before* and *after* showed a significant difference with the laboratory study. Those which were significant had no logical basis for their explanation and hence were thought to be chance variations. For example, systolic blood pressure for women showed a drop of about three points which is very difficult to explain, although significant. This is particularly puzzling since it was the reverse for men. These values were obtained by analysis of covariance which considered the level before and afterwards and the amount of change made.

The errors made in the attention to detail perceptual test did show a highly significant difference which again was rather difficult to evaluate since the results were not clean-cut. In general it may be said that none of the *before* and *after* tests showed any marked difference which was statistically significant. Nevertheless it did seem that this kind of test might yield something if the performance were made on the road. The simulator was relatively easy to maneuver and did not involve all of the tasks on the highway which are met in actual driving. It was considered more an index of continued performance efficiency.

Of the intransit tests made while the person was actually driving, certain measurements did show considerable promise. One was steering efficiency. Steering efficiency changed consistently for men and women (10). Of the 58 subjects, proportions of men and women were chosen approximately as found among drivers. Approximately the same percentage of women were chosen for subjects and their results were analyzed separately. We shall not refer to this group (women) specifically since it was a much smaller group and since the results were in general quite close to those of men.

Error time decreased considerably for the no-pause group which was significant at the 5% level. Steering, however, showed continued higher efficiency throughout the test periods in favor of the rest-pause group. Figure 9, at the right, shows the nature of the trends during the six-hour experimental period. It seems, in general, there was a letdown in effort, physical effort at least.

Hence, little can be said for the various tests made intransit, except for steering which showed a marked tendency to deteriorate consistently as shown.

In order to test the effect of practice and to eliminate this effect the three-hour preliminary run was made. Figure 9, at the left, shows the steering efficiency curves during this practice period which was set up to familiarize the person with the problem and to improve the efficiency as far as possible to offset practice effects. Both groups tended to drop off after an hour or so of driving. Since most of the practice is shown during the first half hour, and

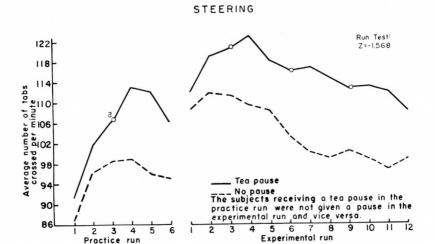

Fig. 9. Steering Efficiency.

since the curves had started to deteriorate in performance, it was thought that three hours was enough for practice before starting the experimental run of six hours shown at the right hand side of the graph. The rise of both curves at the beginning of the experimental run would be expected as an effect of reminiscence. Thus both the no-pause and the tea-pause groups started out nearly the same at the beginning of the experimental run, the no-pause group showing a slight superiority. During the successive periods up to 12 half hours, or six hours of driving, the curves both tended to deteriorate, changing at the end of the second half hour. The decrement gradually became greater down through the experimental period. There were some fluctuations, of course, but the curves in general paralleled fairly close. Hence it may be stated with considerable degree of assurance, steering efficiency does deteriorate and that it held up better for the tea-pause group, running to approximately the fourth half hour. The no-pause group shows deterioration after the second hour. Thus the interpolation of a rest-refreshment pause would tend to maintain steering efficiency level for at least one hour. The curves show a gradual deterioration after the first two, and two and one-half hours. Thus a rest pause seems to improve performance and to prevent an early work decrement to the extent shown.

Summary and Conclusions of Experiment A

In experiment A measures were made while the person was performing at a simulated driving task. The *before* and *after* tests, although sufficiently reliable, did not show any marked decrease or change in efficiency that was consistent. The intransit tests, those which had to do with steering particularly and which were the most nearly like those of actual driving, showed a tendency to deteriorate after one and one-half to two hours for both groups. The introduction of rest pauses seemed to increase or hold the level of efficiency from about one to one and one-half hours and the results were consistent throughout the experimental run. After the first hour the difference would amount to from 10 to 20%. Broadly interpreted, this would seem to indicate that the driver tends to fatigue normally after the first half hour and gradually decreases in efficiency. Hence without the rest pause and refreshment he would lose approximately 15% over the period of six hours. With a pause he would lose only about 5% over his initial performance.

This, in general, summarizes study A made in the laboratory on effects of a rest pause on driving. We shall now proceed to Experiment B which was carried out subsequently in an attempt to determine what would happen on the road proper in actual driving.

EXPERIMENT B

The results from Experiment A showed rather definitely that some change in efficiency does take place consistently from the time when one starts to drive on a trip until the end of a three hour practice or six hour experimental period. It seems to build up for the first hour and then gradually deteriorates. It was not found that there were any significant differences in the individual as measured by two types of tests made *before* and *after*. It was felt that the intransit measures were the most important parts of the study insofar as the Experiment A indicated. That such a need for the study of rest periods exist was emphasized by the National Safety Council as early as 1935 (8). Therefore an attempt was made to duplicate the laboratory study as nearly as possible, or at least to adapt it to a road driving experiment such as had been developed (3).

Because of the fact that traffic varies and conditions cannot be duplicated in the laboratory which might introduce greater fatigue, it was felt that a simplified set of *before* and *after* tests should be included along with the regular intransit studies of the driver. The same general plan of approach was used throughout except that the subjects were given the order of control or experimental runs by a restricted random choice. Since time was an element and the study was quite expensive, the number of subjects had to be limited, as well as the time for driving. As most accidents occur within the first three hours, and since in the laboratory study this time was sufficient to indicate trends the curves would take, the study was originally set up to include only three hours of driving. This included three trips over a 50-mile route selected on U.S. Interstate Highway 30 and Iowa State Highway 60 which extended from Ames, Iowa to Stanhope, Iowa. To make the complete trip required about an hour and was very close to 50 miles.

The study was set up on a progressive analysis basis so that subjects could be run until the desired number could be included. This part of the experiment included 18 drivers, each acting as his own control in two test runs which covered 7,500 miles of driving, a total of 36 trips in all. The groups were designated as rest-pause and no-pause groups. The former had tea as a refreshment given each hour. The initial ingestion of tea was made just after the beginning tests had been completed and before the first run. Subsequently the rest pause and serving of tea was given each subject every hour on the experimental run but not given on the days he did the control run.

Since the *before* and *after* test had shown no significant results in the laboratory phase, a great deal of care was taken in sifting out to utilize only those which were thought to be the most likely to give useful results.

Of the first 12 subjects, 26 such tests were given *before* and *after*. After analyzing the data, 12 of these tests were dropped as being impractical or irrelevant. Of the 12 tests remaining an analysis of the significance was made and the logic of choice was more or less confirmed by the fact that 7 of the 14 turned out to be significant. The differences found were in the expected direction since it was felt that a choice had been reasonably made with respect to those to be included.

Since a study of this type assumes quite extensive proportions it was thought that a run of 18 subjects on double runs each, or 36 runs, would yield enough data to establish whether or not such a road test were feasible and if results could be obtained. At the end of the description of this study, comparisons between the two will be discussed to indicate the possible net results which were obtained.

The general hypothesis set up to be investigated was whether the technique used in the laboratory could be adapted for a road driving experiment which would differentiate the degrees of skill in driving, with and without a rest-refreshment pause.

A secondary hypothesis in null form was that *before* and *after* tests in a driving experiment will not differentiate the effects of decrement in efficiency with or without refreshment pause.

As stated, the design of the study was set up so that each individual acted as his own control, driving once under one set of conditions and another time, the rotation being drawn at random, under another set. Comparison was made of the two runs. The first 12 subjects drove only 3 hours each, while the final 6 drove 4 hours each. The experimental trip included refreshments and a 15-minute rest pause each hour upon completing a cycle of driving. Tea in any form preferred was used as a refreshment.

Method and Procedure

Each subject reported to the laboratory at about 8:30 in the morning. The *before* tests were then administered which included the following:

1. Subjective evaluation of the subject as used by McNelly (6). The aim was to secure an index of the subject's personal evalua-

tion of his general feelings and fitness for the trip. Any such thing as a headache, illness, or indisposition, was thereby spotted and indicated. As a matter of fact, no subject showed any particular symptom of illness during the total driving time and no records were spoiled for this or other reasons.

2. Group of pencil-and-paper tests designed to measure mental alertness were then administered which included the following:

a. Perceptual efficiency or attention-to-detail type of test which has shown a relationship to driving from studies of Army personnel (2).

b. Simple addition or speed and accuracy in this function. Reed (9) has found a 27% loss in this function over a 10-hour practice period.

c. Lateral vision perception. It has been alleged that the field of vision tends to narrow during a period of exertion or fatigue-producing situation. Consequently it was felt this might be an indicator.

d. A test of speed of observation similar to an attention-to-detail test described in 2a but using specific characters.

e. Error detection — a type of attention-to-detail test.

3. A short battery of sensory-motor tests was used.

a. The lateral field of vision tests made by the Maddox-Lloyd Cheiroscope was given. This is a quick method of plotting the visual and form fields. Only forms were used as target stimuli in the present study. Actually the test was conducted merely to note the size of the visual field in the horizontal meridian.

b. Discriminative reaction time. This form of reaction time is usually found most useful in checking differences in certain psychological functions. Fernberger used a tachistoscope to measure time to react to judgment. Cattell earlier had used it as a measure of intelligence. However, Fernberger's results seemed to apply more to driving in that judgment is known to be an important factor in driving (2). If one takes longer to make a judgment it is likely that his efficiency has deteriorated. In this particular test the subject reacts to different colors of light and to the pattern of lights presented. The pattern is relatively simple and the subject reacts with the right or left hand, depending upon the lights which appear on the panel.

c. Modified steadiness. Steadiness has been used by Ryan and others to measure fatigue in driving. They found differences after a trip of several miles north of Chicago. Involuntary tremor (1) had also been used in measuring the effects of fatigue with a certain amount of exercise.

d. Sight Screener Test. Lateral and vertical phorias were measured by the Sight Screener as possible indicators of fatigue.

It is known that drivers frequently tend to see double when fatigued if heterophoria exists.

4. Parking efficiency. Students of automobile driving have always used parking as a critical test of efficiency at the wheel. It involves turning, placement, and effective control of the vehicle to make a proper parking. In the present study a detailed plan was worked out to allow careful scoring of the steps and movements in the process of parking. A special stall was built (see Fig. 2) where all subjects would have an equal chance under controlled conditions.

5. Criterion rating. After the four tests were given each driver was given a rating on the Rogers-Lauer Scale (3). This scale had been standardized on 349 subjects over an 8-mile test run previously. The scale has a reliability of about .9 and therefore gives quite a reliable index of the person's efficiency at the wheel. The validity has been found to be high enough to warrant its use in evaluating drivers. It is relatively simple and easy to use and therefore was included in this battery of the *before* and *after* tests. Each driver was scored over approximately ¾ mile to the edge of the city where tea was served to the experimental group. Each subject drove over the same roadway irrespective of the trip he was making.

After these *before* tests had been administered and the subjects running on an experimental drive had been served tea, they were started on the regular road trip west from Ames, Iowa, on U.S. Highway 30. Each was told to drive as he ordinarily did and not try to make a record trip nor to daudle along. Every effort was made to make the driver feel at ease and to feel that he was out on a simple drive for the purpose of checking his performance. He was not instructed as to what was expected of him, other than to do a good job of driving. Thus it is assumed that he followed the directions and performed more or less as he would when driving alone. No harness or other gear was attached to hi-- directly and he was only asked to respond occasionally to the reaction light which was attached to the windshield at such an angle and of such size as to be approximately the equivalent of a STOP light at 150 feet distance. This will be described further under the proper heading of intransit measurements.

Intransit Measurements

Intransit measurements are those made while driving the car. In the criterion study (3) a number of relationships in driving performance had been derived through correlational procedures and from these a rationale was developed for nine measurable phases of driving which might be expected to yield some clues on driving efficiency. These are classified in a Table I with a word of explanation indicating which direction a certain score might be expected to take. All categories are supposed to operate as indicated within the framework of a reasonable and proper speed and are not supposed to hold for situations where the driver needs to speed up or to slow down in handling of the car unless by voluntary choice. In other words, they hold for normal driving conditions.

TABLE I

INTRANSIT MEASUREMENTS

	Good Performance	Poor Performance
1. Trip time (note limitations stated above)	shorter time	longer time
2. Brake applications	fewer	more
3. Accelerator movements	fewer	more
4. Modal speed (tachograph)	higher	lower
5. Jerk recorder (sidewise to measure swerves)	low score	higher score
6. Fluctuations in speed (tachograph)	fewer	more
7. Reaction time to stop light on car windshield (attention light)	shorter	longer
8. General consistency rating (considering all around performance)	more consistent	less consistent
9. Lateral placement (in lane)	higher score	lower score
10. Intransit rating scale (description above)	higher score	lower score

Since some of these including the last two sets of measurements in the table were especially devised for this study, the assumptions underlying them will be described briefly.

A small attention light with red lens approximately the size of a ɔ ΓOP light at 150 feet was flashed through the windshield at the proper angle at specific points in each lap. It should be stated that the total trip was divided into a series of eight laps of approximately six miles each known only to the experimenter. By prearrangement signals were exhibited to the subject at given points unknown to him within these laps. When the light appeared the subject was instructed to say, "Light," as soon as first noticed. The experimenter started a stop watch at the moment the light appeared and shut if off the instant the subject responded, "Light."

In a like manner, markings were made of the subject such as placement in the lane, etc., within each of the segments so that an objective rating could be made of the driver's performance by the experimenter at the time. The subject had no notion that he was being marked at these times and was not given an indication of whether he was doing the right thing or the wrong thing, so long as there was no danger involved. The markings were made at suitable locations.

The experimenter reports that in no case was the driver especially instructed to slow down or perform other than as he preferred because of faulty maneuvers of any kind. It is assumed by the rationale (Table I) that a superior driver stays near the center of the lane and passes only when no risk is involved. It is further assumed the risks are evenly distributed along the route and that a person who makes 50 passes in driving 200 miles is taking more risk than one who makes only 10 passes. Thus we assume that the person making more passes shows poor judgment at times. This assumption was questioned at one time but a checkup showed the assumption to be thoroughly sound, even though exceptions were occasionally found. It is noted that a judgment made at a designated place and under the conditions met would be valid and could be impartially recorded (compare Figs. 10 and 11). Some practices are more dangerous than others and deserve greater penalties. A prearranged system of weighting was used so that differential marks could be given for different types of behavior.

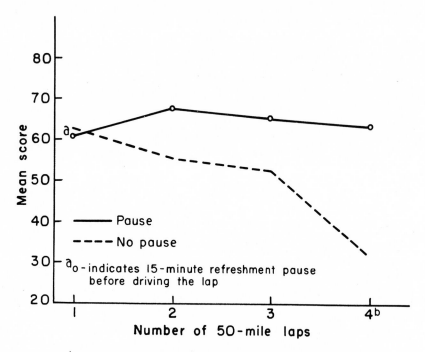

INTRANSIT EVALUATION

———— Pause

- - - - No pause

a_o - indicates 15-minute refreshment pause before driving the lap

Number of 50-mile laps

bOnly the last 6 subjects drove the 4th lap

Fig. 10. Intransit Evaluation with Deductions for Passing.

For example, greater risk is known to exist if the driver crowds the center line of the road which may cause a side swipe or a serious accident. However, there is some danger in crowding the shoulder of the road. Therefore, more penalty was given for crowding the center of the road at the marking point than for crowding at the shoulder. The highest marking was made when the subject was in the proper place in the lane at the point where the marking was to be made.

The intransit measures thus involved two types of observations about the performance of the driver. One type of markings had to do with keeping in the lane. By checking the driver 1 point for being too far right, 2 points for being too far left, or 3 points for being in the center, a score was obtained. The other several items listed as intransit driving measures were scored by deducting points for bad practices. Each driver was allowed 100 points to start each section of the roadway. He was marked down on faulty behavior as follows: 10 points for risky passes; 5 points for unnecessary passes; 10 points for being over the center line when *not* passing; 5 points for being on the shoulder unnecessarily; 10 points for following too closely; 10 points for failure to watch for crosstraffic; 10 points for not slowing down for animals; 5 points for overrunning stop signs; 5 points for holding up traffic; 3 points for holding the steering wheel improperly. These markings were recorded whenever noted on the record sheet.

INTRANSIT EVALUATION

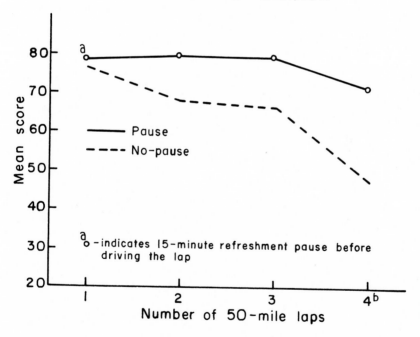

Fig. 11. Intransit Evaluation.

While the lateral placement markings were made at certain points on each lap of the trip, it was necessary to make the markings of the ten items given above at the time they occurred. Thus the experimenter could review his score sheet afterwards and tell exactly where the driver had made a bad maneuver and possibly from the study of the terrain could explain some of the reasons for it.

From the description of the method of scoring it is obvious that high scores are desirable and would indicate better performance. There were enough different types of events to be rated and sufficient variety of performance so that the rater could not very well keep tab on what had been rated or how many markings the subject had. In other words, the rater was more or less in the dark with respect to the subject's performance barring unnecessary or particularly bad records. The experimenter made every effort to be fair and to mark only those points which were violated and to ignore the particular run that was being made at the time.

The remaining points after these deductions from 100 were taken as the driver's score in each section of the route. Consistency of the ratings could be assigned by comparing the eight sections of the route which were travelled three to eight times each way. The evaluations used are from two runs each for 18 drivers, making a total of 36 trips covering about 7,500 miles of highway driving. This was in normal traffic in this section of the country which would be approximately normal for an average U.S. highway in the United States.

Preliminary studies were made of all the measurements used on the various subjects. Analysis of the first 12 regular subject's results seemed to indicate that certain of the *before* and *after* tests could be omitted since they did not contribute to the results by differentiating the groups in any way. Some others were kept for special reasons. Reliabilities of those retained varied from as high as .97 for those with perceptual efficiency to low as .1 for brake movements. Most of the reliabilities, however, were satisfactory and ranged from .70 to .85. The reliability of the Rogers-Lauer Scale was found to be .86 in this study. By the reliability of the test is meant the degree to which it can be repeated with similar results. A reliability of 1.00 means the test given a second time will give the same results as the first time given. A reliability of 0, of course, would mean that it is no better than chance. It is expected that any test should range around .70 to .80 to be satisfactory.

LATERAL PLACEMENT

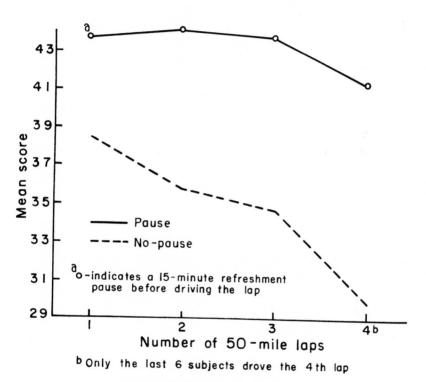

Fig. 12. Lateral Placement.

The intransit measures generally were quite reliable. Accelerator movements gave a reliability of .74; attention to the light, .57; jerk recorder, .90; lateral placement, .81; tachograph record, approximately .60. Two measures were used from the tachograph record — the modal or the most common speed, and the number of fluctuations in speed. These have been found to be indicative of driving ability in the criterion test (3) made with 249 subjects. This was done over an 8-mile stretch of road and had nothing to do with the experiments reported in this study, except in that the results formed the logic for the rationale set up and the devices used for checking drivers.

It should be emphasized that only a limited amount of driving can be done in hours of daylight and under fairly uniform traffic conditions during certain seasons of the year. A typical experiment would take one and one-half to two hours for the *pretest*, three or four hours of driving, and one and one-half to two hours for the *after* tests, not including the time for refreshments, etc. Thus six to eight hours at least were required for each subject during each test run. For the two trips each driver was paid and this ran from $12 up, at $1 per hour.

Selection of the Route for Driving

Before the study was begun several routes were explored and considered. The one finally chosen embraces 10 miles west of Ames on U.S. Highway 30, 15 miles north to Stanhope on Iowa State Highway 60, as previously described. The return was made over the same route. This took the drivers over a fairly uniform type of road on which scorings could be made most advantageously and rest pauses accomplished with a minimum of change in traffic and other conditions.

Eighteen male subjects were used, being recruited from lay drivers in the vicinity of Ames and surrounding towns. Although paid a moderate honorarium on an hourly basis it is difficult to find enough subjects willing to spend two days and from 12 to 15 hours time on an experiment.

The age range was from 19 to 69 years with a median of 29.5 years. Three years driving experience, or at least 10,000 miles of driving, were set up as a minimum criterion for accepting the subject. The subjects had driven a mean of 239 thousand and some miles with a median of 126 thousand miles. For the most part they tended to be older or in the 20-year age group. The older subjects included some retired men who were available for such type of experiment. No attempt, of course, was made to check the driver's mileage which was given on the evaluation blanks reported at the beginning of the experiment.

Each subject of those in the control run did *pretests* after which he was given the criterion rating and then proceeded on the several laps of 50 miles each. The score markings for the section ratings were made in the eight sections of the record form for each lap. Periodic readings of the instruments were made at the end of each lap.

The experimental group went through the same procedure and was given a rest pause and tea with additives as the refreshment at the beginning of each lap. It is to be remembered that the experimental group consisted of the same subjects as the control group, but the order of their trips was varied. In other words, if one were drawn to do the experimental trip first, he was given refreshments on the first trip, but no refreshment and rest pause on the second trip. This procedure was standardized so that all subjects received the same treatment throughout.

Results

As already stated, the *before* and *after* tests were studied carefully at first and 14 selected. This was done after 12 subjects had been run over the route. To complete the experiment, the 12 tests were given to all 18 subjects and at the end a statistical evaluation was made. Those tests which were eliminated will not be reported here. Table II gives the results of the *before* and *after* tests which were retained throughout the experiment.

TABLE II

Before and After Tests

| | *Mean* | | | | | |
| | No Pause | | Pause | | | |
	Before	After	Before	After	F	P*
Discriminative reaction time						
Actual time	98.989	90.733	89.550	84.822	.171	.685
Time corrected for practice effect	115.600	119.594	108.150	114.150	1.159	.289
Modified steadiness test	17.439	14.261	17.622	15.200	.676	.419
Parking efficiency						
Score	139.167	150.278	137.222	153.889	.284	.600
Time	55.778	47.500	63.556	53.111	.002	.968

(*TABLE II continued on page 166*)

Perceptual efficiency						
Number attempted	46.722	47.444	46.111	48.222	.984	.330
Number right	39.000	40.722	37.667	40.833	1.213	.280
Rogers-Lauer Scale						
Part 1	47.389	46.833	47.556	47.944	4.385	.050
Part 2	90.222	89.778	90.611	93.278	17.960	.010
Total	137.611	136.611	138.167	141.222	15.066	.010

*Indicates the chances in 100 that the results might be reversed if repeated.

Under heading "P" is indicated the chances in 100 that the results might be reversed if repeated. In other words, discriminative reaction time of *before* and *after* tests showed 68 chances out of 100 that this is a chance observation and therefore not a valid measure. The best way to interpret Table II is to look for the small probabilities or confidence levels. For example, the Rogers-Lauer Scale is substantial at the 5% level which means that there are 19 chances out of 100 that this is a true indication of the results. These were the most consistent measures obtained. One such as parking time which is .96 shows practically no relationship at all. The parking score, however, did have a fair degree of validity showing a "P" of .6.

These are derived by a method of covariance in which the scores on the tests given *before* were taken as the covariate. By and large it may be said that the *before* and *after* tests did not all hold up well. They were not valid in other words. Those showing fair possibilities were "reaction time corrected for practice," "number attempted in perceptual efficiency," and the "Rogers-Lauer Scale." The latter, however, would be expected to be fairly valid since it had had a great deal of work done on it before this study was attempted.

Intransit Evaluations

The intransit measurements have already been described in a general way. In connection with the table of intransit measurements we shall merely say that for the seven measures used for evaluating the driver's performance while on the route, only one, "accelerator movements," turned out to be of no particular value. The "time for making the trip" was only slightly diagnostic, but was in the right direction. Two other measures taken from the tachograph record did not show results sufficiently stable to warrant inclusion.

TABLE III

INTRANSIT MEASUREMENTS

	Mean				
	No Pause	*Pause*	*Difference*	*t*	*P*
Accelerator movements	35.5000	35.3500	.1500	.094	.9250
Attention light	.0285	.0252	.0033	2.414	.0100
Brake movements	11.5000	10.8500	.6500	1.090	.2800
Driving time	59.0800	59.4300	—.3500	—.833	.4100
Intransit evaluation	68.0330	78.4170	—10.3840	—4.273	.0050
Jerk recorder	305.3670	255.9170	49.4500	1.775	.0500
Lateral placement	35.6830	43.6000	—7.9170	—11.887	.0005

Consideration of the tables on *before* and *after* tests and *intransit* measures seemed to indicate that a road test should be included in any driving efficiency study. The other measures which apparently warrant inclusion are:

1. A reliable criterion rating which in this study was found to be significant beyond the 5% level, showing an advantage for the pause group for *before* and *after* measurements.

2. Possibly a "discriminative reaction test with correction for practice effects" should be used. It showed the pause group most efficient at the 29% level of confidence. While not outstanding this shows a correlation somewhat favorable to the pause group.

3. Some form of perceptual efficiency test should be used which in this study was significant at the 30% level of confidence. While not spectacular, this could be more or less prognostic.

4. Some form of attention light or signal should be included. This test showed the pause group to be superior at the 1% level of confidence throughout the trip in noting signals quicker. In other words, they seemed to be driving at a higher state of attention. In an earlier study it seemed the effect of tea had tended to relax a person. This would probably be consistent with the observation noted in this study. One can relax and yet have a high level of attention if at ease performing the task.

5. Brake movements would be useful if a reliable score could be obtained. Even though the reliability was low this showed the pause group to be superior according to the rationale set up at the

8% level of confidence.

6. A system of general intransit evaluation should be included similar to that discussed here. It was significant beyond the 1% level of confidence showing the pause group superior.

7. Some form of lateral placement measurement should be used. It was significant beyond the 1% level showing the pause group superior.

Whereas the lateral placement showed very consistent trends, some discussion as to whether this should be recorded by objective measures, such as photography, were discussed. There are two points of view, and while we are strongly in support of objective measures whenever such are possible, it is our firm belief that in this instance a photographic record might be misleading. In other words, unless one had the whole photographic picture in hand, he could not interpret any particular marking or set of markings. For example, in case of an oncoming car crowding the center, the driver might show a tendency to take the shoulder. A literal interpretation of such a maneuver would be derogatory to the subject. Actually the maneuver shows good common sense and should be given due credit or the location not marked at all. While this point may be argued either way, the system shows a consistent evaluation of the study in Figures 10 and 11. Some objection was raised to the method of using deductions for passing. The two graphs were constructed and showed the same general characteristics with practically no difference at all. Thus we still contend that deductions made for undesirable and risky passing is necessary and the sole method of getting this is to rely on the judgment of the experimenter.

What the Results Show

It might be well to discuss the various graphic accounts of the different measures used in the *intransit* study.

Accelerator movements: The pause and no-pause results overlap somewhat. As a probability value of .92 indicates, this measure had very little, if any, significance.

The attention factor, or ability of the subject to respond when seeing a light, showed a marked superiority for the pause group during the first hour of driving. After that time, for some reason, the pause group seemed to improve during the first two hours of driving. The results showed the pause group and the no-pause group to be about equal at the end of the third hour. During the fourth period the curves again separated with the pause group requiring less time to respond. While the values are greater for the first two hours of driving, they were all statistically substantial. During the first two hours of driving after a refreshment pause, the efficiency seemed to be greatly improved. During the third hour efficiency gradually deteriorated for the pause group until there was really no difference at the end of the third hour. In other words, the slight practice effect of the no-pause group seemed to offset the efficiency obtained by the pause group. At no time, however, did the pause group regularly react as quickly as the no-pause group.

The brake movements showed the no-pause group to be consistently better, or superior, in this function. Again the greatest superiority was noted during the first and second hours and there was a gradual reversion to near equality toward the end of the third hour.

While driving time, or time for the trip, showed a statistical significance slightly in favor of the pause group, both showed a consistent tendency to reduce the time of the trip after the first increase in speed or initial start. The pause group reduced the time for the first two hours and then levelled off and held about the same speed for the third hour, and then reduced the time somewhat during the third to fourth hour. No very illuminating conclusions can be drawn from the driving time with respect to the effect on driving. The only consistent trend is that driving will tend to increase the speed of the driver. The average speed may increase up to 10% during the three or four hour period of driving. This happened for both groups alike. While not verified experimentally until the present study, it has long been believed by those who are students of driving, that as one becomes accustomed to the sound of his car, as he drives further on a trip, he tends to speed up. This shows experimental verification and there is some slight evidence that rest pauses would tend to offset this tendency beginning with the third and fourth hour of driving. During the first two hours there didn't seem to be a great deal of difference between the two groups.

The intransit evaluations and two graphs made of each, Figures 10 and 11, are most illuminating. The graphs are very nearly identical in trend and one could easily be confused by looking at one and then being shown the other graph at a later time.

Deductions for bad passing tends to increase the differences in the curves. Analysis of the trends and differences noted shows the pause group tends to maintain efficiency up through the third and fourth hour of driving quite well. The loss from the first to the last hour was not found to be more than 4 or 5% for the pause group. For the no-pause group, however, the loss from the first to the end of the fourth hour ran about 25%. The trends of the curves indicate that this was quite consistent throughout and increased gradually.

The argument that this was a subjective measure and therefore might be biased is not borne out by the trends of the curves. Actually one would expect any bias to show up at the end of the first hour. It would also be expected to wear off in any experiment of this type, the experimenter might become confused and more or less forgetful of what particular run included was being made. Since the curves show a very consistent tendency to digress, and the pause group showed a tendency to hold up throughout, we would have to discount any argument that such a marking is not valid.

The jerk recorder, or the number of swerves and partial stops which are made, showed consistently that the no-pause group had more tendency to turn suddenly to the side than the pause group. It occurred consistently throughout with the pause group showing fewer tendencies in this way.

The most striking graphic account, and perhaps as diagnostic as any, is the lateral placement (see Fig. 12). These markings showed the pause group to consistently retain a higher level and to lose probably approximately 4%. The rest-pause group started out with an index around .39 and dropped at the end of the fourth hour of driving to .30. This would be about 20% loss in efficiency during four hours of driving. The pause group showed a decrease likewise, but starting with an index of about .44 they came down to something like .42. The higher score here is the better performance. Hence, the inference is that for the no-pause drivers, driving efficiency will gradually drop off at about the rate of 5% an hour for the first three hours and then drop perhaps 10% an hour from there on. Pauses reduce the decrement appreciably.

Conclusions

The conclusions drawn from Experiment B of this series may be summarized best by the following statements:

1. The hypothesis that a road test can be developed to function as the laboratory test used is sustained and promises to be more useful even than the laboratory test. The secondary hypothesis that *before* and *after* tests will not differentiate the pause and no-pause subjects is rejected at a substantial level of confidence for selected tests. It was definitely rejected for the criterion rating which seems should be used in any *before* and *after* study of driving efficiency. Findings from the laboratory study of intransit measures seemed to show them to be more useful than the *before* and *after* tests and this was supported throughout the experiment.

Some form of lateral placement test should be used for indicating the performance of the driver enroute. This should be objective in the sense that certain definite markings of the driver can be made by the experimenter. The objectivity here is not to be interpreted as an automatic recording of position without respect to conditions surrounding the event. If all traffic conditions could be controlled so that every instance of marking was the same as every other, then an objective type of scoring would be desired. However, since this is not possible and since conditions are constantly changing, we must resort to the intelligence of the experimenter to judge when and when not to make a marking and to allow for any irregularities which may develop.

REFERENCES

1. Eagles, J. W., Halliday, A. M. and Redfearn, J. W. T., The effect of fatigue on tremor. Paper presented at the Symposium on Fatigue held by the Ergonomics Research Society at the College of Aeronautics, Cranfield, March 1952.
2. Lauer, A. R., et al, Selection tests for Army operators of light and heavy motor vehicles. U. S. Army, PRB Technical Research Report 1091, 1953.
3. Lauer, A. R., Suhr, Virtus W., and Allgaier, Earl, Development of a criterion for driving performance. Highway Research Board Bull. 172, p. 158, 1958.
4. Lauer, A. R. and Suhr, V. W., The effect of rest pauses and refreshment on driving efficiency. Traffic Safety and Research Review, 1958, 2, 4-9.
5. Lauer, A. R. and McMonagle, Carl, Do road signs affect accidents? Traffic Quarterly, 9, #3, 322-330, 1955.
6. McNelly, George Winfield, The development and laboratory validation of a subjective fatigue scale. Dissertation Abstracts, 14:2135, 1954.
7. Miles, W. R., The reaction time of the eye. Psychological Monographs, 47(No. 2):268-293, 1936.
8. National Safety Council. Too long at the wheel; a study of exhaustion and drowsiness as they affect traffic accidents. Chicago, the Council, 1935.
9. Reed, H. B., Fatigue and work curve from a ten-hour day in addition. Jour. of Ed. Psych., 15:371-376, 1924.
10. Suhr, Virtus W., Driving efficiency over a six-hour period by simulated driving performance. Unpublished Doctoral Dissertation. Iowa State College Library, 1956.
11. Suhr, V. W., The effect of rest pauses and refreshment on driving efficiency. 1956, Doctoral Thesis (ms), Iowa State College Library.
12. Tuttle, W. W., Wilson, Marjorie, and Daum, Kate, Effects of altered breakfast habits on physiologic response. Jour. of Applied Physiology, 1(No. 8):545-559, Feb. 1949.
13. Woodworth, Robert E., Experimental Psychology. New York, Henry Holt and Company, 1938.

CHAPTER XI

ABOUT DRIVER TESTING PROCEDURES

INTRODUCTION

Most any field in which newer methods are being used, such as in automobile driving, many opinions are usually expressed. Some would-be authorities have one panacea for all driving situations to avoid accidents. This panacea usually is associated with some interest the persons may have. Many times interests are mercenary, and other times they are still in the experimental stage.

Studies (9, 12) have been going on in this field to determine the factors of safe driving since the 1920's, but only a few tests have been definitely recommended for use in driver's examinations (7). Practically no high validity coefficients have been obtained (6), but this is partly due to the fact that there has not been a satisfactory criterion of driving set up. However, many users of the methods of evaluating driving are not interested in validity, except the so-called face validity.

Accidents are not reliable when used as a criterion. Ratings have been used with fair success by the Army and others but frequently they are not available as a criterion against which to check results with the average driver. Classification made by patrolmen in the driver's license examination has been found to have a low reliability.

In general, more has been found out regarding the limitations of tests conventionally used for improving the driver's license examination (6) than of the specific nature of tests for identifying accident-prone drivers. Most tests and procedures are not new in spite of the claims of those who advocate them or who are

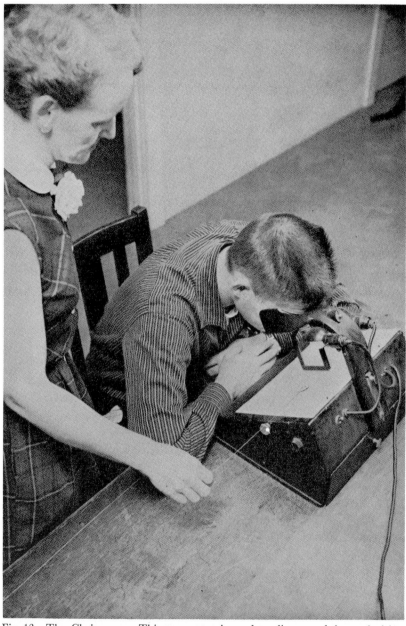

Fig. 13. The Cheiroscope. This apparatus is used to diagnose defects of vision such as scotoma and use of the eyes together. It may also be used to determine blind spots in the visual field.

constructing them. Many are copied from earlier apparatus or forms which are held to be original (13). For example, an early test was developed to measure street car manipulation (11). Later those interested in automotive driving, taxi cab service, etc., built forms of driver testing equipment from the earlier devices or copied them with modifications. Since that time other devices such as the Drivometer (7) built for experimental work at Iowa State College, the Auto Trainer made by the American Automobile Association, and the Drivotrainer sponsored by the Aetna Insurance Company, and others, were developed from these earlier models used to measure street car operators.

In Paris, France (9), special tests were used to measure performance of bus operators and have been used for many years. Marbe and Lippman in Germany employed mechanical tests for classifying drivers also. Other work has been done in Spain and England, and in other countries similar efforts to evaluate driving efficiency have been made.

In Chicago a great deal has been done by some taxi cab companies (12) as well as the Rapid Transit Company to develop devices for measuring the aptitude of operators. In Washington, D. C., and other cities, the transit companies have been particularly active in developing ways and means of measuring characteristics of operators in conjunction with their selection and training.

During our first explorations in the field (14), inquiries were made of work done in Canada, Italy, Denmark, Holland, Sweden, Japan, China, Australia, and South America, besides the countries already mentioned. Replies were received from about half of these places describing the work of this nature that had been carried on. It suffices to say that testing procedures are not new and have a long background of development. Some of the work was not intended to be scientific in nature but did yield results of importance by stimulating the imagination of investigators (12) as well as the applicants.

The value of tests in the selection and training of drivers may be summarized in the following paragraphs:

1. Tests attract the attention of drivers and if properly admin-

istered they tend to give some information on characteristics which are useful in driving (7).

2. Tests, even though some are not particularly scientifically devised, tend to make a greater impression on the examinee and develops a more wholesome respect for the procedures of examination.

An evaluation of tests for drivers used early has been summarized as follows: There is considerable evidence of sporadic attempts made to test drivers of various types, usually for the purpose of meeting some immediate practical situation. One example is that of reaction time as a measure. Investigators become greatly interested for a time but eventually gave up the work for other problems. It is likely that they had overrated the testing procedures at first (1) and found that they were subject to some source of classifying various elements of behavior. Reaction time, for instance, does not measure speed of action but rather the ability to get started into action. Very little research had been done on driving performance as such. No definite ground work had been established from which to proceed and no criterion of driving was available. Perhaps the most consistent study that had been released was a series of researches made at the Ohio State University (14) for the purpose of investigating fundamental factors of automotive manipulation. You will note that, as in most other instances, the first stage of such development was that of practical explorations based on a rational approach to the problems of driving. Later some study was done to establish the reliability and validity of the various test procedures used at that time (6). More is known about the reliability of tests than of the validity. In other words, more is known of the consistency of measuring tests than of their ability to measure driving.

The same is true of the present day efforts of similar nature. There are a number of systems which are being used throughout the country for training drivers, or for retraining them, with the idea of reducing accidents. No doubt some of these are good, but again, are not new. The so-called Smith System of teaching drivers to observe well is good and one of the specific items emphasized is to "aim high in steering." This sounds revolutionary and new, but as a matter of fact in the training of drivers during the past 25 years or more this has been one of the cardinal points in teaching the beginner to drive. Do not look down at the road immediately in front of your radiator, look ahead. The idea is not new, but it has been revised and formulated into an elaborate system of training drivers based on a five-point system.

The second item advocated in the so-called Smith System is that of "getting the big picture." This is tantamount to emphasizing what has been taught in driver education all the time as "watch closely all around you — at the sides and ahead, as well as behind." It has been known for several years that drivers do not fixate on the road but observe around them. It is human nature to move the eyes. Even the special interest groups which are very much down on roadside stimuli, such as business places and advertising signs, have missed the point. Therefore, the Smith System has formalized this notion of looking around when you are driving — "get the big picture." It is well known that when the driver has nothing to see when traveling along he is more likely to get into trouble than when he has something to look at. Interesting things to look at keep him alert and awake. They counteract highway hypnosis.

Another idea taught in this system is to "keep your eyes moving." This is another concept that has been used in driver education throughout the years — to keep the eyes moving about to pick up cues for efficient driving. Let them fixate on one object and then on another. The advertising people know this is important and try to keep the legend on their sign boards down to a very short eye span so that the driver will instantaneously pick up the message intended when his eyes scan the road ahead. The eyes are certain to move and could not be kept stationary even if the driver wanted to keep them so.

The Smith System has another trite injunction which is very good and which has also been emphasized for a long while. They call it "leave yourself an out," which means allowing for hazards that may turn up. It has been generally known as a phase of defensive driving. These teaching points of the film are mentioned to illustrate the fact that many of the so-called new systems and ideas of driving performance are not new at all, but have been used for years. Good drivers tend to practice them and they help keep the operator out of trouble.

ASSUMPTIONS MADE IN MEASURING DRIVING

The assumptions made in developing tests of driving performance are usually as follows:

1. The most practical approach to problems of driving safety is through experimental studies of traits, response pattern habits and skills related to driving.

2. Successful performance of an operator is dependent upon a minimum level of abilities or skills. Below this level, accident risk becomes greater and more acidents are likely to occur. This assumption may be questioned.

3. Reliable measures of certain behavior characteristics should give some indication of one's ability to maneuver an automobile or a motor vehicle.

4. Specific traits or characteristics of driving are only a part of the general pattern of responses necessary for successful performance. Many other factors relate to automobile driving and highway safety such as design features, regulations, effective enforcement, training of drivers, general public cooperation, and good attitudes toward safe driving. Each driver must be willing to police his own performance.

5. Certain existing measures of human traits are well standardized and require only application to the problem at hand. In other words, measures of reaction time, visual acuity and strength have been well established and if applied to driving will be found useful in describing a driver's potential ability. They will not, however, prognosticate his ability to keep out of accidents.

6. It must be assumed that the fundamental processes of psychological testing must be observed to obtain satisfactory results. Further explanation of this assumption may be set down as follows:

a. The test must be as nearly like the basic responses or trait as possible. This does not mean that they are the same types of performance.

b. Measures used must be reliable or consistent when given a second time. The results must agree closely on a test re-test situation.

c. The measures must be valid when checked against a genuine or a satisfactory criterion of driving (8).

d. Measures used for scientific studies should be as simple as possible. Addition of glamorous exteriors will not make a poor test good.

As stated, these are assumptions and some may be subject to modification. It might be well to re-examine them with a view toward critical analysis.

The first seems reasonable and it would appear that any measurements used to evaluate driving should be related to the performance. However, the fact that it is closely related does not necessarily guarantee that it will be a critical indicator. An observational approach may seem reasonable but may not be strictly valid. It is doubtful whether enough basic research has been done on many so-called related activities to guarantee a valid account of a driver from tests of the type often used.

The second assumption holds only under certain conditions. Lack of ability in some respects may not be a handicap but an asset to a driver if he knows about it and compensates for the deficiency. By compensate we mean that he performs in such a manner as to rise above or overcome the deficiency he has. On the other hand, one may be well above a certain minimum level of performance and through improper responses of various types may be likely to get into considerable difficulty while at the wheel. He may do the proper things at the wrong time.

The third assumption is valid to a certain extent. While a test must be reliable, the mere fact of its reliability or consistency in measurement from one time to another does not guarantee that it will be useful in classifying driving performance. It is valid only insofar as it states that a measurement of any trait should be dependable or representative.

The fourth assumption, that driving is dependent upon an efficient general pattern of responses, for the most part is sound. However, there are times when the best organized behavior pattern may deviate momentarily and cause a lapse in efficiency. From various studies that have been made it would seem that the average driver meets about three times as many accident potential situations as accident situations. In other words, his behavior organization is fairly sound for two of the situations he meets, but for some reason or other it fails him in the third which results in an accident.

Assumption five, that any existing measurements of human traits may be applied to the problem of driving, is open to some question. The relationship here is often rationalized and sometimes erroneously. Some reasoning does not always turn out as was intended. For example, in an attempt to explain the curving of a ball when thrown, one amateur's explanation was that the pressure of the atmosphere against the side of the rotating ball would tend to produce a curve by friction on the dense air. Actually, if the ball does curve, which has been questioned, tendency of the ball has been found to move in the opposite direction from that of the explanation offered. A similar example occurs in reaction time. One might conclude that the driver who acts quickest is the safest driver. This is only true if the driving reaction made is correct. If the driver reacts quickly and does the wrong thing he might be more efficient if he didn't react so quickly. As a matter of fact, studies in general have shown that consistency of reaction time, that is, whether a person reacts quickly each time or slow each time, is more important than the actual amount of time necessary to react. Only in extreme cases, which in most instances would be pathological where the reaction time would run exceedingly long, could any general conclusion be made that the length of reaction time is indicative of performance efficiency.

The sixth assumption is a sort of a review which has several facets that might be discussed separately. It is questionable whether the test must be as near like the performance it measures as is possible to make it. It may possibly be entirely different and yet be quite indicative. That it should be consistent is generally accepted and yet does not cover the whole problem. The validity, of course, is necessary, but only when a suitable criterion has not been set up against which to judge it. Therefore this assumption is very hard to evaluate. Simplicity of a test is necessary and it would seem that this assumption is particularly useful when measuring a practical situation where time is limited. It involves an application of the law of parsimony which states that other things being equal the most simple explanation of a phenomenon is the best. This would suggest that the most direct method of explaining or of measuring a performance would probably be the most useful, but selected elements of the situation must be considered.

With respect to the background of these assumptions, several studies have been carried out in different parts of the country as exploratory in the field of machine operation testing. A few of these will be mentioned. While there were studies by Shellow and others done in Milwaukee on street car operators, as well as those done by Cleeton in Pittsburgh on motormen, very little continuous early work had been done in the way of tests for drivers. Snow (12), in Chicago, has devised some simple tests for separating the good drivers from the bad ones for the Yellow Cab Company. His efforts were largely that of setting up scare tests which would frighten job applicants away who had some question about their own ability. The plan seemed to work quite well and he reported excellent results in driving records. Another study by Wechsler (13) with Yellow Cab operators was made early. It was a practical kind of test made in a stationary automobile body.

The most extensive set of researches probably done prior to 1930 were carried out at the Ohio State University (14) with various cooperating agencies in East Lansing, Michigan, and similar locations. This work was transferred to Iowa State College in 1931 (7) and an interest in the problem has been developing here and elsewhere since that time. The American Automobile Association and several instrument manufacturers have gone into the production of measuring devices on a rather extensive scale. These have been largely of mechanical nature.

We should not forget to mention some early studies at Purdue University. Projects on psychology of the highway and driving clinics have been run in Milwaukee, Pittsburgh, Cleveland, Detroit, and Hartford, Connecticut, exploring different phases of the testing procedures.

Another project at Massachusetts State College (1) was later developed by the Aetna Insurance Company and a set of instruments of an imposing nature was constructed and used to evaluate driving. One of these was the Reactometer which was a forerunner of the Drivotrainer.

For practical purposes equipment of a simple type can be constructed for a rather nominal fee from plans available from the American Automobile Association. However, some types of testing equipment have been very elaborately constructed. In fact some were so elaborate that it is impractical to move them about (14). Their use was limited because of the cost of the equipment.

During the depression period much confidence was put in these devices. In fairness to those who contributed to the studies at that time a few explanations should be made along with the presentation of known facts and limitations of the studies. In the first place, statements were made which may be open somewhat to question. For example, one writer on the subject in a scientific journal inferred that the results obtained from validation studies were only one-sixth better than chance in the prediction of accidents (6). Considering perfect prediction this may be true. Inadvertently the word "predict" has been used when perhaps the word "estimate" would have been better. It is true that when one is shooting at a target he usually makes a small percentage of bull's eyes; however, many of the near hits cluster close around the bull's eyes. Therefore, to predict the number of perfect hits may not be more than one-sixth better than chance, but this is rather a meaningless concept. What is one-sixth better than chance? Does it mean that non-hits will be scattered in all directions and distances from the mark?

To resort to prediction of specific results may be somewhat out of the true realm of science. We like to make close estimates, but in some fields it is impossible to make them exact. In other words, improvement in any system for predicting accidents will be very difficult to evaluate. The investigation in Connecticut revealed a driver's accidents for two three-year periods were not highly related. Compiled and correlated the results showed a very low relationship. If one strives for perfection he sometimes misses the mark but will gradually move toward the goal sought. Organized society is run on the premise that improvement, even in a minor way, is desirable. If testing is a refinement over crude judgment it should be encouraged, even if the validity is lower than desired.

Thus we may say that the various results of driver testing over the years have progressed gradually in the way of improvement of earlier techniques but they have not reached perfection as yet. At the present time there are two general types of such equipment being manufactured and sold. One set has to do with the training of drivers principally, and many persons consider the other type to be that of evaluating driving or for selecting drivers. The first usage seems most practical and successful, but sometimes the advantages are taken for granted or overestimated.

The pragmatic value of a test or training device will have to be determined by a long period of usage or by definite research. Therefore we are not able to say at the present how effective any given device may be for training. It looks as though some would save considerable time, although there are conflicting experimental results obtained in the field of aviation as well as in driving. The value of simulated performance has both its proponents and opponents.

It is generally conceded now that the selection of superior drivers based on road testing procedures is questionable. Perhaps the best approach is the use of evaluation or selection devices in connection with training. Here it is not a question so much as to whether the person can or cannot do a thing, but rather an evaluation of his strong and weak points as a driver. After 30 years of study of psychological problems of driving there are certain definite facts which may be given with some degree of certainty. The applications may be made by one inexperienced with the problems.

1. Training devices of the simulative type have their place in aviation and in automobile driving. Probably from one-fourth to one-half the time for training could be saved in learning automobile driving if some simple devices are properly used for teach-

ing the fundamentals.

It is next to impossible to pick good drivers from bad drivers by the use of psychophysical tests (14) . In one study done with the Army it was found that a good set of pencil-and-paper tests would do as good a job of selection as psychophysical tests and at considerable less expense in that they could be administered to a group or several persons at one time and would have slightly higher prognostic value.

The third aspect of the employment of some simple tests has to do with that of using them as an ordinary clinical instrument in connection with training (3) . For example, if a person has poor vision he should know about it so that he can allow for his weaknesses in vision by giving special attention when he drives. If he is slow to react he should know it so that he may be able to adjust his reactions accordingly and allow himself more time. If he is variable in his reaction, if he acts very slow one time and very fast the next time, he should know about this in order to make suitable compensation. This third phase of driver testing technique has been overlooked by many persons who should be in a position to make use of such principles. Too few have been trained to understand the basic significance and the limitations of tests. It is hoped that training courses will be offered to instructors and teachers of driving so that they may be able to make the best use of such tests for training purposes.

Analysis of the various studies of psychological factors of automobile driving indicate there are three groups of persons who are interested. First, there are those who are doing the basic research and have been interested in devising instruments that could be used for measuring certain aspects of behavior in which they were interested. They have resorted mostly to home built devices of the ordinary laboratory type in which conditions can be controlled and which yield fairly reliable and dependable results. The validity of the tests of course depends upon what is being measured and the device used. The idea sometimes was not to devise tests as such, but to devise some kind of measuring instrument.

The second group of persons who are interested in tests have been those who are dealing with problems of driving, driver selection and driver evaluation. This would include the transportation companies, the insurance people and, to some extent, the drivers' licensing personnel. Their interest is primarily in devices which can make quick measurements to determine certain things about drivers that they wish to know. They are interested only in tests from the standpoint of their usability and oftentimes they neglect the scientific aspects of a measuring device. They are likely to grasp at a straw, so to speak, in order to accomplish some immediate result which they have in mind. Face validity is the only important item.

The third group of persons who are interested in tests, for the most part, are those who have an interest in devising and selling the instrument commercially, while at the same time promoting safety. While they may be associated with some organization, such as the motor club, insurance companies, etc., their primary interest is in devising some instrument which will give examiners or testing people something that will be serviceable and give consistent results. Usually these people are interested in building up the quality of their equipment and its performance. They are likely to lean more on the engineering side when it comes to mechanical devices.

It might be stated that all tests would probably come under two headings: (1) those of a mechanical nature, and (2) those of the pencil-and-paper variety. This is true in driver testing as well as in regular psychological laboratory devices for testing other abilities and traits.

So far as tests proper are concerned, they are really the product of various investigations which have been carried on and which have attracted considerable public attention. With these facts in mind let us proceed to discuss some of the results which have been noted during several years of sudy. They are based on a great many observations, although no attempt will be made to bring in the various data at this time.

First and foremost, let us discuss what is commonly called face validity. If you are measuring automobile driving and use a device which looks as much like automobile driving as is possible to devise for experimental use, the test is said to have good face validity because it looks like what you are trying to measure. For example, in industrial research in a psychological laboratory, many times packing or handling of small objects is a function to be measured. One type of test is called spool packing in which a box accommodating a certain number of spools is used. In another measure of dexterity, a larger number of small pins are handled with tweezers and are placed in small receptacles on a tray. The transfer, or the moving of these pins from one to another, or from the table to the receptacle is a measure of finer dexterity and therefore such test would be said to have high face validity for certain types of work. If the purpose is to measure automobile driving, then the simulated test would be supposed to have a number of reactions closely related to automobile driving such as steering, braking, clutching, observing, etc.

There has always been a question as to whether a test needs to have high face validity in order to be serviceable. This, of course, has been disputed and perhaps the only argument for high face validity is that it appeals to the person taking the test, and also was the most logical approach to the problem. It is not only the most logical, but perhaps the most practical, insofar as it would seem reasonable that a direct approach to measuring some function desired to be measured, should in some degree at least represent those functions. Therefore, the assumption that a test should have high face validity is a practical working hypothesis, at least, although it may not necessarily be sound.

One of the earmarks of lack of experience in the field of safety is a ready made formula or panacea for all ailments. In other words, persons who believe that one remedy will stop all accidents on the highway, in the home, on the farm, or otherwise, usually have not studied the problem of safety very long.

ABOUT ACCIDENT FREQUENCY

One major concept that is important in the whole matter of driving safety is whether a person has accidents repeatedly, whether most accidents are due to repeaters, or whether most accidents happen to persons who have never had a mishap before. The proper analysis of this problem is important in all matters pertaining to the philosophy of development and use of tests. A few of the facts seem to warrant the following conclusions. It must be kept in mind that any statement regarding a percentage of drivers having accidents must also have with it the qualifying statement as to the length of time considered. If one takes one-half minute as his base of consideration it is doubtful whether any one person would ever have more than one accident. If one takes a year as a base of consideration, then a certain number of persons are likely to have more than one accident. Over a ten-year period of driving various studies have shown that between 20 and 30% of ordinary or lay drivers have all of the accidents in a given area. With commercial companies over a 15-year period, a study of 1,014 drivers shows that 43% had all the accidents.

Considering such periods of time and numerous nonlinear relationships which have been found, it seems that the accident group may be further divided into two categories: (a) a small percentage, perhaps 2 to 4%, who are accident prone, and (b) the remainder of the 20 to 30% who may be designated as accident liable. The latter term is used with reservation, meaning those who need not have accidents, but who for one reason or another do have a few mishaps. Usually these accidents are experienced early in life after which there is a relatively long accident-free period of driving.

Although the concept of accident proneness has been questioned, studies made in Connecticut (6) and other places have shown that the probabilities of a person having over a certain number of accidents in a given period and due to chance is very remote, and the frequency of accidents is much higher for this group or greater than one would expect from chance alone. This concept of accident proneness is introduced here since all testing must rest quite heavily for its *raison d'etre* on the concept of accident proneness. Otherwise there would be no use to attempt to determine characteristics related to accidents if they happen on a purely fortuitous basis. In other words, persons who have accidents must have certain characteristics related to safe driving which have been assumed to be poor eyesight, poor reaction time, carelessness, poor attitudes, tendency to perseverate or stay at one mode of reaction over quite a length of time, etc. Having established the fact that accident proneness does depend upon deficiencies in these traits, then the necessity for devising a test of such trait becomes reasonable. Many times this has not been done except on a rational basis.

Consider one trait which is quite widely understood at present. Color blindness has long been suspected of being a cause of traffic accidents. Railroads bar color blind persons from regular employment. The Army and the Navy have strict requirements for color vision. The Air Force is more or less strict about accurate color perception for pilots. It is known that about one person out of six of the worst color blind persons of any population may confuse colored lights. There is a difference in the intensity of red and green lights ordinarily and unless the strength is controlled the person may be distinguishing on the basis of intensity. On a percentage basis this means that less than 0.33% of the population will ever miss a stop light through faulty color perception. Actually, checked against accident records, only a very slight relationship, if any, is shown between color perception and accident liability. During several years of study of accident records the writer found no case which was traceable to color blindness. Some few violations were found, although the driver was careful. Only one or two cases were found who admitted going through red lights and being unable to distinguish them, but report no accidents from the practice. This does not mean that one could not get into trouble if he were color blind. It simply indicates that the likelihood of having an accident due to faulty color perception is very remote. The implication that since railroads require good color vision it is important to traffic is not sound. On railroads, using a block system, it is very essential that the engineer be able to distinguish a red from a green light to know whether he has a clear road ahead for a considerable distance. Whereas the driver of an automobile coming up to an intersection can usually tell from the movement of other traffic whether or not he has a clear signal to go ahead. In fact, color blind persons report that this is the cue they use mostly to compensate for this deficiency. Knowing they have trouble with lights, by observing the traffic carefully, they have less trouble perhaps than a normal individual who is not so careful.

Another type of trait which would rationally be expected to be associated with accidents is reaction time. There are several kinds of reaction time which we might describe, but simple reaction time as such, irrespective of all discussion about it, does not seem to correlate with accident frequency. In spite of validity coefficients of nearly zero, several advocates of driving tests are basing practically their whole experimental approach, or testing philosophy, on this one trait. Complex reaction time does show somewhat better results but it would seem that the consistency of response generally is more important than the length of time required to respond. Therefore, it is safe to say that the variability in successive reactions has more diagnostic value than absolute reaction time per se.

Since numerous devices have been built to measure reaction time it is suggested that any attempt to measure this form of the ability to get into motion quickly should be done by means of a complex reaction time apparatus, if it is to be used.

There is evidence developing to support the statement that marked ocular dominance is a factor of importance in safe driving. It seems to depend upon the number of lanes or direction of traffic being used. A right-eyed person seems to have an advantage on two-way streets, whereas a left-eyed person seems to have some advantage on one-way streets. No clearly defined reason for this can be given at present. The fact that eye dominance is important is logical enough when it can be shown that the use of one eye only reduces the horopter, or total field of vision, by as much as 20 to 30%. Cases can be cited in which it is shown that the person looking around at a glance to one side or the other misses an approaching car or train because marked ocular dominance renders the side of the approaching car more or less restricted. An old professional driver called our attention to this and gave instances where it had helped him to turn the head to look. His notion was that one should turn the head and look at the intersection, rather than to glance with the eyes. Since it is generally stated that one's moving eyes do not see, that they see only after they fixate, this would support the driver's explanation. Thus some device which can be used to determine the degree of ocular dominance would tend to alert the driver to this condition and render him safer, at least give him the advantage from the standpoint of driving safely.

Another finding in this area is that visual acuity below 40% seems to be associated slightly with the higher accident rate, and a curve of higher accident frequency raises somewhat for acuity levels below 60%. Visual acuity of 40% in Clason notation is conventionally designated as 20/50, and 60% would be about 20/33. The exact level of acuity which favors safer driving has not been well established and probably never will for several reasons. In the first place, there are so many reasons why a person may have an accident, reasons other than vision, that it is difficult to assign any level of vision as the absolute lower limit. The best fitting glasses will not necessarily guarantee vision above 20/40 but most persons having 20/40 could be corrected to a much higher level by wearing glasses. One writer has placed it at 9 out of 10 or greater.

Still one other measurable characteristic of an individual related to driving is his activity. Activity differs from reaction time in that the latter is the time necessary to get into motion, whereas activity involves the ability to move once one is in motion. The best known measure of activity is the Ream Tapping test which is a measure of how fast one can make repeated movements for a period of 5 or 10 seconds. A 10-second period has been widely used as the interval and individuals vary from 40 to over 100 movements in 10 seconds.

Another device made by the Allgaier Shops, Arlington, Virginia, is known as the Allgaier-Lauer Rotary Activity test. This correlates reasonably closely with the Ream test and has a high reliability but is not subject to the same drawbacks as the Ream test. When tapping the subject may be able to tense his arm and thus increase the movement rate considerably in an artificial manner. The rotary activity is built and used in such a manner that it is not possible for the subject to do this.

From the standpoint of testing procedures and training of drivers, as well as training in other skills, the active person, other things being equal, has an advantage in certain skills such as tennis, driving, baseball and basketball. There are some forms of sports and skills where strength is much more important than speed. Strength may be measured by means of a hand dynamometer which is taken as an index of the general strength of the individual. This is only relatively true, but some notion of the person's basic strength can be obtained by use of a test of grip. Power steering tends to vitiate the need for strength.

Further explanation should be made regarding "safe driving" and what many people call "good driving." These are not necessarily the same. Many safe drivers are not good drivers, that is, skillful in the sense of mechanical and general aptitude. A zero correlation was obtained between company ratings and accident records of their drivers. A racing driver is usually a good driver but we would hardly call him a safe driver on the race track. At least we would hesitate to let the family ride with a racing driver in a contest. He may be a safe driver when on the road, since many of these men drive at a conservative rate of speed when not making time records. They realize the hazards one takes when driving at high speeds unnecessarily.

For the numerous reasons listed it is very difficult to separate superior performance from safe driving records. It may be said that tests developed measure four aspects of performance of a complex nature. These are: (a) manipulation of controls as such, a form of eye, foot and hand coordination; (b) observation, the correct interpretation of and reaction to serially presented stimuli. The emphasis here is upon correct interpretation rather than speed of interpretation with limits of $\frac{1}{2}$ second duration. This is longer than the average reaction time. In other words, a test having a high face validity or resembling driving performance need not involve any of the split-second reactions to be a good test of driving ability. However, a test of skill in driving will not necessarily determine whether the driver is likely to take chances. (c) The time taken for performance of a given task is sort of an overall measure of the person's aptitude at doing it. The time taken for a child to tie a bow knot at a certain age is taken as one measure of his intelligence. However, all persons do not work efficiently at the same rate of speed. Each one should be allowed to set his own record. The time taken to perform a task may also be taken as a measure of the person's caution. Rhythmic control of action may also be a factor but has not been studied in this connection. (d) The fourth aspect of measuring driving performance is that of measuring alertness or observation time. By observation time we mean the time taken to observe a new stimulus which is presented, or which is experienced, when driving along the road or in performing a test. Observation time thus is much more important than reaction time as such. It may be measured in larger units such as several seconds, rather than in terms of split seconds which are often meaningless and may be compared to measuring the size of one's head with a micrometer in being fitted for a hat. It is well known that a hair cut, or the shrinkage of the hat due to temperature, might vary much more than the smaller units of differentiation on the scale.

Enough experimental work has been done on these various phases of skilled performance that it is fair to state that we may use manipulation, observation accuracy, the time to complete a task, and the time necessary to apprehend a new stimulus as basic entities which may be incorporated to evaluate driving. It seems clear at present that the last two are important and accuracy of observation seems to be an important cue to sizing up a situation and driving in such a manner as to avoid accidents. The results have been similar in outdoor field studies and laboratory tests involving simulated performance.

OTHER FACTORS AND HOW THEY RELATE TO DRIVING

Considerable data has been obtained on hearing but this seems to be important only at extreme ranges. Any relationship which has been found could easily be traced to some associated phenomenon. For example, a person who is deaf to a noticeable degree will by virtue of his condition be more likely to observe carefully. Some studies reported have shown that deaf drivers have fewer accidents per mile of driving than do persons with normal hearing.

Extremes of high and low blood pressure seem to be somehow related to accident frequency. An explanation of this relationship has not been found for medium high blood pressure. Drivers with a systolic blood pressure of 175 should be carefully scrutinized. Standard instrumentation is available for determining this condition. Those with low blood pressure seem to go to sleep easily and lack the vitality necessary for alertness and long, continued driving. Lower systolic limits would seem to be around 96 to 100. Of course age must be considered when checking blood pressure, but the old axiom to add 100 plus your age as a reasonable blood pressure is not sound. Our studies have shown that on the average blood pressures do not change greatly between the ages of 20 and 45 or slightly above. It would not be practical to use blood pressure for a driver's license examination, although a self-recording measure of blood pressure may be used in a driving clinic for commercial companies or to check special cases.

Some other factors, which seem important at the present time and in which further studies are being carried out, have to do with several of these and are as follows:

1. Perseveration or the tendency to continue in an activity after it is once started. For example, a tune running through one's head may continue for several minutes or for some time. Thus, repetitions or continuation of a mental image or action is an example of perseveration. In Boston, street car operators driving only a certain type of car during the week were found to have trouble if changed to another type of car over the weekend. In other words, they could not adapt their movements to the new type of operation apparently because of perseveration from driving their regular vehicle.

2. Attitudes toward law enforcement and safe driving practices in general seem important. This would also include attitudes toward people. It is believed by scientific investigators, as well as by enforcement people and the public at large, that one's attitudes have more to do with his being able to stay out of accidents than skill itself. Thus, measures of attitudes have been variously developed and explored, but so far defects have been found in

those that have been used. One weakness is that persons tend to mark the form the way they think it ought to be marked. Only the incorporation of some gimmick to detect such attempts will bring these tests into general usage. Most examiners will not do this.

3. Another factor accepted by most laymen is the importance of knowledge and understanding of traffic hazards and safety principles. Particularly the driver's license is predicated on the theory that if one knows traffic laws which are presumably based on the importance of safe practices, he will be less likely to have accidents. This seems reasonable on the face of it but there is evidence that knowledge of traffic hazards and safety principles is not as important as it was once believed. Compensation and specific attitudes, commonly described under the heading of recklessness, is widely accepted as an important aspect of safe driving. In other words, a reckless driver is likely to get into trouble. The reckless driver does not compensate sufficiently for his weaknesses and therefore may get into trouble.

Adequate tests have not been devised for these last four functions although there has been some exploration in each field. The Army has developed some quite satisfactory tests of driving judgment which seem to be important in keeping the driver out of trouble. In fact, from studies we have carried out up to date, it would seem that judgment is the most important factor in the whole driving performance pattern and a road test in the driver's examination is supposed to measure to some extent the judgment of the driver.

It seems quite clear that any validation of test results which does not take into consideration the factor of compensation is likely to be inadequate, although there may be other explanations of unsatisfactory results. In this connection, the various results obtained up to the present suggest that accidents are possibly due to mental and physical conditions which might be called major or minor susceptibilities. One major susceptibility may have as much weight as several minor susceptibilities. Again, one minor susceptibility may not be operative except in the presence of another minor susceptibility. For example, clumsiness at the wheel may be a minor susceptibility. Clumsiness coupled with nervousness may become a serious handicap while alone it may be easily combated by the driver making the necessary compensations in driving. By compensation we mean that the driver may try to be especially careful if his vision is not good. By driving slowly and being careful vision may not be an important factor to his driving. On the average it may be very important to drivers under certain conditions.

WHAT ARE DRIVING TESTS ULTIMATELY TO BE LIKE?

This leads to a further conclusion that the most likely method of evaluating driving ability will probably be that of identifying patterns of behavior which may prognosticate accident susceptibility. Several different types of ability-capacity constellations may be identified which will probably be most useful in diagnosing or prognosticating accident proneness. The concept is not new in that it is similar to that of syndromes identified with certain diseases. Until this is done no highly valid method of picking out accident-prone drivers from a random sampling of population can be made. This cannot be done by any single test. By use of simple tests, when properly administered, one may expect to effect some accident reduction by focusing attention on weaknesses in the same way that a physical examination will tend to safeguard the health of an individual by warning him of ways in which he may protect himself.

EPIDEMIOLOGY IN THE EXPLANATION OF ACCIDENTS

In recent years a great deal has been written about the epidemiological approach to the study of accident proneness. Precisely what is meant by epidemiology? It is a highly technical word and has not been defined to our knowledge except by Webster. From the dictionary meanings it would seem that the causes of accidents are implied to be somewhat regional, as a result of local or sectional conditions, and that they may depend upon attitudes, habits, or traits of drivers which are catching or mutually stimulated among drivers. The explanation would render testing less important, if we have made the correct interpretation, since the conditions or the factors involved would tend to be more or less dependent upon local conditions or trends. However, if enough were known about the regional conditions to warrant proper classification it is conceivable that a testing procedure might be worked out which could be of value in explaining or in analyzing the epidemiological factors of accidents.

There are certain things that must be kept in mind in the use of testing procedures. When properly administered they have a certain effect on accident reduction through focusing attention on weaknesses in the same manner that a physical examination will tend to safeguard the health of the individual by warning him of ways in which he should exercise caution. By interpreting the results of test data in this manner a great amount of good may be accomplished. If too much weight is given testing it may not prove as valuable to those using it as expected. Specially trained assistants are necessary and evaluation devices must be used with considerable care. It is not likely that one who is untrained in psychological and biological measures would be a good examiner. Allowances for various psychological differences must always be made. These are practical points that cannot be put into a formula. Charles Kettering once said that his engineers could design some wonderful gears and his machinists could turn them out to perfection so far as the formula prescribed. While theoretically correct and practically perfect, when put into the car they howled so loud that it was necessary to have them removed and given practical touches necessary to remove the noise. Allowances for various psychological differences must be made in the same way and if these adjustments are accounted for, better judgment may be made of the driver's aptitude. Testing methods must be considered as an aid rather than a final court of appeal in driver's license examining. They are of no more value in the hands of a layman than a dentist's tools are of value to one not trained in dentistry. The important thing to be considered is the training of the person in charge of the equipment. It is a special branch of psychology as remote from conventional routine in graduate training as the techniques used in studying the conditioned reflex are different from those used in the perfection of a personality inventory. This fact must be recognized by psychologists if they are to be an asset in solving the accident situation.

SOME NEWER MEASURES OF DRIVING ABILITY

More recently some newer applications of psychological and psychiatric concepts have been made to driving situations. Psychologists have found and have stressed more or less the concept of personality in driving. Such personality traits as over-aggressiveness, lack of conservativeness, a tendency to exhibitionism, stubborness, lack of emotional stability, and others of a similar nature. Psychological and biological causes of accidents are no more alike than the causes of certain other conditions of life. One might as well look for a single cause for early marriage among certain persons as for a cause of accidents. Various and sundry antecedents or antecedent relationships and associate factors must be identified before a response pattern may be predicted with any high degree of accuracy.

High mileage drivers are found to have a lower accident rate generally even when units of time are equal. Experience, hazards, purpose of the driving, time of the day, conditions of the weather, of the roadway and of the car, the type of vehicle, the attitude of the driver, the degree of responsibility for the accident, the seriousness of the accident, and many other factors operate to produce accident situations. Even then some estimates have shown that whereas the average driver meets an accident situation once in about 3,000 miles, he meets two others which do not cause him trouble. This had led some investigators to consider the concept of near accidents.

One study by Forbes (5) has made a rather thorough classification which cannot very well be reviewed here, but the general conclusion is, that although all possible conditions did not occur in the small sample of near accidents, a very large number of combination of incidents which did occur made it impractical to determine those most frequently found. It would be necessary to carry out a special study with a very much larger number of cases than the one made in order to make such a determination. It is concluded generally that a wide range of characteristics such as occupation, age, experience, and training are involved in near accident incidents. This wide range of types of near accidents and a wide range of ages reported for drivers was included. In most cases from two to seven categories of behavior and driving conditions were listed as possible contributors to the accident. Thus it will be seen that since so many factors lead to accidents in actual situations the problem of measuring any characteristics responsible for an accident becomes more difficult. Thus we have pointed out some of the difficulties facing those interested in validation studies, and not the least of these has been the lack of a valid criterion of driving ability. Only recently have attempts to solve this problem been made (8).

In spite of the limitations of the methods used and the results obtained, the only scientific view one may assume is that research should be continued until results are more definite. We do not abandon our sunday schools and churches because some few who attend get into trouble, nor do we abandon aviation because a plane crashes now and then. We do not cease the quest for better methods of education for the reason that some individuals remain illiterate or do not profit by education, nor throw away our automobiles or radios because they fail to function properly at times. We have to face the issues squarely. More research is needed. There has been some unnecessary promotion in the field of driver testing and this should be discouraged by all means. Some large universities and technical schools have established centers and institutes for studying accident prevention and safety in various ways. It seems reasonable that this should be a function of educational and research institutions.

As technical schools become genuinely interested and show initiative of their own the scope of work will be broadened. Interest in a problem should precede aid given. Sporadic interest will be engendered in any field if some grant is established. The real test comes when the funds cease. If those in charge continue studies in which they have shown some interest we may conclude the interest was genuine.

One of the urgent needs now is administrative and financial provision for scientific research on the problems of automobile driving. Some administrators have sensed the need and are allowing time and support for staff members in this field. Others have been very slow to see the need for work along this line and have not aided the program. At present there is enough genuine interest to get things going if the administrative setups are made conducive to productive results.

Unfortunately, some writers have interpreted the space age in such a manner as to discourage results in anything excepting the nuclear and physical areas. This may be a needed gesture in some respects but it has its limitations. Unless certain curbs are placed on this type of thinking and some attention made to solve problems nearer at home, society stands to lose considerably. They may win the cold war but lose the very principles by which they have been able to gain a highly developed technology.

SUMMARY

In this discussion we have attempted to point out certain facts regarding driver testing procedures. First, we have tried to explain the philosophy back of the testing movement; second, we have tried to point out the various groups and sub-groups interested in testing; and third, we have tried to indicate some of the factors of which there have been attempts to measure and the reasons for development of tests. We have tried to show that all of the testing procedures being used have limitations, and that sporadic attempts to solve the problems of safe driving are inadequate. A thorough-going program is needed.

The problems of highway and traffic safety are going to require the efforts of many workers to show fruitful results. Those adverse to work and discouragement are not likely to stay in the field. And yet there must be a solution; our rate trends during the past two decades would indicate that progress is being made. In the meantime we must be on the lookout for new avenues of approach. Testing procedures have their place in this battle to reduce unnecessary losses of life, resources and personal injury by traffic accidents, but tests cannot be considered a cure-all for the situation.

REFERENCES

1. De Silva, H. R., Why We Have Automobile Accidents. John Wiley and Sons, Inc., 1942, pp. 394.
2. Eno Foundation for Highway Traffic Control. The Motor Vehicle Driver, His Nature and Improvement. 1949, pp. 165.
3. Fletcher, E. D., Effect of special tests on driving performance. The California Highway Patrolman, 1939, 3, No. 7.
4. Forbes, T. W., The normal automobile driver as a traffic problem. Jour. of General Psychology, 1939, 471-474.
5. Forbes, T. W., Analysis of "near-accident" reports. Highway Research Board Bull. 152.
6. Johnson, H. M., The detection and treatment of accident prone drivers. Psychological Bulletin, 1946, 43, 6, 482-582.
7. Lauer, A. R., Methods of measuring the ability to drive an automobile. Extension Bulletin 115, 1936, Iowa State College.
8. Lauer, A. R. and Suhr, Virtus W., Development of a criterion for driving performance. HRB Bulletin 172, 1958, 1-8.
9. Lahy, J. M., Psychological selection of employee drivers of tramways and busses. 1927.
10. Selling, L. S., Psychiatric findings in cases of 500 traffic offenders and accident-prone drivers. Amer. Jour. of Psychiatry, 1940, 97, 68-79.
11. Slocombe, C. S. and Brakeman, E. E., Psychological tests and accident proneness. British Jour. of Psychol., 1930, 21, 29-39.
12. Snow, A. J., Tests for Chauffeurs. Industrial Psychology, 1926, 1, 30-45.
13. Wechsler, D., Tests for Taxicab Drivers. Personnel Jour., 1926, 5, 24-30.
14. Weiss, A. P. and Lauer, A. R., Psychological principles of automotive driving. Ohio State University Studies in Psychology, 1930, #11.

CHAPTER XII

IMPROVEMENT OF THE DRIVERS' LICENSING PROGRAM

IMPROVING THE DRIVERS' LICENSE

There can be only one legitimate purpose for a drivers' licensing program and that is to make safer and better drivers on the highways (1). A number of secondary reasons have. been given which in some cases are defensible and in others are not. The only way to improve drivers is, first, to train them and, second, to see that they assume responsibility for applying this training through proper use of their cars on the highways.

PURPOSE OF A LICENSE

While most everyone would agree in theory upon the fundamental requisites for a good driver's license examination, actually those charged with the responsibility of administering examinations often fall short of the primary objective which the license is intended to accomplish (2). Failure to keep the examination up to standard is usually not done deliberately but is the result of heavy pressure which comes from examining a large number of drivers throughout any given geographical area within a limited time period. Sometimes 300 to 500 applicants have to be taken through in a day by one team of examiners.

One of the most useful aids in smoothing the load was the adoption of the birthday law which distributes renewals evenly throughout the year instead of having them pile up at one time every year or so, whenever the renewal time is stated by law.

To consider some of the elementary principles of driver licensing it is axiomatic that a driver's license examination should
accomplish several things. Five of these are:

1. It should screen drivers for physical and mental defects
which might interfere with proven performance at the wheel.
This is universally admitted to be one of the valid aims of the
examining procedure (3).

2. It should attempt to determine whether one knows how to
drive an automobile with reasonable skill.

3. It should determine whether one has a mastery of the local
and state traffic ordinances, regulations and laws, as well as a
knowledge of the accepted principles of safe driving on the highway. The latter category is often neglected, perhaps because of
lack of time. Actually it is one of the most important.

4. It should provide a proper description of the driver so that
he can be recognized on apprehension.

5. Roadability of the car the applicant expects to drive should
be noted.

It is assumed that all these functions are fulfilled by a driver's
license examination if done in a proper manner. These should
be considered minimum essentials. Any attempt to shorten or
by-pass the immediate routine of an examination will likely give
an unreliable account of the driver's qualifications. It would
amount to selling the public short on the basic purposes of an
examination. Other related factors such as attitudes should be
assayed.

The driver's license should not serve as a revenue-raising source
for general purposes. Any money that is taken in at the time the
driver's license is given should be applied to the cost of administering the examination and to improve the examination as such
(2). Any extra funds should be used for driver education or for
improving examiners.

NEED FOR TRAINED PERSONNEL

From what we have said it is to be inferred that the examining
personnel for the drivers' licensing procedure should be well
trained. They must have certain personal qualifications and be

conscientious on the job if the procedure is to have the effect it is supposed to have on licenses. If we continue to tolerate slipshod examinations such as are often being given throughout the country, it might be just as well to go back to the 25-cent drug store license which former President Truman often criticized in his home state of Missouri until the law was changed.

In looking back over the records it would appear that Missouri and South Dakota have probably been two of the least progressive states in adopting and upgrading the standard drivers' licensing program. However they have fairly good accident records when compared with neighboring states. Until recently they have only completely fulfilled the fourth function of the drivers' licensing objectives mentioned above, that is, registering of drivers. This might be done with much less expense than it is, in some states, at present. Others with a more ambitious program, probably would accomplish very little if subjected to rigid evaluation.

Perhaps the most progressive step taken recently in the area of driver preparation and training is that made by Michigan. In 1957 they implemented a program that will require every person getting a driver's license for the first time to have a course of instruction in the public schools and to complete this course satisfactorily. Such a program would be much more effective in accomplishing the first, second and third objectives set forth. These are: (a) screening for mental and physical defects, (b) determining whether the person knows how to drive, as well as (c) the assurance of mastery of certain knowledge of driving laws and practices. Very few persons really study for the driving tests in many states. The written examination should be greatly strengthened.

If all five objectives are to be properly accomplished through a driver's licensing examination it is quite obvious that the person giving the examination should be well trained in methods of examining and be able to discriminate between those who know the subject matter and those who do not. The requirements for a good examiner are not necessarily entirely a matter of formal schooling. Any qualified person with a high school education could be taught to be a good driver's license examiner probably in three months of intensive training. It would help if he had more formal education. He should know something about the theory of the tests that he is giving, what their limitations are, how they can be improved, some short cuts and alternate tests, how they compare with standard medical, dental, and optometric tests, and cerain other things of this type. Further, he should know something about the theory and practice of constructing a good examination. He should be able to recognize the weaknesses of our road driving tests and how they can be improved. If there are ways of beating the tests or cheating he should know about them. This would take at least three months of quite concentrated training and study requiring at least a portion of each day for accomplishing it. In other words, it could be given as inservice training.

Until such preparatory work is made available and examiners are trained under supervision, then sent out as apprentices to work under experienced examiners until they have mastered the art of examining, certainly we cannot hope for a better driver's licensing examination. Public school teachers are required to do practice and supervised teaching for a semester or more before being given full charge of a class. Their responsibilities are not greater than those of driver's license examiners.

At the testing bureau or personnel service department of any standard college or university at this time, elaborate examinations are given to all persons coming into the school as students. It is not a routine matter of a five-minute check, but such examinations may run from one to three hours. In addition, a special medical examination is given to secure information about the student's health and physical fitness. Certain background factors are also considered when the person is entered as a student. Usually transcripts of former course work and character as well as scholarship recommendations are also required.

We are not proposing that such an elaborate examination be given to drivers but we are taking the position that the driver's license examination should not attempt to do more than it can do well (4). It is fairly obvious that in the past drivers' license examinations have included more than examiners can handle with the training they have received and in the time allowed for the examination (3).

LICENSEES TEST WISE

It must be remembered that at present the schools are doing an enormous amount of testing and examining. Every school child has a physical examination, is checked by nurses, eye physicians and dentists, as well as by counsellors and teachers. He is in a position to know what constitutes good and bad examining. Teachers are well trained in methods of psychometric and educational measurement and children go through a series of examinations every semester. Even junior high school youngsters are test wise and know to some extent when an examination is well done and when it is not well done. They are aware of the fact that there can be much confusion from several persons helping one another while being examined in a room at the same time. They know that a proper visual examiantion cannot be given in 20 seconds by a vision specialist, and that it may take up to an hour or more to be fitted for glasses. Thus when a 16-year-old youth steps up to take the driver's license examination the treatment he receives is a send-off on his driving career. If sloppily or shabbily done he will recognize it even though he may not be able to point out specific methods of improvement. In other words, he may lose confidence in the whole procedure unless the examining is well done and impresses him favorably. This may account in part for his lack of respect for traffic laws in general. It has been shown that accidents of commercial drivers may be reduced by a careful examination.

Another reason that the quality of the driver's license program should be stepped up appreciably is that many driver education courses are merely geared to coaching students to pass the driver's license examination. Since millions of persons secure a license to drive every year without special instruction this is certainly a low ideal to be established for a course. Therefore the drivers' examination should present a real hurdle that would tend to improve the driver education courses that are geared at the level of passing for a license.

There are many driver education courses in the country which have quite a high-level proficiency standard. Course grades may, or may not, be sufficient to warrant issuance of a drivers' license depending upon the thoroughness of the training. The states can do a great deal with respect to upgrading the standards of driver education by giving a more thorough driver examination (2).

PRESTIGE OF LICENSE NECESSARY

A driver's license examination should have prestige and should be respected by those who take it. One only needs to travel about through certain states and quiz persons he meets, or perhaps visit some of the examining bureaus and note comments, to learn that the prestige of the driver's license examination is about as low as it could possibly be. This is due largely to the fact that the personnel in charge are frequently not adequately trained for the job. They are also attempting to do more than can be done in the time available. The examination would have much more prestige if it were limited to fewer features and these were done extremely well (4). In the next section we shall discuss the possibilities of improvement in procedures which might be made. It isn't so much a matter of making the tests more elaborate as it is a problem of getting a reasonable and valid answer to the questions that are posed by the state when a person applies for a driver's license. Does the applicant qualify as a responsible driver on the highway?

Perhaps the first and foremost item that should be brought up is that of the visual and so-called physical examination. At the present time, in many states, about all the driver's license examination tells us is whether the person can move or see. In fact, a few persons with a blind pension have been found to hold a driver's license.

If the objective is only to screen out those with vision below a certain level there is no reason to have anything more elaborate than a few charts of $3/4$-inch block letters hung on the wall at a distance of 20 feet. This test could be made more or less foolproof by having several lines on a rotary cylinder which could be turned as desired so that persons taking the examination are unable to memorize it. Needless to say one person should not watch another take the test. Under the present system this precept is frequently violated.

For driving there seems to be only interest in distance vision of a driver. If a person can read ¾-inch lines or words at 20 feet he can see well enough to pass any driver's license examination in the country, the highest standards of which require only 20/40 vision.

So far as other factors are concerned it would be fairly easy by inspection to note whether the person has one arm or two arms, whether he is undersized or oversized or has any superficial physical defects. Even these could be gotten through a written application by mail. Does the information we get from the drivers' examination as now given justify the expense?

GET PROFESSIONAL JUDGMENT

However, it might save the state considerable money if instead of attempting to cover all phases in the driver's license examination, each one presenting himself would be required to bring a certified statement of his background showing that he is normal mentally, has no background of epilepsy or other black-out conditions, has at least 20/40 vision and is in good physical condition. If laws were set up which would make the physician or person signing such document responsible for their statements, any application signed would likely be given careful consideration. If it were understood that any trouble the driver might get into would partly be their responsibility, licensing could be controlled much better than it is in the cursory way it is being administered at present. Responsible professional people usually feel an obligation to the public as well as to their patients, clients or patrons. The visual examination could be handled in the manner suggested by Form 1. It includes a statement on physical fitness and other matters of interest to the state when granting a driver's license.

A third objective of the driver's license examination which we would consider legitimate is that of determining whether or not the applicant knows how to drive. This, again, can be determined much quicker and easier by merely having a person park a car parallel to the curb in a space six feet longer than the car. Devices could be built which might be set up in front of the place of examination and the degree of skill established in much less time than can be done by a short drive. It is a scientific fact that conventional road driving tests are particularly untrustworthy.

Some persons get nervous during the examination and make a poor showing yet are fairly good drivers. In fact a certain amount of emotion is desirable for safe driving. Others may be brazen and bluff their way through. Also, the "watched" driver becomes a "careful" driver and very little is found out from riding a block or even several blocks with him. The same information could be obtained very simply by having the applicant park. If he can park satisfactorily, let him drive up to the end of the block, turn around and come back. If he gives his hand signals, stays on his side of the road, and observes traffic, this is about as much as anyone can learn by driving with one for any reasonable period of time.

The chance of meeting an accident situation in a short drive is very remote. It requires around 3,000 hours of regular driving before a person meets a genuine accident situation in which he will need to exercise more than ordinary ability to stay out of trouble. The examiner does not have time to drive long enough with an applicant to be able to judge properly.

LET THE SCHOOLS HELP

If the applicant has had a course in driver education in the schools and could show a card or statement to this effect it should be recognized as prima facie evidence that he knows how to drive (see Form 1). If this training were mandatory, as it has been in Michigan since February 1957, the schools would refuse to sign an application for persons who do not know how to handle a car properly. This would strengthen the preparation of applicants.

WHO HAS TROUBLE ON THE HIGHWAYS?

It is not the beginning drivers who usually give the most trouble on the highways. In a study of 59,125 drivers of known experience in Minnesota it was shown that 61% had been driving more than 10 years; 21% had been driving from 6-10 years and 17%

had been licensed from 1-5 years. Less than 1% had been driving less than a year. Any person who has not driven before would certainly pick up most of the basic fundamentals of driving within a year. It seems persons get into trouble because of the more complicated factors of driving. These can best be assayed by a form of driving inventory. Special written tests are being used by the Armed Forces to evaluate and select military drivers.

Another study in Oklahoma showed that 45% of the drivers involved in accidents had been driving 11 years or more. Drivers with five years or more experience accounted for 405 of the 518 traffic deaths in Oklahoma in 1949. Thus it would appear that the problem of determining whether the applicant knows the bare essentials of maneuvering a car is not the most important part of the driver's examination. What is needed is more insight into what the driver will do four, five or ten years hence. Several written inventories have been developed which will do this reasonably well, at least better than any known techniques of rating the ability to maneuver the car, by a road test, and with much less expense. Instead of examining one at a time, an examiner could take 50 to 100 at one time by using written forms. Colleges examine up to 2,000 persons together in the administration of freshmen entrance tests. This is largely a matter of satisfactory seating space.

The use of a form of classification application and a long-range prognostication test would not only give information about the general qualifications, skill and knowledge of the applicant, but something about his or her attitudes and predispositions of much deeper nature than are ever acquired from superficial accounts now obtained. Such an inventory should have probably around 40 to 50 items.

We now come to the matter of the knowledge of the road laws and traffic regulations. This is important of course but a test will require about 50 items or so to give anything like a reasonable account. In the schools and in driver education classes it has been found that anything shorter is not reliable or dependable and of little value. In schools and colleges no examination of 10 to 20 questions of the objective type would be considered very revealing by a competent teacher. This is about as far as we go in our driver's license examination in most states by written tests.

Also matters of defensive driving, emergency driving situations, and safe driving habits are usually not stressed in a drivers' license examination. Most of the motor vehicle examinations have emphasized principally the road laws and regulations which should be known but these should be studied in a systematic manner in a course, or at least from a manual which could be given out by the state in advance of the examination. Most states have such a manual.

The matter of driver registry is more or less taken care of by any procedure used. Even writing into the department for a blank would take care of this feature. There is no need for considerable expenditure of money to merely register drivers.

So far as information relating to the applicant's readiness to drive and so on, such is not usually obtained on the driver's license examination as given. It would seem that some kind of a qualified statement or endorsement might be requested which could be signed by the parent, the school superintendent, the minister, the police or others in the community as suggested in Form 1. This could be presented along with the doctor's certificate which would have much more value in this regard than anything we get from the driver's examination as it is usually given.

Form 1

PROPOSED APPLICATION BLANK FOR SECURING AND RENEWING THE DRIVER'S LICENSE

Name.. Age............ Sex....................

Address...Yr. first licensed......................
          Street or RFD   City   State

Height............ Weight .... Hair color............ Eye color............ Date....................
(This might well be copied from the driver's license set up in the same form. See Form 2. The present outline is only suggestive.)

1. *Driving Competency*—The person named above is known by the undersigned to:

   a. Have passed a regular course in driver education satisfac-
   torily, including behind-the-wheel driving........................... Yes........No........
   b. Has at least one year of experience driving a car with
   skill and discretion.. Yes........No........
   Competency is........OK ....Not OK for driving. Mark one. If not OK give
   recommendation ....

   Signed by one of the following: Instructor..

   School ....

   Endorsed by...
                                        Prominent citizen & title

   Address ....

2. *Physical Fitness*—I, the undersigned, have examined the above applicant and make the following report. (Check and enter exceptions.)

   c. Health: Excellent...

   Average...................................

   Doubtful..............................

   Exception noted (c)...

   d. Physical Capacities: Excellent...................................

   Average...................................

   Doubtful..............................

   Exception noted (d)...

   Physical fitness including (c) and (d) is............OK ....Not OK for
   driving. Mark one.

   ....
                    Physician   Title

   ....
                              Address

   ....
                              Date

Form 1, *continued*

3. *Visual Condition*—The above applicant has been examined by me and found
   to have the following visual qualifications. (Mark and note exceptions.)
   e. Acuity (Snellen notation):

   R.........................

   L.........................

   B.........................

   f. Lateral field in degrees:

   R.........................

   L.........................

   B.........................

   Exceptions noted (e) and (f)...
   g. Muscle balance: Check only one of each divergence from normal.

   Lateral within 4 prism diopters.........................

   over 4 prism diopters.........................

   Vertical within 3 prism diopters.........................

   over 3 prism diopters.........................

   h. Night vision: Excellent...

   Average..................................

   Doubtful................................

   Exceptions noted (g) and (h)...
   Visual conditions OK............ Not OK............ for driving. Mark one.

   ....
   Vision Specialist   Title

   ....
   Address

   ....
   Date

4. *Citizenship**—The above named person is known to me as (i) a responsible
   person, is (j) a prudent and careful driver and is a law abiding citizen.
   I endorse his application for a driver's license with respect to (i) and (j)
   of this paragraph.

   ....
   Name   Position

   ....
   Address

   ....
   Date

Form 1, *continued*

5. *Roadability of the Car*—The person described in this application appeared at

   the place of business designated and his car...

   Year   Make   Model

   was inspected by us and put in (k) roadable condition as described by law.

   The car is OK............ Not OK............ for driving.

   ....

   Name

   ....

   Place of business

   ....

   Date

6. *Insurance*—At present I carry (1) adequate public liability insurance in the

   form of Personal Injury........................ and Property Damage........................

   ....

   Applicant

   ....

   Address

   ....

   Date

....

Notary's signature and seal

No one would be given a license unless all six paragraphs were filled out properly and items (a) to (1) were marked as satisfactory. Examiners would need only be concerned about those not completed or blanks. This would probably be only about five per cent of the population.

---

*No. 4 may be signed by a police officer, businessman, minister, or any well-known citizen or public official.

A WELL-ROUNDED DRIVER IMPROVEMENT PROGRAM

The proposals herein made are something of the nature of a generalized driver improvement program in which the initial steps would be made at the time of the driver's license examination. Follow-up would be made in case of accidents, violations, or at the time of license renewal. The first license examination would be conducted very much as at present except for the following points of differentiation.

The applicant would appear for examination or inspection and if trained would present his application blank stating that he has had a course in driver education, knows the local regulations and laws, and knows how to operate a motor vehicle carefully.

The second phase would be a doctor's statement vouching for the person's physical condition and health which would be much more satisfactory than the evaluation of the driver physically as the examination is now conducted in many states. A part of the application having to do with visual efficiency would be certified by a vision specialist. This would be the third phase.

The fourth part would be a character statement which would be sort of an endorsement of the application for the driver's license signed by the school superintendent, the local police, minister, or other responsible parties. This would indicate that the person was of good character, that he had stayed out of trouble in general, and as being a worthy person who could drive an automobile in the community with responsibility.

Fifth would be a statement by an authorized garage or testing station as to the roadability of the car.

The sixth item would be a statement of the extent of insurance carried by the applicant.

The Motor Vehicle Department should have a list of the acceptable technical and professional consultants.

Form 2

DRIVER INVENTORY
(Suggested Form)
(See reference 5)

To be filled out by the applicant at the time of licensing or renewal and retained by the Department of Motor Vehicles as a permanent record. Clerk would fill in the left-hand box at top which would be photostated for license.

(Photo and thumb print here)
OPERATORS LICENSE

Name..
Street or RFD...............................
City.................... Co. No.................
Date Issued........License Expires........
Sex........Eyes......Height........Race.......
Weight......Hair......Occupation...........
Restrictions.....................................
Signature...............................
Above person is hereby licensed to operate motor vehicles.

....
Commissioner of Public Safety
See Reverse Side
(Fill out above from driver's license)

CHAUFFEURS LICENSE
Yes............ No.........

LICENSE SUSPENDED BEFORE
Yes............ No.........

LICENSE REVOKED BEFORE
Yes............ No.........

WHERE WERE YOU RAISED?
Farm........ Village........ City........

MARITAL STATUS:
Married........ Single........ Other.........

DEPENDENTS:
1 2 3 4 5 6 7 or more....................

HOW DID YOU LEARN TO DRIVE?
Taught in school...............................
Learned out of school........................

DRIVING EXPERIENCE:
Years driven.......... Cars driven...........

YEAR FIRST LICENSED TO DRIVE:
Year.................... Age......................

MILES YOU DRIVE A YEAR:
Miles.............................

NUMBER OF CARS DRIVEN:
Number............ Types........................

EDUCATION
1 2 3 4 5 6 7 8 9 10 11 12
13 14 15 16 17+

SPECIAL SCHOOLS ATTENDED
(Name)...
....
Time Attended..................

WHAT DO YOU THINK OF SITUATIONS YOU MEET IN EVERYDAY DRIVING EXPERIENCE? Read the following list and give your first reaction to each. Think of each word or phrase in terms of driving situations. Put a cross through the letter which suits you best for each item.

Schedule of Responses for First 18 Items
H—Disturbs me very much (very displeasing)
J—Bothers me some (displeasing)
K—Makes no impression on me (indifferent)
L—All right at times (pleasing)
M—Highly approve (very pleasing)

Form 2, *continued*

For example, if "pleasing" best describes how you feel about an item, mark it heavily with a cross like this: H J K L M. A few are to be marked as 0 1 2 3 4. Put a cross over the number which pertains to you. Draw a cross through the number or letter as shown in letter "L" above. If more than 4 put cross through 4. You may refer back to "Schedule of Responses" at any time.

1. Railroad crossing
   gates   H J K L M
2. One-way streets   H J K L M
3. 14-year-old drivers   H J K L M
4. Not having a job   H J K L M
5. Meeting large trucks
   and busses   H J K L M
6. Having people fly off
   the handle   H J K L M
7. My employer's
   methods   H J K L M
8. Being promoted before
   I expected   H J K L M
9. Dislike being told
   what to do   H J K L M
10. Saving my money for
    a rainy day   H J K L M
11. Traffic regulations   H J K L M
12. Seeing a young girl
    drink liquor   H J K L M

13. Driving 14-15 hours
    a day   H J K L M
14. Riding a motor cycle   H J K L M
15. Finding others getting
    promotions
    I deserve   H J K L M
16. Working at a desk job   H J K L M
17. Meeting nerve-racking
    situations   H J K L M
18. Having people mis-
    understand me   H J K L M
19. Cars driven this year   0 1 2 3 4+
20. Headaches I have
    occasionally   0 1 2 3 4+
21. Times my glasses were
    changed this year   0 1 2 3 4+
22. Age of my present
    car in years   0 1 2 3 4+

Signature...   Score.............. Decile..............

Finally, the applicant would be given a rather thorough driving inventory (Form 2) to ascertain his attitudes and basic tendencies as an operator. This could be kept in the state files and used for future reference. It would not only be a measure of the applicant's attitudes and psychological makeup but would indicate a desire to comply and obey the traffic laws and follow all the ordinances and regulations of his state and community, as well as the rules of safe driving.

There is only one other consideration. In case the applicant has not had a driving course in school, which is mandatory in the State of Michigan and could be made so in other states, it might be possible to have a parking stall and have each park his or her

car. The applicant might also be asked to drive to the end of the
block, give hand signals, and turn around to show that he maneuvers properly in traffic situations. This could be used in lieu of
the requirement of a driving course for older persons.

SALIENT POINTS FOR IMPROVING THE DRIVER'S LICENSE PROCEDURES

It is contended that the drivers' license examination has five
legitimate objectives which are not always being adequately determined by the driver's license examination as it is now given.
With a system set up similar to that established in Michigan one
examiner could probably process many more applicants per day
than by any existing system. He would have the cooperation of
a large group of professionally trained people in the state who
would cooperate by endorsing the applicant's petition and vouch
for his competency and responsibility. The latter would not be
at the expense of the state. It should tend to put the driver in
a more responsible state of mind for receiving a license. The state
would act as the final inspector or judge of the evidence presented
and issue the license.

GRADATION OF LICENSES AN AID

In addition to the improvement of the driver's license examination, the matter of graded licenses should be carefully reviewed.
It is asinine to think that one should have no privileges at all at
15 years and 364 days of age, then go to the licensing station the
next morning and within five minutes be able to drive away with
the full privileges associated with driving a motor vehicle practically any place in the free world.

Since most states already have a regular school permit it would
seem more reasonable to set up the drivers' license requirements
somewhat in the following fashion. A beginners license might
be issued at the age of 14, 15 or whatever age is thought desirable
to license youths. This could be set to fit the needs of the local,
state, or community. The beginners license would function very
much as a school permit does at the present. It would allow the
person to drive to and from school, to drive with other licensed

persons in the car, but not to drive at night unless accompanied by an instructor or parent. This license would be valid up to the age of 16. It should have a distinctive color.

LIMITED LICENSE

From 16 to 21 a provisional or limited license would be issued which would place the responsibility for keeping out of trouble squarely upon the applicant's shoulders. It should be mandatory that any violation or accident would automatically recall the provisional license upon request by law enforcement agencies. This practice we believe is in force in North Carolina and possibly some other states at present. If anyone has an accident or flagrant violation it is not necessary to have a hearing but simply to request that the license be surrendered at once. It may be returned when the charge is investigated at a hearing. All the evidence points toward an advantage in nipping violations in the bud.

A provisional license would be issued from 16 to 21 as indicated but might not be extended beyond 21 if the driver did not keep himself in good standing. This would place responsibility squarely on the operator. It would be up to him to demonstrate that he can drive properly and stay out of trouble. The provisional license should be of a color to be easily recognized.

These are two different types of fundamental requirements for driving successfully. Some persons can drive who cannot stay out of trouble; others follow regulations but cannot drive.

REGULAR DRIVER'S LICENSE

At the age of 21 a person would be given a full-fledged license which would then be handled very much as it is at the present time. This license should be still another color. It could be revoked or suspended through the regular procedures prescribed by law. The driver's licensing program should be supported by a good driver improvement program to pick up the persons who tend to backslide from their earlier good records. As shown in the Minnesota and Oklahoma studies, there are people who know how to drive but who later get into much trouble. It would seem that the application of such a system as proposed could be used very successfully for renewals with some modification.

This follow-up through a driver improvement program is very essential and is more or less inherent in most driver's license statutes at the present time. Not all states are active in the program but the 15 most active ones are reported to be Massachusetts, North Carolina, New York, New Hampshire, North Dakota, Maine, Florida, California, Utah, Iowa, New Mexico, Texas, Washington and Oklahoma. Most others are doing something about driver improvement.

It is hoped that this short account may help to orient and stimulate some thinking with respect to a more suitable method of evaluation and licensing drivers. It is felt that such a system would materially reduce accidents. The administration of a good driver improvement program alone apparently does help to reduce the fatality rate. Nine of the states reported to have the best program of driver improvement are found in the best one-fourth on the basis of fatal accident records. This, in itself, speaks quite well for the program as it stands. Either the states that are active in this respect or the program itself may be instrumental in helping keep down fatalities. A predriver education course would greatly aid in this matter also. It would place the teaching of driving where it is most likely to be effective over a long period of time. These systems might well be used in connection with a point system.

SUMMARY

This chapter is a critique of the conventional driver's license examination and sets forth five legitimate purposes of the driver's license examination. Other implied functions of the driver's license examination such as raising revenue are not considered legitimate.

It is maintained that functions of the driver's license examination could be accomplished much more efficiently by having medical, optometric, as well as training and character endorsements submitted at the time of application. These would be of standard form and probably should be supplemented by a notorized affidavit that those affixing their signatures are representative persons of the applicant's community. Only the applicant would need sign before a notary.

It is contended that this type of a driver's license examination would not only enormously reduce the cost of carrying on the licensing procedures so far as the state is concerned, but would give much more reliable and valid information regarding the applicant. In addition it would tend to delegate some of the responsibility for checking up on the driver to the local community. If the local police had endorsed an application for a license it is likely the driver would be more careful in driving his car around the community in order to retain the respect of those who had aided him. It is maintained that the whole procedure would tend to place more responsibility upon the driver. At the present time this is one of the greatest weaknesses of the driver's license examination. As given now it fails to develop a feeling of responsibility in the driver and by the nature of administration under which it is given, through pressure of the number of applicants, it does not command the respect of the general driving public. This tends to weaken its prestige and effectiveness for certain individuals. About 10 to 20% of younger male drivers are found to be wanton violators of the traffic code.

At the present time revocation or suspension of an individual's license is likely not to be known in the local community. If such notices were posted, when the community had been partly responsible for granting the license, such local publicity would be much more likely to elicit cooperation between local authorities and the state.

Unquestionably many persons today are driving without a license and often one gets caught. Probably no one knows what percentage of drivers who have forfeited their licenses are still operating vehicles on the highways and are not apprehended. About 5% of drivers on the road have no license.

The foregoing proposals are in no sense ideas developed over a short period of time. They represent a reversal of the writer's point of view developed during the first 20 years of a 25-year research on drivers, driving and driving examinations. While the overall proposals may need to be modified, simplified, and adapted to local conditions, the essense of a much more effective and economical driver's license examination are herein described.

REFERENCES

1. A.M.A. Medical guide for physicians in determining fitness to drive a motor vehicle. 1959, J.A.M.A., 169, #11, 1195-1211.
2. A.A.M.V.A., Drivers license fees duration and expiration dates. 1946, Washington, D. C.
3. A.A.M.V.A., Minimum driver license examination standards. 1949, Washington, D. C.
4. A.A.A.M.V. and A.O.A., Manual on Drivers' Vision Tests. 1949, St. Louis, pp. 36.
5. Lauer, A. R., Driving Reaction Inventory. Iowa State University Press, Ames, Iowa.

CHAPTER XIII

IN DEFENSE OF THE YOUTHFUL DRIVER

Several rather stirring articles have appeared in which the so-called teen-age driver has been most strongly indicted. These articles, of course, have some basis of fact, but the writer feels it is time someone comes to the defense of the youthful driver, since the picture seems to have been somewhat overdrawn in light of scientific studies of age groups, particularly at the lower age levels.

WHO ARE TEEN-AGE DRIVERS?

In the first place, the age group frequently designated as teen-agers runs up to 24 years of age. It is stretching the cloak of semantics slightly to include those above 20 as being teen-agers. They were capable and responsible enough to win one of the most far-flung, potentially disastrous and vicious wars of history with a casualty list one-third that of traffic casualties perpetuated by the folks at home during the same period. There is reason to believe that one who can hedge-hop his way to Berlin or Bagdad on a hundred missions and return all in one piece can drive a car safely at home, assuming he has the proper attitude and training. While a few exceptions spoil the record of the majority, this should by no means stereotype the whole group.

First, let us distinguish between the true teen-age driver — those between 14 and 19 inclusive — and the third decaders above 19, i.e., from 20 to 30. This distinction should be clearly drawn on several bases. Those below 21 are minors and, therefore, subject to guardianship in the eyes of the law. Those 21 or above have reached their majority, are full-fledged citizens, and are raising families with corresponding duties, obligations and responsibil-

222

ities. While our studies during the past 21 years would indicate that they are inexperienced and, from a commercial point of view, are not desirable as professional drivers, their natural physical and mental characteristics are at a peak. In fact, these researches have indicated that persons between 32 and 37 are the safest age while those between 18 and 22 are the most skillful at performance of various types including the ability to handle automobiles. Their accident records by percentage are shown in Table I for 1958. These figures were carried out to three places.

TABLE I

PERCENTAGES OF ALL LICENSEES IN IOWA IN 1953 AND 1958 WITH INDICATED INCREASES OR DECREASES BY FIVE-YEAR AGE GROUPS

Age Group (Years) (1)	1953 % of All Licensees (2)	1958 % of All Licensees (3)	Increase or Decrease from 1953 (4)
15-19	7.133	7.695	+0.562
20-24	11.893	10.471	—1.422
25-29	13.292	10.665	—2.627
30-34	12.617	11.199	—1.418
35-39	10.499	10.571	+0.072
40-44	8.903	10.111	+0.072
45-49	8.422	9.217	+0.795
50-54	6.999	8.195	+1.196
55-59	6.209	7.007	+0.798
60-64	4.841	5.426	+0.585
65-69	3.969	4.431	+0.462
70-74	2.198	2.997	+0.799
75-79	1.569	1.475	—0.094
80-84	0.656	0.387	—0.269
85+	0.252	0.154	—0.098
Totals	99.452	100.000	+0.548

Percentages given in column (4) are the algebraic differences of the values of column (3). 1958 distributions, contrasted to column (2), 1953 distributions. The total plus value in column (4) is equal to the difference between totals of column (2) and (3).

SOME FUNDAMENTAL FACTS FOR CONSIDERATION

Returning to the true teen-agers, there are in reality two groups. Those 14 and above, up to the legal licensing age, who can drive only with a limited permit, and those above the age at which a license is granted. The latter group varies in age from 15-18 among the various states, depending upon the motor vehicle laws (1,3).

So far the writer has been able to obtain only sketchy data as to who among these groups, and what per cent of any specific group or age level, is having the most accidents. That obscure fact is creating all the furor. *Accident Facts for 1948* (6) published by the National Safety Council shows the age group 15-24 to have a death rate of 30.9 due to motor vehicles, against 20.1 for those between 25-44, 25.1 for those 45-64 and 50.3 for those over 65. Here again it is not stated who was at the wheel at the time and true facts are masked by the wide age groups considered. The average index is 22.5 for all ages when corrected for numbers.

Even though those between 14-24 have both high injury and death rate, when corrected for the population, it is not at all clear whether the true teen-age drivers are highest, whether it is the below legal age drivers or whether it is the third decaders.

It is undoubtedly true that the number of passengers per car will average higher when younger drivers are in control. They think nothing of crowding in two or three extra passengers. This again might well affect the injuries sustained and could possibly be a contributing factor in vehicle accidents as such.

One state reports 50% of all fatal accidents between 12 midnight and 6 A.M. involve drivers 20 and below. They fail to tell us whether it involves those who hold licenses, those who do not have a regular license, those who have licenses revoked or suspended, or at what specific age levels most accidents occur. Nor do they tell us what percentage of the respective groups are involved in 50% of the fatal accidents during hours of darkness after midnight. Again we do not know who was driving at the time.

In one sampling study (5) it was found that there were more young drivers on the road after midnight, particularly at the most dangerous hours from 12 to 3 A.M. However, only about 10-20% of these drivers were driving at careless speeds. Speed was checked by a radar speed meter and age of the driver was ascertained as soon after the observation as possible by reference to the county registration files and by a post card sent to the owner to verify the driver of the car at the time.

SPIKING SOME GENERAL POINTS OF CONFUSION

We should at least identify the three groups mentioned, that is, (a) those below the legal age for driving, (b) those from the legal driving age to 20, and (c) those between 20 and 30 inclusive with the subdivisions mentioned. Still another classification might well be made — those who have been trained to drive by systematic instruction and those who have learned to drive in a "by ear" fashion. Again, we might consider those whose parents are good and safe drivers and those whose parents have a bad record. Likewise we might study the driving habits of adults and others with whom these youthful drivers associate. A careful research on some of these points might be revealing and until scientific evidence is forthcoming, some of the "band-wagon" attempts to crucify low-age groups of drivers en masse may be entirely incorrect and misleading.

It is true that some young drivers are bad actors in many ways (3). They are behavior problems behind the wheel as much as in any other type of juvenile delinquency, but this should not condemn the whole group. Figures are available to show that Iowa has more violations and intoxication charges between the ages of 35-45 than any other 10 year group, but that does not mean that everyone in this group is an alcoholic or an habitual violator.

It must be remembered also that safe driving and good driving are not necessarily synonomous. Most racing drivers are very skillful at the wheel, but we would not care to ride with them, and they are frequently involved in serious accidents.

Safe driving involves at least three categories or types of satisfactory behavior traits:

1. Basic alertness, or intelligence, and a certain amount of mechanical aptitude, both of which are largely inherited.

2. Skill and knowledge which come through careful and systematic training.

3. Proper judgment and attitudes which are developed only

through proper training, coaching, association, and experience of a general nature.

The opportunities afforded for proper development of such behavior patterns must be carefully evaluated before we blame too sharply any particular group for the conduct of its extreme mal-behavior types.

WHO IS TO BLAME?

Assuming a case can be made against the pooled accident record of the younger generation of drivers, we need first to look into our system of licensing and training of drivers before allocating the blame. The railroads have an enviable record for safe operation. Every engineer must not only pass rigorous tests to first qualify as a fireman, but he must also serve an apprenticeship of several years before he is given charge of an engine. Yet his locomotive requires no steering and is provided with all the known safety controls.

Last summer we observed a young driver in a new car overtake and pass the Burlington's crack streamliner on a level stretch of highway in Nebraska that paralleled the tracks. The driver may have had no qualifications whatever except that he had paid a license fee and knew his way to the corner drug store to purchase his license. Nebraska has an average system of licensing, but the driver may have been licensed in one of the states where lower standards are maintained.

There are only a few types of machines or devices which we allow and expect persons to have and use without training. One is the automobile and the other is a gun. The use of firearms is very carefully controlled and restricted to use in certain rural areas where the dangers are minimized. Also the hunting season is open only a very small portion of the year, yet there are about 60% as many deaths annually from firearms as to all employees, passengers, and others by the combined railroads in the United States.

It seems the height of nonsense to grant a person of 15 or 16 years a learners permit which he may use within two weeks to make his application for a drivers license with no indication that he has been instructed or has studied in any way. He goes to the licensing bureau without legal rights of any kind, drives around the block and leaves with all the privileges of the most expert driver. He may drive his car practically anywhere in the civilized world to which he can transport it. By way of comparison, parents would not trust the judgment of an average youngster to go out and make a $20,000 deal for real estate or a business, but they will trust him to go on the road and flirt with a $100,000 lawsuit. Judgment develops very slowly unless aided by expert coaching and instruction.

The written examination given by most states can be passed by anyone with practically no study of the motor laws. Few of the examinations given touch on safe operation of a motor vehicle other than the superficial items brought out in the law such as how many headlights are required for driving, what color they should be, etc. Only a few states, among them California, make any pretense of giving a rigorous examination. Unfortunately some states still hold to the philosophy that the driver's license fees are a revenue raising device.

Through the efforts of the American Automobile Association, the insurance companies, and to some extent, the motor vehicle manufacturers, driving courses have been introduced into the schools. Unfortunately these courses are not available to all high school youngsters in the schools where they are given. Many who drop out before they reach high school, or who do not finish grade school, will never have a chance to get the course. Somewhat more than half of the young people between 5 and 24 were attending school. At present the number in school is increasing but to be fully effective, out-of-school driving courses should be established. Only 10.2% of the population studied were between 20 and 24 and had 4 years of high school. Driving instruction might well be given as a vocational subject during the summer months.

One report has shown that somewhat over 92% of 14-15 year, 68.5% of 16-17 year, and 27% of 18-19 year groups are in school.

A PROGRESSIVE PROGRAM FOR MOTOR VEHICLE ACCIDENT PREVENTION

Since we know what type of training is necessary and what should be taught to improve drivers, it seems reasonable that certain minimum standards should be set up which would improve our methods of licensing drivers. No one would think of buying an airplane and teaching himself to fly since he would soon run afoul of the law. It would seem that we should now be ready to set up much more rigid requirements for licensing, at least for younger drivers. There would be just as many persons receiving a license after they had actually made some preparation for driving. It is our firm conviction that an eight-point accident prevention program would greatly reduce our highway mishaps at all ages, but be particularly effective for the younger driver. The eight-point accident prevention program is as follows:

1. Grant a learner's permit one year before the license examination is given with a definitely outlined program of instruction to be followed.

2. Man our drivers' license bureaus with sufficiently *well trained* personnel to construct and give comprehensive examinations only after the applicant presents bona fide evidence of at least 25 hours of authorized instruction. Doctors, lawyers, barbers and beautitions, as well as others, are allowed to practice only after taking rigid tests following a period of authorized training.

3. Grant a provisional license to everyone of legal age and under 21 who passes the test for a period of at least two years. It might, or might not, be renewed by a regular license at the expiration of this period. Make driving a privilege and not a pre-ordained right.

4. Grant a regular license only to those with an accident-free record at the age of 21. Those with an accident record would need to complete another two-year period without accidents or violations before receiving a permanent license.

5. Handle flagrant violators on the same basis as other persons who infringe upon the rights of others. A boy who steals five dollars from a cash register may be sent to the reform school. A motor vehicle driver can do several thousand dollars worth of damage

and even kill several persons, yet never even be arrested if he is not primarily at fault. We tend to be especially lenient excusing so-called accidents. There is no more reason to believe the petty thief more responsible for his behavior than the automobile driver. Accidents are caused or "committed" and don't just happen.

6. Make those riding in a car responsible in some degree, along with the driver or owner of a car. Many times the driver is "egged on" to "strut his stuff" at "chicken," "spider," "swerve," or some similar asocial and moronic games. Parents who know their children would be liable for damage would be more careful with whom they ride. Under criminal law, an accomplice or observer of the commitment of a crime is also guilty to some extent and may be prosecuted.

7. Revoke licenses of those who maliciously or otherwise repeatedly violate a motor vehicle code in such a way as to endanger the life and limb of others. The license would be returned only after a period of three to six months during which time the person would secure further training and counsel and pass tests on attitudes and other possible characteristics before the license would be reinstated. A young lady was recently given a sentence of banishment from California for five years when convicted of reckless driving.

8. Make driving instruction a vocational subject along with agriculture, home economics and trades and industries courses.

WHY DON'T WE DO SOMETHING ABOUT IT?

The main reason is that facts are not available, words are bandied, and loose opinions are expressed which carry little weight. Another reason is that it would cost money and effort to change our system, and there is always resistance to change.

So far as cost is concerned, there is no valid argument when overall economic factors are considered. In 1949 our total educational system was estimated to cost around $4,000,000,000 annually, while motor vehicle accidents were estimated to cost us about $2,265,000,000, or almost 56.7% as much as we are spending on all education. The cost now is even higher. It would only cost $50,000,000 to teach every boy and girl in the United States to drive at the age of 15, 16 or 17.

Of course some things are being done to reduce accidents, but not enough. Highway accidents are down to about 60% of the expected from 1941 figures when the number of vehicles, mileage driven, gasoline consumption, and the number of drivers are taken into consideration. Industry, however, has reduced accidents to less than one-seventh of the expected number on the basis of 1913 figures of man-hours work. The best estimates from various studies of traffic and driving would indicate that, as a conservative statement, we could cut fatalities well below 8,000 a year, or about one-fifth of what they are now, with a workable and effective program such as outlined above.

A few years hence we will look back with as much abhorrence on present highway accident rates as we now look upon the high mortality rates from childbirth, smallpox, and other diseases before the time of Pasteur. Why don't we do something about it? Well, it costs money. In time we will, but unfortunately not until the death toll reaches a staggering total far beyond that of all our wars — past, present or future. No one has ever calculated or begrudged what we spend for sanitation, hygiene and germ control. We accept it as a part of our civilization.

WILL THE YOUNG PEOPLE SUPPORT SUCH A PROGRAM?

Our youth are very enthusiastic about learning to drive safely. It is the general experience of schools offering driving instruction that there are many more applicants for training than facilities available for teaching. So long as this condition prevails we cannot justly point an accusing finger at the neophyte driver who must teach himself incorrectly by hit-and-miss methods, if he learns at all. It is for this reason that we come to the defense of the youthful driver — the rank and file of teen-agers and not the small group of abnormal individuals who are involved in a majority of the accidents. For the most part, the latter group are no more typical of the average teen-age driver than the inmates of the reform schools are representative of the great mass of idealist youth who make our nation great. It is poor psychology to tell any person in a group that he is bad. After a time he begins to believe it and tries to live the part. It is time we begin to find out some good things about younger drivers and attempt to build up their pride in trying to keep down accidents, thus making our highways safer for all.

Controlled studies in various parts of the country have shown that training alone, the last mentioned in our eight-point program, has reduced accidents of those learning in this manner to less than one-half and down to one-fourth of that of the untrained group. Coupled with the other provisions outlined in the proposed program, a minimum of 8,000 fatalities a year is probably a high estimate. It would not be surprising if we could cut down well below 5,000 fatalities a year with a reduction of $2,500,000,-000 or more unnecessary economic loss. Thus such a training program would show a saving for every dollar spent.

Many of us are basically opposed to increased federal spending, but here seems to be a case where our national wealth would be greatly increased by wise spending. It could easily be made a part of the federal aid vocational education program which already has a well organized administrative staff. About all that is needed is a ruling or regulation that driving be classified as a vocational subject and that such training offered meet certain well-accepted standards.

In any case there is no point in laying the blame for accidents at the wrong door. A few smart alecs do increase the fatalities and general accidents of this age group, but in no sense is the accusation general.

SUMMARY

Criticism is levelled at the attempt to smear the driving of teen-agers. First, the ages of the group are not used with discretion and ages up to 24 have been classified as teen-agers. Second, the records of actual teen-age drivers are better than those of the group in the early 1920's. This was found true even on a mileage basis about the time young drivers were under fire. Insurance companies are alleged to have lost money since 1955, about the time the campaign subsided. It may very well have been that the fault was due in part to previous emphasis on the wrong age groups, but is no doubt largely due to increases in repairs of flamboyantly styled cars and inflation. The miles per fatal accident index has decreased which should be an index of cost to insurance companies, other things being equal.

REFERENCES

1. Keller, H. W., Age and sex of operators licensed and in accidents. 1941-1947. Bull. State Dept. of Motor Vehicles, Hartford, Conn. (ms.)
2. King, Gerald E., The age characteristics of Michigan drivers. Bull. Highway Traffic Center, 1958, pp. 11.
3. Lauer, A. R., Characteristics of the driving population with respect to age, sex, driving habits and accident involvement. Proc. Iowa Academy of Science, 1954, 61, 89-98.
4. Lauer, A. R., Age and sex in relation tó accidents. Highway Research Board Bull., 1952, 60, 24-35.
5. Lauer, A. R., A sampling study of drivers on the highway for the 24-hour period. Bull. Highway Research Board, 73, 14-31.
6. National Safety Council, Accident Facts (any year).
7. Swanson, C. O. and Lauer, A. R., Relative changes in percentage of Iowa driver licensees and traffic involvement by age groups between 1953 and 1958. Proc. Iowa Academy of Science, 1958, 65, 427-431.

CHAPTER XIV

MAKING LICENSE PLATES MORE LEGIBLE

INTRODUCTION

Periodically the problem of license plate legibility comes up as being important to certain groups of state officials interested in changing or improving their license plate numbers and car identification. There are a number of psychological factors involved in the make-up of the automobile license plate construction. The moving plate involves dynamic vision and therefore must be fairly easy to read. We cannot touch on all the items of interest here, but we shall discuss a few and give examples from experimental studies with some suggestions for improvement.

First are those characteristics which are inherent within the license plate. There are outside factors, such as the amount of light falling on the plate, roughness of the road, and extraneous influences which cannot be considered as belonging to the plate itself.

CHARACTERISTICS OF THE PLATE

A number of design elements that affect legibility as far as the plate itself is concerned are: (a) height of the digits, (b) number of items on the plate, (c) spacing of the numbers, (d) width of the numerals, (e) grouping, (f) shape of the digits, (g) thickness of stroke of the numerals, (h) ratio of width to height of the digits, (i) amount of background surrounding the number, (j) reflection factors of the legend and the background, (k) wavelengths or the colors of the number and the background, (l) color of light with which the plate is illuminated, (m) ratio of the legend to the background, (n) number of conflicting items, as well as (o) amount of gloss on the surface of the plate. Some of these factors are closely related while others are independent of each other.

We shall confine this chapter to the discussion of some of these elements in a brief manner so as to give the highlights of information which has been derived from a set of experiments done on plates from each state in the union that were collected and studied. Certain of these factors will be discussed in relation to license plate efficiency. They will not be considered in the order listed above.

RATIO OF WIDTH TO LENGTH OF PLATE

Instead of considering the width and length as such we shall consider the width to length ratios and the extremes found in shapes. The plates measured had a width-length ratio of approximately .45 on the average. In other words, plates were slightly less than half as broad as they were long. This varied considerably and ranged from narrow plates which were .305 to the broadest plate which was .601. Most of the plates ran in between and were not far from .45 either way. This is important with respect to the space on the plate and the way the legend or the number is written. Of the 114 plates measured, only one ratio ran .601 and one .305.

Instead of speaking of the height of the numeral or letter in this discussion, we shall consider the visibility distance of the extremes and the average. With respect to the width-height ratio of the numeral, about the same proportions held as for the width-length of the plate. Most of them were approximately 40 to 45% as wide as they were tall, having a ratio of .40 to .45. Lower values obtained in the 114 plates measured were about .31. The highest value obtained was .605. Thus common practice is to use numerals slightly less than half as wide as they are tall. The slender numeral tends to be used most since more numbers can be put in a row on the plate.

NUMBER OF ITEMS ON THE PLATE

Some plates had an inordinate number of items — not digits. The median was four items, although they ranged from three to five. Besides the group of digits in the number this included such things as the state, year or date, certain insignia used by some states, etc. The plates most efficient had fewer digits in the groups as well as fewer items on the plate in general. The 12 most efficient plates had a median number of three items on the plate such as state, date, etc. Of the 12 most efficient plates six had letters combined with numbers and most of them were either one and four, or two and three numerals to the group. Numbers like 32-3773, or groups of two and four, were superior to those with more numbers however grouped.

Of the 12 least efficient plates, seven had a combination of numbers and letters. However, the efficiency seemed to depend not so much on whether they were a combination of letters and num-
:rs, but how many items were on the plate. Crowding reduced the efficiency. The 12 least efficient plates have numbers running up to five in a group, with one letter, making six characters in all. The more units in the group seemed to reduce legibility considerably. Efficiency was figured on the basis of the width-height ratio and legibility distance in daylight.

A Snellen letter is as broad as it is tall, or a block letter. Narrowed down it tends to be seen at a shorter distance. A few plates were actually seen further than expected, although most were not. An index was determined by dividing the expected visibility distance by the actual distance read properly. Efficiency was found to run from 120, or 20% above what would be expected, down to as low as 65% which was about two-thirds of that expected. In other words, some numbers were almost twice as efficient as others.

HEIGHT AND WIDTH OF NUMERALS

Height of the letters varied from four inches for the tallest ones found down to three inches and in one case letters were only $2\frac{3}{4}$ inches high.

The widest letter found was $2\frac{3}{8}$ inches. The narrowest one found was $1\frac{3}{8}$ inches. The modal width was somewhat less than 2 inches. Only one plate was found that was $2\frac{3}{8}$ inches wide.

A block letter one inch high is legible at 56 to 57 feet. By calculating the expected legibility distance by equating the digit with a block type, a fairly reliable index can be obtained. This is done by adding the width to the height and dividing by two, using the result as a standard of comparison.

Thus the tallest digit, 4 inches, of average width, 2 inches, would be equivalent to a block digit or letter 3 inches on a side. It should be legible at 3 x 56 or 168 feet distance.

GROUPING OF THE DIGITS

Many different combinations of groupings were found. We shall discuss them in the order of their efficiency. For numbers we shall indicate n and for letters l. The most efficient groupings found were: 2n-3n, 1l-4n, 1n-3n, 1l-2n-2n, 1l-2n-3n, 4n-3n, 1l-2n-3n, 3n-3n. The most efficient plates were conspicuously devoid of conflicting items, i.e., vertically inserted rows of small characters. Any items which were put on such as state and date were either at the top or at the bottom of the most efficient plates.

Conversely the 12 plates which were found the least efficient may be described as follows: 1l-5n, 3n-3n-1l, 2n-3n-1l, 3n-3n, 2l-5n, 1l-2n-2n, 1n-4n, 1l-3n, 1l-2n-3n. Some instances of identity were found in the most efficient as well as in the least efficient plates. This was probably due to factors other than groupings. The least efficient plates had various markings and state insignia running vertically on the plate. The latter tended to clutter up the number and make it difficult to read. The plates that are described as most efficient usually were read at greater distances. Those that are described as least efficient were read at the shorter distances.

In summary, those plates most efficient were grouped in digits of twos and threes. Very few had more than one letter which seemed to work very well with numbers grouped in twos and threes. Groups of more than three numbers were not as efficient as those with smaller groups. There was about an equal number of plates having letters in the most efficient group as there were in the least efficient group. Letters as such do not reduce legibility. Use of letters like *B* used with other digits are a source of confusion. A group such as 1B2 may be read as 182.

SHAPE OF THE DIGITS

The shape of the digits has considerable to do with the efficiency of the plate. We shall try to describe some of the characteristics of digit shape in the most efficient numerals as contrasted with the least efficient ones.

One (1) was seen best with a slight backward bend in the middle and a smaller top extension. Just a straight line was also good.

Two (2) seemed to be most efficient with a short base and rather open top.

Three (3) was found to be read best when the curles were short, rather an open type of 3.

Four (4) when formed like the commonly used script 4 was best. The open top seemed to give it an advantage in legibility.

Five (5) which may be described best as a two (2) turned over and upside down was most efficient.

Six (6) having a rather straight top was legible. Curling the top would tend to make it look like an eight (8).

Seven (7) having a straight top with a straight line at the side was best.

Eight (8) was not a good number generally, but when used should have rather large open segments. Those made like a script numeral were good, using a slight extension at the upper right.

Nine (9) made like a six (6) upside down seemed best.

These characteristics of the shape of letters seemed to make them most efficient. Any crowding of units, extra curls and additions seemed to be detrimental to efficiency.

THICKNESS OF STROKE OF THE DIGIT

One of the very important elements for legibility of digits on the license plate is width of the stroke. It makes a difference whether white numerals on black are used, or a black numeral on white. Because white tends to spread out or seem larger if placed on black, and vice versa, the stroke of black numerals or letters tend to seem thinner when spread on a white background. Thus the stroke of a black legend on a white background can be heavier than the stroke of a white legend on a black background. The thickness of the stroke on plates measured was found to average close to half an inch. One of the thinnest strokes found was

.38 inch, whereas the thickest stroke found was .61 inch. In general, the letters with the thinner strokes were more efficient than those with thicker strokes. The latter seemed to run together, and particularly the 8's and 6's which were confusing. Reflection factor seemed to make a difference. The observation of the effect of stroke width would be particularly applicable to reflectorized signs.

AMOUNT OF BACKGROUND SURROUNDING
THE NUMBER

Quite a wide difference was found between the percent of legend coverage of the plate. Some plates had as low as 18.8% covered by legend, whereas others were found that ran as high as 47% covered by numerals and characters. Those with a high percentage of the plate covered by legend were found less efficient in general with respect to legibility. The only exceptions were one plate having 17% covered by legend which was found to be 86% efficient, and one with 43.6% legend being 89% efficient. In general, those with a high efficiency rating showed a fairly low per cent of legend coverage on the plate.

REFLECTION FACTORS OF THE LEGEND
AND BACKGROUND

Detailed analysis was made of the effect of reflection factors of the legend and the background. It may be stated that reflection may result from either contrast in amount of light reflected, or of the contrast in wavelength. The two are sometimes confounded. We shall only say that most plates had both contrast of wavelength and reflection factor. For example, green and red were satisfactory as long as the contrast in reflection factor was high.

White numbers on black seem to be the most legible. White or yellow numbers on dark blue are also good. The differences in reflection factor for legend and background varied from 8% to 68%. In other words, a black number on a white background would give a large difference in reflection factor. A black number on a dark green background has only a small difference in reflection factor. The most undesirable colors on plates were those in which there was a low reflection factor difference. The only exception was white on light blue which was quite effective in high illumination, but less effective in low illumination. Dark red or dark green on black was particularly inefficient in low illumination. The mean values for all plates ran about 50% difference between legend and background. We may generalize by saying that any plate in which these factors differ by as much as 50% between legend and background, or vice versa, is usually efficient if other factors are favorable. If less than this difference exists there is some question as to desirability of the combination of colors.

A point should be made concerning the gloss of plates. Dull plates were found to be more efficient than glossy plates. If there is a choice between the gloss and nongloss it is best to use the nongloss surfaces.

It may be well to state that color of the numeral and background is not as important as the amount of contrast between the reflection factor of the legend and background. Size and distinctness of the characters of the legend are of fundamental importance.

COLOR OF LIGHT WITH WHICH THE LETTERS ARE ILLUMINATED

Not enough data were obtained on this factor to make a statement but it seems that the white illuminating light would give the greatest visibility. Any coloring of impinging light would tend to render plates of the same color inefficient by a masking influence.

THE RATIO OF LEGEND TO THE BACKGROUND

This has been discussed under the heading of amount of background surrounding the number. We shall only emphasize the statement that plates having the least amount of space covered by numbers are more efficient than those which have greater amounts of surface covered by legend.

NUMBER OF CONFLICTING ITEMS

The fewer items such as date, state, etc. on the plate, the better.

The most efficient plates studied usually had a minimum of items. Auxiliary items found are usually placed either at the bottom or at the top of the plate. Particularly bad are state designations which often run vertically and may be confused with numerals such as 1 or any slender digit. Items at the top are also bad since details of character discrimination at the top of letters are most useful in reading. State slogans included in the license plate render them less efficient.

The observations cited here were made from a study of 114 plates made under the auspices of the National Research Council. When all of the factors were correlated, efficiency of the plate and visibility distance showed a correlation of .55. The beta values from a multiple correlation for the various factors in order from highest to lowest were: (1) the width-height ratio of the characters, the broader the numeral the better the legibility; (2) the legend-background ratio, the lower the percentage of space covered by legend on the plate the higher the efficiency; (3) the stroke of the numerals gave a minus correlation with legibility indicating the broader stroke gave desired legibility; (4) spacing of legend which gave a positive correlation indicating the greater the spacing the higher the efficiency of the plate; (5) wave length difference between legend and background seemd to be important if the reflection factor also varied. Analogous colors seemed to have some advantage in this respect, such as combinations of blue and red. There was no advantage shown by having contrasting colors for number and background unless the wave length differences were greater for those plates using contrasting colors.

A SYSTEM FOR LICENSE PLATE ROTATION

A plan was developed whereby using the nine most effective combinations each year a rotation scheme could be used for license plates in the United States. With such a system every state would have a different color of plate each year. This plan would probably not have universal support but would avoid confusion of license plates of adjoining states. Details are described under another heading.

The basic purpose of license plates is to identify automobiles.

Not only must the number be clear and easily read but should be recognized as belonging to a certain state. With one or two exceptions there has been no general agreement among states as to what colors they use each year. Some correspondence is often carried on between administrators of adjacent states in order to reach a decision as to numbers to be used.

New York and California have arbitrarily decided to alternate background and legend every other year, using the same two colors. California uses orange background with black letters one year and the next year changes to black background with orange letters. New York uses a reverse system, or combination of colors, each year. So far as we know no other general agreement between states has been reached with respect to the use of colors and background. While studying the general problem of license plate legibility the unscientific method of selecting color combinations of automobile license plates was forcibly brought to our attention.

While it is true that a few of the states have adopted a scheme of alternating colors, the majority use what might be termed a "grab bag" method of selection. They adopt what they consider in their opinion a good color combination without regard to its efficiency and many times without reference to plates selected by neighboring states. Even though a desirable compromise could be made the method of selection makes it practically impossible to do so. Some states use several colors each year for different types of vehicles such as busses, trucks, and other vehicles.

The efficiency of color schemes of different types of plates varies considerably. Inquiry regarding the reasons for using different colors were sent to several states known to be progressive in this respect. Replies were received from nine motor vehicle departments. A few statements are quoted. Excerpts from letters are given in numbered sections and direct quotations made from them.

1. "The different color arrangement of license tags are for the purpose of assigning tags to various types of vehicles, such as passenger cars, trucks, motor cycles, dealer's cars, commercial and official cars. The color for the year is decided upon for the passenger car. For example, if a maroon background with white numerals is selected, perhaps a combination of these colors are

used for other vehicles. For example, a white background with maroon numbers for trucks or dealer's cars, etc. may be selected.

"An effort is made to have a decided contrast in color arrangement in states contiguous to one another. This is desirable from the standpoint of law enforcement. Officers can tell at a glance to which state the car belongs. While this is given as a statement there has been no systematic attempt to develop a nationwide system which would guarantee that such a plan would be used."

2. Another reply was received which went as follows: "We use different colors for our license plates each year. I think the reason for using a different color is to discourage the use of last year's license plates during the succeeding year. I think there are very good reasons for adjoining states to use different colors for license plates."

3. "A different color scheme is used each year as the motor vehicle law provides that the color scheme cannot be repeated for a period of five years and this practice is also to aid the enforcement officers in determining whether new plates have been secured or not. Attempts have been made by this state so that the colors will not conflict with the colors used by bordering states, and it is my opinion that the bordering states likewise make an attempt to avoid confusion which would prevail if the plates of all bordering states were of the same color."

4. "We wish to advise that we have adopted state colors which are blue and gold for automobile license plates, alternating colors each year." It is not stated what is alternated but presumably the background and numerals are alternated.

5. "Our practice has been to use the same color scheme each year except in connection with registering some classes of vehicles and we have the colors in reverse on these vehicles from what we have on others. The advantage in adopting a different color scheme each year for number plates is that it makes any illegal use more difficult than if the same color scheme were used all the time. It is presumed the chief reason why adjacent states use different color schemes on their number plates is that it makes identification of cars easier for enforcement officers as soon as they become accustomed to the colors in use in the several states

and this is sometimes a help in a difficult case of identification where it is not always possible to read the inscription upon the plates at a glance."

6. "We alternate the colors on the plates each year. The colors for one year being orange background and black figures and for the next year being black background and orange numerals. It is our opinion that it is preferable to have adjoining states use different colors as identification as it would be easier to identify them when operating in the same territory which is frequently the case along the borders."

7. "Different colors are used on various license plates for the reason that it is easier for the inspectors, the state highway patrolmen and local officers to locate stolen cars as they can tell immediately whether or not it is a current year license plate. Ordinarily the same colors are not used on the same class of vehicles within a period of five years. Our license plates also show the class of vehicles. For example, C-M for commercial plates, M-B for motor bus plates, and T-R for trailer and tractor plates."

8. "We have never used two colors during the same year, but we have used a different color each year. In this way we endeavor to have our plates of a distinctive color from adjacent states for easy identification." It is not stated in the letter the method by which the effort to keep plates of distinctive color from adjacent states is accomplished.

9. "We are very much interested in the approach you are making. Most of our practices in use today have been the results of a cut and try method of finding the most practical way to handle certain situations.

"The reason that we change the color of our plates each year is that if we did not do so it would be impossible for the highway patrolmen of the various states to determine who were resident and who were nonresident users of the highways of various states. Our state alternates with another state in the color scheme of its plates. We have done this for several years and it works out very nicely.

"For one or two years there were two different colors of plates used in this state in the same year. One was used for one type of vehicle and the other for another. At present we designate the different vehicles by letters. Exempt plates given to public service vehicles have the letter PS in front of the figures."

Thus it will be seen there are a number of reasons given by states for choice of plates and they all seem to be slightly different. In a review of these comments it is noted that most of the states: (1) change colors each year, (2) try to have colors different from adjacent states, and (3) have no definite system for either. A few have standard color combinations which they alternate as background and numerals. One or two states use more than one color each year to designate different types of cars. The reason given in practically all cases is to facilitate identification and discourage illegal use of plates.

THE NEED FOR A UNIFORM SYSTEM

It seems necessary to call attention to the inadequacy of the methods used by the separate states in selecting color combinations for license plates. It may be helpful also to suggest a means whereby each state may have one of the most efficient color schemes that it is possible to find. By using a standard national system each motor vehicle department would know several years in advance just what combination was to be used for any given year. This would assure the use of plates which are not identical in color by states which adjoin. By such a plan the color combination of automobile license plates could be uniform and standard throughout the United States from year to year.

The system proposed involves nine different combinations. Any state which wishes to use other colors than those recommended, particularly for use with different types of vehicles, would be privileged to do so. Passenger cars would use the recommended color. Auxiliary colors should be different from the colors of adjoining states. Maroon and white, red and metallic gold, or some other secondary color combination could be used for this purpose.

WHAT ARE THE BEST COLORS?

From the study of one group of 114 license plates it was noted that 51 color combinations were used during one year. It is possible even more have been used at one time. The most frequent combination was black figures on a white background. We shall designate this as black on white. It made up about 10% of the total number. The next most frequent was white numbers on a violet-blue background. The third most frequent combination was black numbers on an orange background. This combination was used in about 5% of the cases. The fifth most frequent combination was yellow-orange letters on a black background. The yellow-orange was lighter yellow than the orange-yellow. This combination was used on nearly 5% of the plates. The sixth most common colors used was white numbers on a green-blue background. This was used in about 4% of the cases. White on a light green was used in 4% of the combinations. Several other color combinations were used on other plates and the frequencies shaded down to something less than 1% for each type. The table of combinations used is too long for reproduction here and we can only indicate some of the possibilities. Reds and greens were used in various combinations with white and yellow. Both combine quite well with white. In at least two instances very *undesirable* combinations were found. One state used a dark green plate with black numbers. These colors are difficult to read in low illumination. Another state used dark red legend on a black background. This was extremely difficult to read since red tends to get darker in low illumination. Blues tend to appear brighter and are relatively more conspicuous in poor light.

There is also a tendency for some states to use two very light colors together. For example, a light blue background with white figures. This is not bad in daylight, in fact it held up quite well in efficiency, but it was very bad in low illumination — there was not enough contrast.

Ignoring the shadings of colors there were at least 26 fundamental color combinations used in one year. While 13 states were reported to have adopted the practice of alternating standard combinations of colors it was not stated exactly what they meant by alternating. Many of the color combinations used are very inefficient apart from other features of the plate.

In some instances it is noted that neighboring states have identical colors. Two nearby states had color schemes white and blue in one year. Two other adjacent states had black on white the same year. Even though the color combinations are efficient they defeat the purpose of using colors for designating license plates as stated by motor vehicle departments quoted. No doubt many more cases of identical colors could be found. As is known, the reds, oranges, yellows, greens, blues, etc. used are quite variable. Final choice of license plate colors should be based on their legibility.

CHARACTERISTICS OF COLORS USED

There are two methods for the description of colors that are in common use. One is by subjective comparison with standards such as the Bradley color scheme or some other. Another is to use one of several commercial color analyzers that are available to determine the exact wavelength of colors. One of these standard methods should be used rather than to simply stipulate a color as blue, green, yellow, or some other. Considerable variation is found between various greens, blues, yellows, oranges, reds, or others. Such general descriptions have slight meaning.

Along with variations in color is that of reflection factor. Reflection factor refers to the amount of light that is reflected by components of the plate. If a light is thrown on a white paper, approximately 85 to 90% will be reflected. If a light is thrown on a black surface of a plate as little as 4 or 5% may be reflected. The difference between the reflection factors gives the amount of contrast and it is very important in making a plate efficient. Thus the reflection factor of plates can be described quite exactly if one cares to go into the details of doing so. This probably is not always necessary and we shall describe the colors by the use of common words which will give a fair idea of hues found most efficient on the plates studied (Table I).

TABLE I

Most Efficient Combinations

	Combination Background	Number	Difference in Reflection Factor in Per Cent—Numerical-Background
1	white	black	80
2	medium green of bluish cast—very light color	black	40
3	light gold	black	40
4	metallic aluminum	dark blue	40
5	bright yellow	dark blue	40
6	medium blue—light	black	40
7	yellow-orange	black	40
8	white	dark red	60
9	black	yellow	50

By a careful study made both in the laboratory and outside, it was found that the most efficient colors could be determined. We shall list these under three headings. We shall not attempt to go into the details of why the differences exist but merely list the order which they ranked in efficiency.

Some other combinations have been used for trucks and other vehicles which might be designated as secondary value colors, but need not be discussed at this time. All were less efficient than those given in the table.

It will be noted that some of these colors do not appear as being the best that could be picked. The reader may also note that in general the difference in reflection factor between legend and background of efficient plates is between 40 and 50%. It seems to require about this degree of difference in reflection factor for an efficient plate.

The reasons for using some of the less efficient colors in those selected was to get enough combinations which might be worked into a system. Thus white on black, black on white, are by all odds the best combination that can be used. However, since the states might want to reverse their colors on certain commercial vehicles we tried to select nine combinations which were entirely different so that states with the most boundary states need not have the same colors in one year. For example, #1 is white with black letters, whereas #8 is white with dark red letters (see Table I). Actually white on black is the most efficient combination but in order of selection the white with dark red gives a very close second rating to white on black. The recommended colors were not perfectly matched for ease in reading, but were found to be superior to many others that are in common use.

THE ROTATION SYSTEM

A check of the practicability of using a rotation system for the United States was made by using maps and assigning numbers to each state. By a careful comparison of the map it was noted that states differ considerably. While the rectangular states, such as Colorado and Iowa, tend to be bordered by four or five states on the average, certain states like Tennessee and Kentucky have several others touching them. Tennessee is bordered by eight other states. This would mean that in order to have color combinations differ each year there would need to be nine different color combinations in effect as shown in the Table II. Kentucky has seven neighboring states, but eight states border Tennessee as described. Eight states also touch the border of Missouri.

Thus the nine best color combinations found by experimental testing would be sufficient to establish a scheme for use of all of the states. By an elaborate process of trial and error it was possible to determine how many combinations would be needed to rotate every year. The number as representing the nine different combinations were carefully allocated for each of nine years and arranged in such a manner that the color combinations were systematically distributed among the states.

These nine combinations were given to the different states in rotation in such a way that no two alike were given adjoining states. For the second year the states having color combinations for #1 were given #2 and those having #2 were given #3, and so on. In other words, each state was given the succeeding color combinations in rotation. When the ninth year is reached the cycle is repeated.

In order to check the accuracy of the system, United States maps were made for each of the nine years using one color combination in the scheme for each state. This was done empirically and the results are entirely satisfactory. Such a plan for rotation is shown in Table II.

TABLE II

ROTATION SCHEME FOR AUTOMOBILE LICENSE PLATES IN THE UNITED STATES

	*1957 1st Year	1958 2nd Year	1959 3rd Year	1960 4th Year	1961 5th Year	1962 6th Year	1963 7th Year	1964 8th Year	1965 9th Year
Alabama	7	8	9	1	2	3	4	5	6
Arizona	6	7	8	9	1	2	3	4	5
Arkansas	8	9	1	2	3	4	5	6	7
California	7	8	8	1	2	3	4	5	6
Colorado	4	5	6	7	8	9	1	2	3
Connecticut	3	4	5	6	7	8	9	1	2
Delaware	9	1	2	3	4	5	6	7	8
Dist. of Columbia	1	2	3	4	5	6	7	8	9
Florida	2	3	4	5	6	7	8	9	1
Georgia	5	6	7	8	9	1	2	3	4
Idaho	3	4	5	6	7	8	9	1	2
Illinois	4	5	6	7	8	9	1	2	3
Indiana	5	6	7	8	9	1	2	3	4
Iowa	6	7	8	9	1	2	3	4	5
Kansas	3	4	5	6	7	8	9	1	2
Kentucky	2	3	4	5	6	7	8	9	1
Louisiana	4	5	6	7	8	9	1	2	3
Maine	9	1	2	3	4	5	6	7	8
Maryland	8	9	1	2	3	4	5	6	7
Massachusetts	1	2	3	4	5	6	7	8	9
Michigan	1	2	3	4	5	6	7	8	9
Minnesota	3	4	5	6	7	8	9	1	2
Mississippi	3	4	5	6	7	8	9	1	2
Missouri	9	1	2	3	4	5	6	7	8
Montana	9	1	2	3	4	5	6	7	8
Nebraska	7	8	9	1	2	3	4	5	6
Nevada	5	6	7	8	9	1	2	3	4
New Hampshire	7	8	9	1	2	3	4	5	6
New Jersey	2	3	4	5	6	7	8	9	1
New Mexico	1	2	3	4	5	6	7	8	9
New York	6	7	8	9	1	2	3	4	5
North Carolina	4	5	6	7	8	9	1	2	3
North Dakota	4	5	6	7	8	9	1	2	3
Ohio	7	8	9	1	2	3	4	5	6
Oklahoma	5	6	7	8	9	1	2	3	4
Oregon	4	5	6	7	8	9	1	2	3
Pennsylvania	4	5	6	7	8	9	1	2	3

Rhode Island	5	6	7	8	9	1	2	3	4
South Carolina	8	9	1	2	3	4	5	6	7
South Dakota	5	6	7	8	9	1	2	3	4
Tennessee	1	2	3	4	5	6	7	8	9
Texas	7	8	9	1	2	3	4	5	6
Utah	2	3	4	5	6	7	8	9	1
Vermont	8	9	1	2	3	4	5	6	7
Virginia	6	7	8	9	1	2	3	4	5
Washington	1	2	3	4	5	6	7	8	9
West Virginia	3	4	5	6	7	8	9	1	2
Wisconsin	8	9	1	2	3	4	5	6	7
Wyoming	8	9	1	2	3	4	5	6	7

*Any state can adopt the system by starting on the year with the number listed.

ADVANTAGES AND USE OF A SYSTEM

A method for systematic use of license plate combinations is presented. Motor vehicle departments of each state could adopt such a scheme of rotation of the most efficient color combinations described and could eliminate the "grab bag" method of selecting colors for automobile license plates. Nine number combinations would need be used in the United States. The size of plates, the shape, the numbering, grouping system, or any other variables might be standardized to help distinguish one state from another. The use of reflectorized letters or background would make plates more efficient at night. It is possible that the stroke of the numerals should be reduced.

The same color scheme could be used by a state every nine years. This would not be contrary to regulations which make mandatory a change every five years in some states. If other colors for one year were needed they could be chosen for local use. In this way there would be no confusion between local vehicles and those from other states. In other words, they would use colors not normally selected for the regular rotation system. No state would use similar plates on successive years.

If such a system could be adopted it would: (1) eliminate the use of the same or similar colors by adjoining states in one year, (2) avoid tedious negotiations and conserve the time of motor vehicle administrations, (3) guarantee the use of the most efficient color combinations, (4) make for economy in license plate construction by making possible the placing of large orders for plates to be used by a state over a period of years. Our 49th state, Alaska and 50th state, Hawaii, could use any efficient color combination since there would be no conflict with adjoining states.

The system could be used even if not adopted by all states. For example, Delaware might have adopted her state colors of blue and gold which were reversed on alternate years. If she insisted upon keeping this combination it would be troublesome only on certain years. The plate could be changed slightly so as not to be confused with the regular combinations used in adjoining states. Their color is not one of the standard combinations suggested. States surrounding Delaware could use the regular rotation assigned to them. Each year a state's color would be used only by those whose turn for this color in the cycle of rotation had arrived. If other colors were used than those in the rotation it would make no difference.

While it would be advisable for all states to cooperate, the scheme could be adopted by any group or a minority of states. After it were once put into operation some other states could adopt the system as confusions become troublesome. If there were no confusions the state might well keep any preferred colors as in the case of Delaware, for example.

MAKING NUMBERS MORE LEGIBLE

In order to make license plates more legible there are certain principles of construction of numbers which could be set up for use. We shall review this set of principles for improving license plate legibility. They are set down as originally noted without any order of preference.

1. Cut off the side of the sharp corner of 4 when used.
2. Make 1 with a slight base but no top.
3. Make 7 with a slight base but a heavy top.
4. Make 9 straight and not curled. It should be more like a longhand 9 is usually made.
5. Use single letters mixed with numbers only for coding and spacing them apart for numerals. Letters not easily confused with numbers should be used. Examples are X, M, Y, etc.

6. Avoid printing the state or year vertically between groups in small digits or letters. They are often mistaken for 1's.

7. Make 6 and 9 the same, but one the reverse of the other. Both should be more like a script nine.

8. Use a narrower stroke for numerals and letters. For the most part broad stroke numerals do not show up well on a license plate. This is particularly true of slender digits.

9. Space numerals or characters as generously as possible.

10. Keep the plate clear of unnecessary writing. Various emblems, state slogans, and signs have been used. They are not good, reduce efficiency, and should be avoided.

11. Use letters and numerals of the same size for primary numbers. It is best to space the letter if one of a different size is used.

12. Keep 5 open at the bottom and make the top heavier.

13. Keep numerals open. An example is that of a 3.

14. Make the base of 2 heavy. In this way it will not be confused with a 6 or an 8. Make lower part of 8 larger.

15. Make 0's more nearly round. Long 0's fuse and may be read as 1 at a distance, particularly if the stroke is heavy. Make 8 more like a script 8. In general, draw the middle in and allow one end to project slightly higher.

16. Set groups as far apart as possible. Crowding reduced legibility.

17. Press down sides of plate instead of making a raised beading. A flatter edge tends to make for better illumination of the number.

18. Make characters used uniform in size if possible. Irregularities tend to lower efficiency.

19. Make top of 8 different from 9 by the method described. Also let the lower part of 9 be straight and not curled.

The use of these principles would greatly increase the legibility of license plate numbers regardless of colors used. Reading distances could be increased as much as 25 to 30% on the average.

REFERENCES

1. Helwig, Don, and Lauer, A. R., Improvement in highway signs. American Highways, 1933, 11, No. 2, 14-15-19.
2. Lauer, A. R., Factors which influence visibility of license plates in daylight and under artificial illumination. Iowa Acad. of Science, 1944, 50, 185.

CHAPTER XV

A PROGRAM FOR HIGHWAY ACCIDENT REDUCTION

While there has been a gradual reduction in the rate of motor vehicle deaths per 100 million passenger miles, the actual number of fatalities has been greatly increasing due to the increased numbers of licensed drivers and car registrations. The rate has also been decreasing at a slackened pace and the curve which best fits the last 20-year trend seems to be approaching an asymptotic or parallel position to the base line. Various studies are now being made to determine the causes of the tendency toward diminishing returns from accident prevention measures. This might be expected since in most any field as progress is noted the going becomes harder. A slowing down in accomplishment usually takes place unless an entirely new outlook on the problem is taken. The old mechanical scanning process in television became sterile. It took electronics to give us modern television perfection.

NEED FOR NEW APPROACHES

The purpose of the present chapter is to introduce certain facts, figures and novel ideas in an attempt to stimulate original thinking and, if possible, to improve methods of accident reduction which may establish a basis of progress. In most any field there is danger of getting into a rut and of thinking along conventional lines so intently that some ways of improving the situation are neglected.

This presentation may be considered mostly as an outline for the convenience of those who may be interested in considering

possible improvements of methods of traffic accident prevention
or reduction. Something should be done soon to orient the thinking of our legislative and law-making groups. There are those
who will feel that 50 billion dollars put into cross-country limited-
access highways may make us highway poor. Particularly if
the construction is a pump-priming venture. One foreign observer
noted that we already have good roads. As a friend has recently
put it in a review, "Everyone is in favor of such things as driver
education and good roads in the same way that they are in favor
of kindness to children and animals, matrimony, mother love,
and lower taxes." Unfortunately good roads and low taxes are in
conflict with one another. They are at the opposite ends of the
scale. Unless they show a good return on the investment with
the trends now toward increased costs of living, higher taxes and
inflationary tendencies, the public may feel we have reached a
point of diminishing returns in travel facilities. Like polar flying,
we may have to set up a new grid on the map and steer our course
with an entirely different plan of operation from what we have
used in the past. The answers are not all available. We are running the gauntlet between two demons — depression and inflation.

While some of the proposals discussed are scheduled to be accomplished in the overall program and will naturally be taken
care of as a matter of routine, there are others which are not likely
to receive attention at all in the process of developing better roads.
They bear a close relation to the results that may be obtained in
the way of safety. One short section of new highway just opened
has acceleration lanes entirely too short and are reported to require
rebuilding. New types of markings are needed.

We are grouping suggestions for increasing highway safety
under four headings, although this classification may need to be
expanded. The order in which the topics are taken up is not
necessarily the order of importance but probably the order in
which they are least likely to be considered so far as conventional
developments and thinking are concerned. Tradition and con-
vention are very strong retarding influences and it will be difficult
to orient persons with respect to topic numbers I, II, and III.

The basic objective of this chapter is to point out ways to de-

velop individual responsibility for careful driving and to establish such conditions that a full realization of responsibility may
become a part of the driving performance of every person on the
highways (3). If this can be done successfully it is believed that
accidents can be cut in half within a few years.

From the information we are able to obtain, about the best
that limited-access highways have done up to date is attempt to
decrease accidents proportional to the decrease in hazards built
into the highways but no further. In fact, some motor vehicle
administrators have doubted that they have done even this and
some comparisons have not established this to be a fact. We agree
that the improvement is commendable but we feel that much more
can be done to increase traffic safety. Here is our formula for
safer highways and substantial reductions in traffic accidents.

I. *The first problem that should be attacked in this schedule
is an overall improvement of the driver's licensing program.* One
approach has been discussed in Chapter XII. This may be summarized under three major headings.

A. Provision in the driver's licensing laws and procedures whereby the state would assume the role of an inspector to see that
the obligations of each individual are followed for qualifying
himself as a driver. The examination would be taken away
from the state department and made a part of the individual's
responsibility by proving his competence. If one can afford
to buy a new automobile every two or three years, he should
be able to afford a first class examination to assure the public
that he can operate the vehicle safely on the highway. At least
such an examination is required in aeronautics, by railroads,
and in certain other transportation areas where very excellent
safety records have been established. Three further subdivisions of this principle may be identified as follows:

1. Delegate the responsibility of giving examinations for qualifying drivers to professional groups trained in their profession.

2. Strengthen the driver's license requirements and set the

standards for passing the examination considerably higher than at present but easily possible to attain by those who try to do so.

3. Inaugurate a system of licenses which would work one into his driving career gradually. In no other field are persons suddenly taken as rank amateurs and plunged into activities in which they are considered professionals. A gradated plan of licensing should take care of this weakness. By such a system one would start with a beginner's or school license, get a provisional license from the ages of 16 to 20, and at the age of 21 would be given a full-fledged license if he maintains a good record. These cards would be issued in different colors so that one could easily be identified if he were apprehended when not driving properly and according to the standards of the type of license he holds.

B. Adoption of the point system and a driver improvement program are essential features of an effective drivers' licensing program. While the point system is not essential to a driver improvement program it probably would help to reduce accidents by pin-pointing responsibility. At least it would give the state something tangible from which to judge performance and driving records and would tend to act as a deterrent to reckless and flagrant violation of the traffic laws on the part of the public, particularly when some points have been lost and the license is in jeopardy. The point system is well enough understood so that it need not be elaborated further here.

C. Driver education in the schools should be linked with the licensing of drivers and the adoption of a state administered driver education program similar to that which went into effect in Michigan in February 1957.

II. *A second phase of this overall traffic accident reduction program is the adoption of more workable speed laws.* Many studies have been done on speed, per se, and it is the general opinion of all of those who have collected data or have attempted to do anything like a scientific study of the problem that reduced absolute speeds should decrease the number of fatalities and the number of serious injuries as well as the amount of economic loss on the highways. Those who have only opinions are likely to be on the side of the no-speed limit group. What we need is more factual data on this from an unbiased point of view.

A. At present the evidence points to a prima facie limit with unequal day and night speeds as being the safest type of speed rule. Further delineation of this principle might even go so far as to include:

    1. Personal speed limits to be stamped on the license of the individual driver might serve to make him assume greater responsibility for the speed he is capable of driving. This is not inconceivable since his license is already restricted in many other ways by most states. Individuals differ in their ability to drive, and at speeds which are safe. If this principle were recognized and applied it would do much to develop individual responsibility at the wheel. Some maintain it would not be workable but this view does not seem tenable.

    2. The evidence that is available seems to indicate that whatever speed limit may be considered safe in daylight should be cut to about 60% at night for equal safety. It will be observed that in no state in the Union has this practice been followed. The differential is much less. Nighttime accidents and fatalities are much higher. It should be pointed out that about 8 or 9 times as many accidents occur during darkness as during daylight per mile of driving. We are considering measures which should be imposed to reduce accidents and yet be reasonable.

B. Our laws should be set up so that speed zoning could be practiced more widely on our highways. There is no reason at all to believe that one can get on an ordinary road and follow a certain speed constantly throughout a trip. There are certain points where speeds have to be reduced for proper safety. This would imply:

    1. Proper marking of speed zones with large reflectorized signs which could be seen in daylight as well as at night.

2. It should also possibly incorporate a system such as is used on the New Jersey Turnpike where posted speeds are changed for different types of weather. This is very essential in reducing accidents.

III. *The whole traffic enforcement program needs complete revision.* At least it needs to be studied with the idea of possible overhauling. Certain points will be considered here.

A. Preventive enforcement. In commercial transportation preventive maintenance has received wide recognition and has been found to be one of the most useful devices for reducing rolling costs. It is predicated on the idea that "an ounce of prevention is worth a pound of cure." Greasing the bearings properly is much cheaper and saves more money for the company than paying good mechanics to replace the bearings on the road. Such a preventive program for reducing accidents would require some systematic investigation, such as:

1. Locating the possible danger points along the highway. When one hunts he expects to flush quail and other game from the underbrush and hiding places. He doesn't just stand out in the field and expect the game to run up to him to be bagged. Too often enforcement policies are of this nature. This flushing-out process to be successful would involve further the compiling of:

    a. Hazard lists of places which should be more carefully observed or policed, based on accident records.

    b. Courtesy reports on motorists in which no summons are made. The apprehension would be reported to the licensing bureau for consideration in the point system only. This might lead to further refinement which would result in better reporting by the local police to the state. This phase of reporting could be greatly improved.

    c. Lists of problem cases within the state such as are now carried under the assigned risk insurance plan but would need to be much more extensive. An assigned risk plan in a state such as Iowa carries 7 or 8 thousand names from about 1½ million drivers. There are some 50 or 60 .thousand reported accidents each year. Each patrolman might have several hundred cases which he would need to follow up. This system would be similar to that used by the FBI in any crusade against narcotics, espionage, subversion or other similar type of case. Enforcement today is too often made on a shotgun basis and not aimed accurately enough. We need a better system rather than more patrolmen for improved enforcement.

2. The criterion of patrol efficiency should not be the number of tickets given or the miles the patrol car travels each week or month. It should be the accident record in a given area as compared with that which could be forecast from records in the area over the past several years. Methods of calculation based on past experience, amount of traffic, type of terrain, exposure risk, and other factors which are fairly well known could be developed (1).

Such a criterion would put each patrolman on his own to accomplish results rather than by the superficial process of putting mileage on his car or writing up tickets which are often ignored by the courts.

3. More studies should be made of the methods used by successful patrolmen. A number of men on any force could be singled out by their supervisors as doing an especially good job. It is doubtful that any set of principles could be listed which would do more to guide administrative personnel or which would tend to motivate members of the patrol to do a better job than by having comparative records kept. These might even be publicized.

IV. *Physical improvements which would increase highway safety fall naturally under two headings* — those which have to do with the car and those pertaining to the highway.

A. The car. The automobile has been very well designed by the manufacturers and certainly it is an engineering accomplishment to be admired. However, certain practices have crept into the manufacture of cars which are not in the best interest of public safety. Neither are they in the best interests of the automotive industry in the overall picture since many people are reaching the point where they take the train or a plane rather than be bothered with a car. It is not uncommon in cities for persons to dispense with the use of an automobile and use taxis. If this tendency continues for a long period of time it is going to reduce the demand for automobiles since longevity is increasing. Especially this would be true if there comes a time when families can scarcely afford to own a car. With present trends in manufacturer's prices this is likely to make quite an inroad on the market. Some points which might be regulated, either internally by the industry or legislatively, are as follows:

1. Establish arbitrary or legal limits of horsepower as we have done with the strength or candlepower of headlights. In some preserves there are legal limits to the caliber of a rifle or hunting weapon which can be used. The length of the blade of knives which can be carried on one's person are regulated. There is much more logic to the idea of legislative control of horsepower than there is perhaps to some of these other factors which are regulated. There is no good reason why it should not be done since the horsepower far exceeds that needed by the present day automobile. Notice the tendency to reduce horsepower for economy and other reasons by certain foreign makers of cars such as the Volkswagen.

   The manufacturers could probably make more money if they would give up the horsepower race and concentrate on other features which the motorist should buy. A dealer recently remarked to the writer that the public will buy speed but they will not buy safety. Perhaps this is due to an advertising weakness on the part of the manufacturers and their merchandising system. Speed and pickup have been overemphasized in advertising. A referendum of the public certainly would not call for increased horsepower and I am quite certain, for various reasons, there will be a tendency to reduce horsepower within the next ten years. Why not do it now and save a great many lives and perhaps increase the dividends of our stockholders in the automobile companies? Retooling for the new models is tremendously expensive and in most instances hardly seems worth the cost.

2. Cars might also be designed to prevent accidents to a greater extent than they are today. Certain items about the controls could be changed which would greatly improve safety as has been done with steering wheels, seat belts and doors. Most manufacturers have concentrated on such features since 1956 and some have put out a number of alleged safety devices. If more of these could be developed and more effort made to sell safety features rather than speed we would probably be much farther advanced from the standpoint of highway safety as well as economically. We might list three specific areas needing further emphasis.

    a. There should be more attention given to safety built into the controls on automobiles. *Coronet Magazine* recently reviewed a number of things that have not been promoted widely by the industry which could and should be developed. Many of these are already on the drawing board of the major companies.

    b. Automobiles should be designed to prevent accidents rather than merely to alleviate the effects of an accident once it occurs. An effort toward reinforcement of the weaker points in the mechanism should be undertaken. No one knows how many accidents are due to failure in the steering linkage on cars which is characterized by very bad design and certainly not protected by safety features which could be incorporated.

    c. Cars should be designed to make it easier for the driver to do a more efficient job at the wheel. There could be better road view. The new raised fins on the tail and the lowered body are not a step in this direction. The windshield should be designed to avoid distortion, etc.

The instruments should be grouped and made to conform to a standard pattern of operation and in keeping with the basic principles of human engineering. Some things have been done in this way but it certainly has not been deeply studied when compared with methods of securing greater horsepower, at least on paper. Brakes could be greatly improved.

    d. There should be warning signals of speed and other hazards. Some designers are considering more devices of this type. Some cars are using a speed warning device on the speedometer. Other types of signals for low tires, bad lights, etc. might very well be incorporated. Plane manufacturers have done a much better job in this respect. It costs money but perhaps not as much as the 200 extra, almost useless, horsepower which many cars are carrying to consume gas.

B. Road characteristics which would tend to reduce accidents are also very important. The Bureau of Roads is greatly interested in this problem now in connection with development of the new interstate system of limited access highways. Some of these features have been well tested and will be designed into the new roads. We can only cite a few of the most outstanding ones.

    1. Divided highways are favored by highway officials. By divided highways we mean lanes of traffic on any section of road which might be separated from one another by as much as a quarter of a mile or more at places. West of St. Louis, Highway 66 is treated in this fashion and many places in the country such construction has been encouraged. It would be advisable to do this wherever possible. On turnpikes it might be more difficult, particularly in mountainous terrain where it is difficult to engineer such construction economically or in areas where the land values are unusually expensive. In the centuries to come we may need to eat as well as travel and therefore must keep one eye on conservation.

2. Limited access, of course, is a standard feature of modern superhighways and should be encouraged. Limited access, however, should not mean taking everything away from the roadsides. In fact there is a tendency to remove many features which are an advantage to the motorist.

3. Built-in control devices for guiding cars on the highway have been seriously considered by highway engineers.

C. There should be greater variety of visual stimuli present along sides of the highway and within an easy view at the side — perhaps not to exceed an angle of 30 degrees. We might add that a certain amount of auditory stimuli is also desirable. One reason given for divided highways is that it would eliminate the swish-swish which is noted by motorists when passing other cars. This would seem the least of the reasons for dividing the highways since it actually is a type of cue or control. The main reason is that should a driver temporarily lose control due to a flat tire, going to sleep, or other reason, his car will not run across the lane into oncoming traffic. The swish-swish or sound reflections that might be experienced along the road may very well be beneficial providing the sound produced is not spaced in rhythm, inducing a hypnotic state. They tend to keep the driver awake and alert through serving as a guide to his speed. Any aperiodic mild distraction of this nature should be looked upon as beneficial to driving efficiency.

There are certain proponents of highway roadside development who would retain only the natural beauty. It is common knowledge that in the wide-open spaces of the western states, where perhaps natural beauty abounds more than any other place in the country, untrammeled by human developments, accident and fatality rates are much higher than in the east where there is a multitude of various types and diversity of stimuli.

In a similar manner one would expect that by reason of reduced landscape stimuli there would be many fewer accidents at night than in daylight since the driver cannot see objects around him. The reverse is true which weakens the alleged distraction theory.

By the same token it would be expected that there would be many more accidents per mile of driving in the city and on the trunk highways than there is on ordinary roads. This is not the case when traffic flow is considered. Apparently the more stimuli the driver experiences along the way, the greater his alertness and consequently the more successfully he drives.

D. Worry, mental anxiety, emotional disturbances, etc., are being looked upon as contributory factors to accidents. If a driver is troubled by lack of places to refuel or service his car, search for something to eat or to secure accommodations for his family at night, the cause of safety is not served. Make it easy and interesting for the motor vehicle driver to travel and avoid traffic hazards.

Well-designed roadside improvements and facilities are an asset to the motorists. Novelty along the highway keeps him alert. Any source of information along the highway is stimulating. It is the monotonous stretches of roads that we need to eliminate by using well designed and interesting roadside stimuli.

Various kinds of developments such as novelty in roadside architecture, highway signs, advertising signs, as well as formal and informal developments, are desirable along the highways. Special limitations placed on any kind of stimuli which reduces variety are undesirable. Anything which lies far to the side to cause the motorist to turn and gaze is questionable. Particularly if the object is located more than 30 degrees from the line of sight.

E. Better roadway and route markings are desirable. Highway builders have done much to improve the markings of highways but still in many places we do not have adequate signs, either in design or size. Those signs that are the most easily understood are pictographic or pictured markings which indicate the volume of traffic or the importance of the road one is about to cross or enter. At one place in Indiana there is a tree where 22 persons were killed on one curve located at the end of a long tangent section. It is located at the end of a very slow downgrade and is not well marked. Most all of these accidents could have been avoided had a large billboard been placed at the end of the curve, particularly if reflectorized. Most of the fatalities occurred at night. Cooperation between the advertising people, the road builders and administrators would greatly help in this respect. Large commercial signs should be encouraged, especially at corners and at the end of curves. Newer interesting designs would be helpful.

SUMMARY

During the past 50 years the United States has sponsored a road-building program which has developed until further expansion may not be economically sound unless the greatest precaution is taken in getting the most for the money in roads. The most for the money would not only mean permanent and useful highways, but also highways that will reduce the great toll of accidents, deaths and economic losses from accidents throughout the country.

It must be kept in mind that in the final analysis the argument for highways has been as avenues of commerce built for travel and transportation, rather than as aesthetic developments for the country. Some aesthetic treatment can be accomplished at junctions, in parks, etc., without any great outlay of money or other economic considerations.

It should go without saying that extensive parks laid out along the 41,000 miles or so of highways throughout the country would impose an enormous burden in various ways. In the first place it would take out of production commercial land which has high potential value and therefore is an asset from the standpoint of raising revenue. In the second place, to take this land out of production and put it into expensive parks, would require excessive expenditures for upkeep and maintenance.

A third reason is that such a plan would not serve the best interests of the motoring public from the standpoint of convenience as well as safe motoring. There must always be a compromise between utilitarian functions and aestheticism. Prohibitions of one are as bad as prohibitions of the other. The two have lived side by side since the dawn of civilization and perhaps will need to continue in such relationship along our highways for some time to come. Fundamentally they are not opposites but parts of an essentially well developed whole. The objective should be to build safer highways and only factors which are definitely contributory to this end should be given consideration.

REFERENCES

1. Berman, Jack, The Highway Engineer and the National Committee on Urban Transportation. Traffic Engineering, 1959, 29, #6, p. 17.
2. Buisson, H., Le nouveau code de la route. Surate Nationale de la Route, 1959, 7 année, p. 25-28.
3. Bendtsen, P. H., All-purpose roads and streets. Int. Road Safety and Traffic, 1959, 7, #1, p. 17-26.

CHAPTER XVI

DRIVING FOR PLEASURE AND PROFIT

Perhaps no other convenience of modern life gives more enjoyment to greater numbers of persons than the automobile. Since the advent and development of fine all-weather highways throughout the country everyone has a desire to go somewhere, be it near or distant. When two or more persons are traveling from one place to another the cost of automobile transportation will compete very favorably with any other type of rapid transportation. Regardless of the purpose for which one may be going, the automobile stands out as one of the preferred methods of travel, unless distance and stress of time make it impractical.

IMPORTANCE OF DRIVING

Driving is important to everyone in practically every walk of life, and it only takes a gasoline shortage, or a strike of some type which ties up delivery facilities of this commodity, to make us realize how much the motor vehicle means to us.

During the last three decades we have come to depend more and more upon automotive transportation. Not only do we drive to and from work, but in many cases we depend upon some form of motor vehicle for delivery of our mail, our milk and other necessities. The foodstuffs on our table are brought to the city by truck frequently, and the grocer uses the motor cycle or small delivery truck for bringing our grocery order. We receive the daily paper from the distant city by rapid transportation afforded by the motor car. When we are ill the doctor rushes to our bedside in his car and again rushes to see another sick person, while relief in the form of drugs and supplies are brought to us by some type of gasoline-propelled vehicle.

Thus in a thousand and one ways we depend upon the smooth operation of the pneumatic tires and the utility of gasoline-propelled type of transportation. The problem, however, is to learn how to operate these vehicles with the greatest efficiency and safety. From our accident record it is quite obvious that we are not always doing this with sufficient skill to insure greatest safety in the widespread usage of this most useful tool of mankind.

VOCATIONAL DRIVING

Practically everyone in modern society needs to drive and it is necessary for a very large percentage of persons to drive in order that they may carry on the important business of making a living. In general we would classify the latter as vocational driving which includes a much wider scope than that of driving buses or trucks for hire. Any industry of magnitude has transportation problems of some type. Employees often do other things for a major part of the working day, but may take the company truck to go to and from jobs. Thus they assume responsibility for handling the vehicle in a safe and efficient manner. The reputation, and even the finances of the company, are to a great degree tied up with his success in manipulating the motor vehicle. If the driver should run off the road and down an underpass, as was the experience of a rural electrification vehicle recently reported in our vicinity, the company is at considerable expense not only of loss in man hours but damage to equipment, to correct the carelessness and inefficiency of the driver.

We would include in vocational driving all of those pursuits which in any way have to do with making a living. That is to say, if it is absolutely necessary for the person to operate the motor vehicle to hold his job, we would consider it vocational driving. This will have a large number of connotations and there will be some overlapping with the next question which we will classify as avocational driving.

AVOCATIONAL DRIVING

By this heading, of course, we mean those types of driving

which are not absolutely essential, but which are a convenience to the driver or to the worker. For instance, going to and from work in a factory. While one may not need to drive since he may be able to ride with others and pool his transportation, the fact remains that someone in the group will need to drive and perhaps in time each must take his turn.

RECREATIONAL VALUE OF THE AUTOMOBILE

We have just emerged from a period of wide-spread employment and perhaps a period of overwork in some respects, but no doubt the problem of leisure time will again command our attention before too many months roll by. Everyone will remember the stress that was being placed upon the use of leisure time during the slack economic period following the last depression. The automobile is one of the finest and perhaps least expensive methods for securing recreation. The person who has been confined to his sick room or to his home through the winter gets more pleasure from going out in the automobile for a drive than perhaps anything else he could do. In the summer when one has a vacation the automobile offers the choice kind of transportation for this period. With the development of tourist camps and motels throughout the country, in addition to existing tourist rooms and regular commercial hotels, one has a wide choice of rooms and places for "putting up" when traveling. He can go most anywhere he likes at his own convenience, stay as long as he cares to and enjoy whatever he is interested in. This in the broadest sense is recreation. In this way it is possible to get away from the cares of everyday life and really relax. It would be interesting if someone could calculate the benefits to mankind that the motor vehicle has brought through this avenue alone. Then, of course, there is the matter of driving on Sundays and holidays. One can visit relatives and friends much more frequently and with greater ease than in the old days when it was necessary to take the train or drive the horse and buggy. This procedure naturally precluded any distant visit on short holidays. Ten or 15 miles was about the maximum distance one could drive a team in a day and return. If children were in the group one needed to take into consideration the fact that they must reach home in time to retire early so they would be physically fit for school the next morning.

EMERGENCY NEED FOR EVERYONE TO DRIVE

In our driving education courses we frequently have wives of business men and others who come to learn to drive because of illness in the family. They have never learned to drive and then suddenly while on a trip the regular driver, the head of the house perhaps, becomes ill. There is no one to take the wheel. The children are too small or inexperienced and the wife finds herself very much at a loss to accomplish the family objectives without the ability to drive an automobile. These emergencies are likely to occur to everyone. In the Army, while there were regularly qualified drivers, the service desired that every man should be able to drive. There was no way to know at what time such demand might arise and the safety of an entire regiment might depend upon whether or not one person could drive a motor vehicle in order to transmit messages, materials or equipment to some specific point. In the ambulance service every person was trained to drive and trained very thoroughly in every phase of motor vehicle operation. This was a very essential part of their work. Thus if for no other reason than for the fact that you might be called upon to take the wheel in an emergency it would be advisable to learn to operate the motor vehicle safely.

THE NEED FOR GREATER COURTESY AND SAFETY IN DRIVING

While it is easy to establish the need for driving an automobile and the necessity of using the automobile in everyday life, it is also equally certain that we are not handling the motor vehicle with adequate precaution and safety. The loss of 30,000 or more persons each year loudly attests this point with reference to motor vehicle operation.

THE INCREASE OF PASSENGER CAR ACCIDENTS

Since the advent of the motor vehicle there has been a constant rise in the number of motor vehicle fatalities each year. An increase would, of course, be expected since the number of motor vehicles increased from a meager few in 1895 to something over 30 million at a given time during the last decade. The number seems to increase greatly as soon as motor vehicle designs change and are manufactured in quantity sufficient to satisfy the existing demand. But the increase in accidents is not inevitable and could be greatly reduced. The volume of traffic alone does not warrant this increase as is shown by the fact that certain eastern states such as Rhode Island have a very low per capita ratio loss due to automobile accidents, while some of the western states have a very high ratio loss. In fact this varies from about as low as 5 per hundred thousand in Connecticut to as high as over 40 in certain of our western states. As a matter of fact, the traffic in Rhode Island, although a small state, is considerably heavier per mile of highway within the state than that of certain of our western states. If the density of traffic alone could account for accidents, this condition would be reversed.

Another distracting feature of the situation is that despite the fact that we tend to blame trucks and buses for highway accidents, actually their rate has improved a great deal. Their accidents on any equivalent mileage basis has decreased in some cases as much as 30% while the increase in passenger car accidents during the same period with the same traffic conditions has increased as much as 30% or more. Therefore we must conclude that our increase in automobile accidents cannot be attributed or blamed entirely on the increase in the number of vehicles. Accidents have even increased out of proportion to the increased number of vehicles. All of these facts point to one salient feature of the whole situation. The average person does not know how to drive. He may be able to "herd" a car, but he actually does not know how to drive safely.

IMPROVED HIGHWAYS DO NOT ALWAYS MEAN GREATER SAFETY

Engineers quite often lead us to believe that super highways and road construction programs tend to solve the accident problem. While we must have good roads and agree they are necessary, the facts show that with the advent of good highways, invariably there is an increase in traffic accidents. One may try to justify this fact by saying that this increase in accidents is due to the increase in traffic over the roadway. Of course this probably is true to a certain extent, but there are cases frequently which do not justify such conclusions at all. One stretch of eight miles on a midwestern highway had been devoid of accidents for a number of years. After the pavement was laid and a beautiful highway built across this section, eight fatalities occurred within a very short period of time, and the stretch of roadway became known as dead-man's lane. The only reason for such accidents seems to be that there were no crossings or otherwise inherent danger points along the way and drivers took advantage of the level stretch and drove too fast. If a tire blew out or any emergency arose they became frightened and ran off the shoulder. Immediately the car went out of control and usually one or two deaths occurred. Another instance in a midwestern state is cited. It was reported that after a series of railway accidents, the city took the precaution to install eight or nine underpasses. Within the next year, twice as many fatalities occurred at these points, caused by drivers running into the piling or peers set up for supporting the overhead crossings. In another locality a viaduct was built at the expense of nearly one-half million dollars at a point where no fatalities had occurred. Two or three serious accidents and fatalities occurred at this point within a space of two years. Naturally some of these happenings may have been the result of chance. However, chance will only operate when conditions are such that there are no counteracting factors. When using loaded dice, the deuce may fall up a number of times in succession, but this is not strictly chance. It is the fact that the dice are loaded such that the heavier part of the cube gravitates to the bottom.

DRIVING BY "EAR"—NOT TRAINED

We have discussed this problem with persons learning to drive by saying those who do not have instruction learn by "ear." In music, a fiddler will perhaps learn to play the *Fisher's Hornpipe* or a certain melody with rhythm. But if this fiddler is placed in a symphony orchestra where he has to watch the conductor, follow, and play the notes that are printed on the music before him, he is about as useless as anyone could be in a complex situation. While operating a motor vehicle is not quite so marked in extremes, it is a fact that most people actually just get in and drive without instruction. Very few persons know the correct procedure when starting a car. It is safe to say that if one would check men who have not been trained to drive by a competent instructor or systematic instruction, many will not do the first thing correctly when starting a car. By doing the first thing correctly we mean doing that thing which will not only be easiest on the car, but which will preclude any possibility of an accident due to the car lurching forward when the motor is started. Such accidents are frequently reported in the accident statistics of the country.

No one would really want to be an ear player on a violin or clarinet if he could actually get musical instruction and read music. Anyone can memorize notes and then play his numbers and even swing a section here and there, that is, ad lib when he pleases, but it is impossible for the fellow who can't read notes to sit in and play with a string quartet or symphony orchestra without having accomplished this ability by careful and systematic study.

EVIDENCE THAT TRAINING INCREASES SAFETY

A few persons are always skeptical in their attitudes toward any statements regarding the results of education. This is perfectly normal and to be encouraged. We need to be scientific in our judgment of results of schooling and have a right to know whether instruction is of value. The answer to this question regarding driver education has been given in two or three instances, and a number of studies are being made which will give us more light in the near future. Professor Amos Neyhart, of Pennsylvania State College, has trained a large number of drivers throughout the country; possibly he has been responsible for training more than any other person in the United States. In one small study which was conducted in cooperation with the Pennsylvania State Police he reports that the accidents of systematically trained drivers as compared with the control group of untrained drivers was about one-fourth as great. In other words, by systematic training the records of these drivers two years following the end of their training was four times better than the records of those who were untrained.

Another study was made in Cleveland, Ohio, where driver training has been given in the schools and in the city for a number of years. In this instance it was revealed that the accidents were decreased about 50% for the trained drivers as compared with untrained drivers. There is also a marked decrease in the violation of the trained drivers. In a study conducted at Iowa State College of about 300 drivers who had first taken the driver training courses, it was shown that the accidents in the ensuing two years was about one-tenth of that to be expected from an unselected group of the population. The unselected group, however, included those from the entire population of the state. The study will be more convincing when it is reduced to a comparable group of the same age and other qualifications, excepting the matter of driver training per se. It seems quite evident that training does help one to stay out of accidents and also to keep out of unnecessary violations. It appears from studies of a clinical nature that most persons do not deliberately violate traffic ordinances, but do not see the lights, the stop signs, parking signs, or whatever may be the reason of their traffic violation. By training in the habit of looking for all signs, instructions and guiding devices along the highway while driving, one becomes more likely to observe them. This has to do with what psychologists call perceptual ability. It is the capacity to interpret, or the ability to interpret, and it is known to be highly developed by training.

Commercial companies have long realized it was necessary to train their drivers for their commercial work, not only for safety but for maintenance. An untrained driver in a commercial company has a tendency to abuse the vehicle and thus run up unnecessary expense in repair bills, consequently shortening the life of the vehicle. This latter aspect of driver training should not be underemphasized.

TRAINING AS AN INSURANCE

One may look on the matter of driver training as an insurance against accidents. However, it is better than the ordinary commercial insurance since the latter pays only after you are injured, have your automobile damaged, have injured someone else, or demolished another vehicle. The training is an insurance which pays dividends by keeping you out of accidents and thus avoiding unnecessary loss of time and life. It also insures one against unhappiness resulting from automotive mishaps. One should undertake the problem of learning to drive scientificlly from this viewpoint. Look on your efforts to learn to drive safely as a type of insurance which will cost you no premiums in the future but which will operate every day of your life to keep you out of trouble.

COURTESY IN DRIVING

Perhaps no other feature of driving is more stressed by interested laymen, the clinic of traffic malpractices and mishaps of various types, than is courtesy. Pamphlets obtained from any insurance company, automobile association or service club that is attempting to reduce accidents, will undoubtedly contain some reference to the lack of courtesy on the highway. Courtesy on the highway, like courtesy at church, in the schools, on the street, in a restaurant, or in the home, is largely a matter of training. We look upon discourteous persons as those who are not properly trained, or who lack some phase of training. Therefore, much that is termed discourtesy on the highway is actually not intentional discourtesy, but lack of information on the part of the driver. In reality he may think he is extremely careful and considerate of others. It is contended that courtesy would follow any training in the principles of safe driving on the highway.

PSYCHOLOGY OF LEARNING AND SKILL

Practically everyone today has read or heard enough about psychology to know that it deals with human behavior and with the principles of how the mind and body work together. This, of course, is established by the nervous system, and particularly with

reference to a skill of any type there is much to be learned about
the most efficient method. Early in the history of applied psychology, Dr. Frank Gilbreath made studies of bricklayers and found
that by reducing the movements made by a bricklayer he could
increase his output as much as 400% or in terms of units used,
they were able to increase from 12 units per unit of time to 47
units per unit of time. The psychology of skill has to do largely
with that of reducing movements necessary to accomplish a certain
result to the minimum, and at the same time relieve the other
capacities or departments of the psychological makeup for observation and self protection.

A PERSON MUST WANT TO LEARN

Before anyone can be taught he must first have a desire to learn.
This is one of the first psychological principles involved. If for
any reason he is in doubt about his desire to learn a certain thing
he should at once stop and take careful consideration of the whole
matter in its entirety. It is a waste of time both for the learner
and the instructor to attempt to develop a skill when the learner
himself has some doubt as to its value.

However, most of the above does not apply to driving an automobile in a general sense. We have found from experience of the
past 10 years that practically everyone wants to drive an automobile. There are very few exceptions and when an opportunity is
given to learn the class for the course is always crowded. However,
the following is probably relevant to the matter of attitudes. Most
persons would be glad to learn to play a piano if that learning
consisted only of sitting down to the piano someday and playing
a concerto. What they do not like is the routine five finger exercises, scales and arpeggios which are necessary to develop a technique for playing the piano. In driving we have a similar situation. To go out on a road and drive a car down the highway is
perhaps the ambition of every boy, girl or grownup, and when he
takes a driving education course the natural thought is that this
will be the first thing to do. Actually it is very uneconomical to
start this way. He will learn much quicker if he goes through the
exercises, the particular types of practices which are necessary to

learn skill at the wheel. For this reason every learner is warned to have patience with the successive steps which he must take in the process of learning to drive. Otherwise he will find his learning considerably delayed due to the fact that it will be necessary to go back and pick up some of the "lost stitches" which will result from undue haste in attempting to get on the highway.

ONE MUST LEARN GRADUALLY AND MASTER STEPS

In the development of any skill it is essential that certain steps be mastered to some degree at least before proceeding to the next step. As was suggested in the foregoing paragraph there is a tendency for a beginner to overlook the essential steps in the learning process. On the other hand an instructor can't spend too much time on simple steps. We shall attempt to point out the parts which must have more practice and where we may eliminate unnecessary practice on the steps which will more or less take care of themselves, as one goes along. It would be a waste of time to attempt to keep one standing still with a vehicle until he can steer perfectly. On the other hand, to allow him to attempt to park and drive in traffic before he has mastered steering is hazardous and a decidedly uneconomical method of learning.

THE NEED FOR UNDERSTANDING

Practically all of our educators stress the importance of understanding in the learning process. This is probably one of the crucial points in any teaching process. The learner must understand what the instructor is trying to show him. Now this understanding in driving an automobile will be largely in the nature of information which will need to be read about the car, the highways, the laws, and in some cases the actual learning process. He will need to know what are the essential things to be learned and to understand why they are essential. A little later when we consider the clutch it will be necessary that he learn why clutching and the control of the clutch is very important in driving. These and many other things will come under the heading of understanding. The more one reads and is attentive in this respect, the easier it will be for one to learn to drive successfully and safely.

OVERCOMING FEAR

Persons as well as animals tend to fear new situations. Grandpa can tell you how his horse acted when the first automobiles appeared on the road. To overcome fear, it is necessary to have experience with the thing you are afraid of. Understanding the problem, inspires confidence.

VALUE OF KNOWLEDGE ABOUT THE CAR AND DRIVING

As already mentioned fear of something is largely due to inadequate information regarding it. In earlier times people were afraid of the eclipse of the moon, of darkness, and of anything portending of danger — that is, anything strange. If you are afraid of an automobile it is usually because you know very little about it. Of course one does not expect to be an automotive mechanic, but he can learn enough about the mechanism of the car to know it is perfectly harmless and will do him no injury unless it is misused. By becoming familiar with the general parts of the automobile, of their functions and what they do to keep the vehicle running, one will tend to forget about the fear of the machine and to enjoy its behavior. In addition, he will be able to appreciate any irregularity in function which might lead to injury to the car. Our various senses aid in this way. Going around a corner we have a feeling of being pulled to the side. This is known as the tactual or touch sense. No doubt the muscle sense operates in this respect, as well as the sense of equilibrium, which has its seat in the semicircular canals adjacent or attached to the inner ear. The sense of smell operates to help one understand the functioning of the car. If the oil is running low you will have a particular odor from the motor. If the water is low you will get a smell that is characteristic only of this particular condition. If your brakes are hot or if there is a "short," or any one of several other things, it may be detected by a more thorough understanding of the car and how it works.

For the above reason we want you to become familiar with the workings of the car — at least, the general differentiations of the vehicle into its component parts or sections. For example, there is the running gear or the chassis as it is called. Then there is the motor proper which is connected to the wheels by means of the transmission and is also considered as a definite part. These devices in turn are controlled by a set of mechanisms. There are certain auxiliary aparatus also, such as the generator, the starter, the oil filters, the temperature indicators and gauges, and so on. Finally, there is a body which is the part in which you ride, called the tonneau. All these parts properly integrated make up the modern automobile. An understanding of this mechanism and its parts is necessary to overcome any fear which you may have with respect to the operation of the motor vehicle.

THE FUNCTIONS OF AN INSTRUCTOR

When one is learning anything the function of an instructor may be divided into three main divisions. Namely, (a) that of giving information or explaining any information. It is naturally the duty of the learner to acquire such information in the learning process. Otherwise, in a sense the instruction is a failure. (b) That of acquiring certain skill. The function of an instructor with respect to skill is to show you the simple way of doing a certain thing. A beginner tends to use all of his muscles to accomplish a very simple trick which may require only the use of one or two muscles. In the case of a sleight-of-hand performer, I have seen an experienced man keep a coin in his hand for an hour as he practiced turning the coin from the front to the back of his hand which required the use of a certain specific muscle. For most of us the attempt to do this would be quite ridiculous because we would drop the coin immediately, due to the fact that too many muscles operate antagonistically against others. An instructor is supposed to observe these unnecessary actions and to try to get the learner to use the muscles which he should use to accomplish the results intended. Finally, (c) the function of an instructor is to develop certain attitudes of the learner. That is, certain ways of thinking regarding a certain situation. Technically, an attitude is an idea which has been brought about through some emotional tendencies. One may have an experience and for some reason have a negative reaction toward it. In other words, he doesn't like it. If he has an experience several times and each time has the same general reaction, it is likely that he will eventually develop an attitude toward it. A stop sign should be considered an aid to traffic and an aid to the individual driver. It should not be considered a barrier to the enjoyment which one may derive from driving. After all, if you go through a stop sign and collide with someone your trip will be cancelled anyway. One might as well stop for a second or so, bring the wheels to a complete stop which is necessary to fulfill the requirements of the law, and then proceed when the way is clear.

Thus in a general way the function of an instructor as an aid to the learner is to help him get further information to improve his skill and to develop the proper attitude toward driving.

NEED FOR MASTERING PRECISION CONTROL IN A SAFE AREA

In connection with acquiring mastery of a motor vehicle and subduing any fears which may arise, it is necessary to practice under conditions which will not be disastrous. The old adage that nothing succeeds like success is a very fundamental principle in teaching driving. There are three reasons why one must be taught to drive in a relatively safe area. We will first consider the problems connected with the automobile itself. Cars are very expensive at present, difficult to get and repair bills are high. If one drives in traffic, parks his car in dangerous places, or drives through hazardous conditions before he has mastered the art of driving, it is not at all conducive to long life of an automobile. In the second place, as already stated, it is necessary to learn how to operate, or do a thing well in order to overcome fear. The best place to practice is under such conditions that no great amount of traffic will be encountered. This is a very essential point in learning to drive scientifically. On a traffic-free area you will have ample opportunity to turn, to back, to steer, to place your wheels on a line, to start, to stop, to turn and to do anything and everything which will be necessary in traffic. This is all done with no danger at all to yourself or to the car. The third reason why it is necessary to practice on a limited area is that the public at large needs to be protected.

Not long ago a young lady who had never had training was taking her driver's license examination. She came to an intersection at the end of an underpass and instead of stopping according to a stop sign, failed to notice the sign and drove on into the intersection. Aside from upsetting a semi-trailer truck and demolishing her car, there was no serious personal injury or damages. However, this young lady was probably so shaken up and frightened that it will be some time before she will attempt to drive again. In addition, she might have been responsible for the death of people who had a right to expect her vehicle to be under control when in traffic. Therefore, one must consider not only the car and himself, but other people. Thus it is essential that beginners have an opportunity for getting experience in a safe area before mixing with traffic.

PERSONALITY AND DRIVING

There is another angle for mastery of any skill or field of knowledge, regardless of what it is, which should be considered by every person, and especially by those who are in the early stages of their educational careers. Personality in driving is receiving a great deal of attention in schools and by the general public. Personality may be defined as a lot of things, but everyone knows that a very essential part of personality is a certain poise or self-confidence. Poise and self-confidence are only to be obtained by mastery of some particular field or skill. If you drive well, persons will give you credit for doing other things well even though perhaps you are mediocre. If you can do nothing well, you will have an inferiority complex, probably, and be more or less a wall flower when mingling with others. One of the important aspects of mental hygiene is to be able to do well those things which you attempt to do. Of course, no one can do everything well. He should specialize in some one or two things, especially those things which are needed in everyday life and do these exceptionally well.

ECONOMICS OF DRIVING

By economics we mean the dollar and cents aspect of operating an automobile and the need for conservation of resources in the field of transportation. It is estimated that our accident costs on the highways today are running around five billion dollars per year. This is a small consideration compared with the national debt, perhaps, but it does mean an amount equal to about 2% interest on the total national debt. This loss in goods and services throughout the country is not entirely but mostly unnecessary. Therefore we should consider some of the specific things which contribute to this particular economic loss.

CARS ARE COMPARATIVELY EXPENSIVE

It has been stated that families spend more for their automobiles than for any other single item in the household or about the house, except the home itself. We have not made calculations to this effect, but several years ago we did calculate the cost of keeping an automobile for a period of three years. This was a relatively small car and included gas, oil, tires, depreciation and other expenses. It was found that it cost approximately $25 a month to own an automobile, not including the investment of a garage. At the present time this cost has undoubtedly risen to thrice that amount. In other words, if you have an automobile and keep it a number of years and trade cars, you will find that it will cost approximately $75 a month for you to own and operate an automobile under conditions such as have been practiced in the recent past. That is to say, you expect to trade your car every so often and keep it in the proper condition. It is well known by commercial companies that the driver has a great deal to do with the upkeep, expenses and overhead on a car. A good driver can get three to five miles more per gallon of gasoline than a poor driver. These are a few of the things that we have to keep in mind and some of the reasons why one should learn to operate a car as economically as possible.

OPERATING COSTS ANALYZED

As suggested above, there are a number of things which go into the cost of an automobile. In the first place there is the original price, or amount paid out. This, of course, varies with the type of car you are driving, and the age of the car at the time you purchased it. If you purchase a new car you have relatively few repair bills as long as you do not damage the car in an accident. Probably you will have very few repair bills, including tires, for two or three years. In the second place there is the matter of actual operating costs including gas and oil. The oil bill for the first two or three years will be negligible because oil is relatively cheap and new cars use very little oil. If you drive your car at moderate speed it is likely that the oil consumption problem will not disturb you. There are many men who have driven 50 to 60 thousand miles without having any major repairs to the motor and yet the car uses very little oil. The use of good oil is important. Gasoline does not vary so much with the condition of the car but a car in bad condition, improperly adjusted or improperly driven, will use considerably more oil than others. Another expense of operating a motor vehicle is the matter of tires and the repairs to the different parts of the car including such work as lubrication of the chassis and working parts, the periodic washing and care of the finish and other items of this type.

The above expenses are largely inherent in the ownership of any piece of mechanism. It is expensive to buy and it costs money to keep it in operating condition. However, there are still other expenses to an automobile which we must consider. There is the problem of insurance. You should be insured in a number of ways, but we will discuss this matter later. Since you are liable to others when you drive your automobile, you should make a careful study to see that the policy is properly made out and in force at all times. Finally we may consider the cost of depreciation. It was formerly the custom, and I presume still is, to consider the depreciation of an automobile for the first year as 40% of the cost price. After the first year deduct 40% of the balance or remainder of the investment for each succeeding year up to 4 years. It is doubtful whether this holds at the present time, but when cars are plentiful it undoubtedly is operative. Therefore it behooves one to use his car carefully and to make it last as long as possible if he is going to get the greatest return on his investment.

TODAY'S AUTOMOBILE AND THOSE OF YESTERDAY

Automobiles today are much more complicated than they were a few years ago. They are much more powerful. In 1925 the breaking horsepower of the average automobile was 32, but in 1940 the horsepower was 85. The tendency is even to build more powerful cars than in 1940, although the change was not marked until 1953. Automobiles are several times more powerful than they were in 1925. This emphasizes the need for more skill at the wheel. Any powerful machine requires a better operator than a less powerful machine, particularly transportation equipment.

The automobile, since the war has risen materially in price. We may be lead to believe this amount is about a 10 or 15% increase, but if you will look on the registration certificate of an old car which was registered perhaps in 1938-40, and compare it with a car which was registered later, you will find that this cost price is nearly 50% higher. We have demanded much more powerful cars today, hence they are much more expensive. There are also many more gadgets and special kinds of equipment, one of the most modern being buttons to press releases the gas tank cap. Some of these are, strictly speaking, merely gadgets, but others are bona fide improvements which we have discussed in other pages of this book. You should read all instructions quite early in your driving course, as it will help you if you happen to own one of the cars with the newer type of equipment.

PROPER MAINTENANCE

Proper maintenance of an automobile means keeping it in repair, properly lubricated, properly housed and used in a reasonable manner. The brakes must be adjusted periodically and any parts which wear or tend to give trouble need to be serviced. Some knowledge of the car will help you a great deal in this respect and when you take the car to a repairman you can tell him what you want done exactly. You will find your repair bills will be much lower than if you merely take the car in and say, "Fix it and send me the bill." Being informed is just good business, however. In order to maintain your car properly, you need have a great deal of knowledge about it.

GAS AND REPAIR OF CAR

We hardly need to discuss this essential item at length, but it might be well to explain why, and specifically how, training would help one cut the cost of repairs and maintenance. In the first place, if you know how to drive a car, you will never jerk it and abuse it unnecessarily. Although very reliable in the strict sense of the word, an automobile does break. You can break a spring by hitting a ditch too hard. You can turn a corner so fast that you damage your tires. You can hit a curb and cut a tire very easily by inability to properly gauge the stopping power of your brakes. As was stated before, you can get a great deal more gas from your car if when starting you press the accelerator very gradually and do not shove it to the floor allowing an undue amount of gas to be drawn up into the cylinder. Any sudden spurts of speed of the motor also draws up more oil into the cylinder than necessary and in this way tends to increase the oil consumption. The fan belt will slip slightly under surges of power. This will tend to wear the fan belt. There is also danger of burning up the generator when the car is speeded up, particularly when it is cold, as the generator tends to throw a little more current under those conditions. Thus in various countless ways training will help cut your gas and repair costs.

DEPRECIATION

We have already given an estimate of the rate of depreciation. The term depreciation, as it is called, when used by dealers, is an average for all types of cars. There are always cars being sold on the used car market which do not nearly bring blue book prices, and again there are others which will bring more than blue book prices. These prices are not set by any regulating agencies, but are merely averages or market prices established by certain associations of used car dealers. Therefore the trade-in value of your car will depend largely on how well you take care of it. Slamming the doors, breaking the glass, hitting the corner of the garage, denting your fenders and otherwise damaging your car will tend to increase depreciation. Knowledge of how to drive, and skill in handling your car will largely eliminate unnecessary damage to the car and thus protect your original investment.

RESPONSIBILITY LAWS AND INSURANCE

Most everyone is aware of the fact that a driver on the highway is liable to the public for proper manipulation and control of his vehicle. It is considered good business on the part of any person who has property, or expects to have anything other than enough to pay his bare living expenses, to carry what is known as public liability and property damage insurance. These insurances should be discussed at length because everyone should understand what these terms mean. However, they do tend to add to the operating cost, thus making one more reason why it is necessary to be able to stay out of trouble while on the highway.

YOUR QUALIFICATIONS AS A DRIVER

In the not too distant past it was thought that everyone was equal and had equal qualifications. Of course we all realize now that this is not true. People differ in their ability to think, to play baseball, to amuse other persons, to speak in public, to act, and any one of a thousand other things which we might mention. In other words, each person has his basic qualifications for certain types of activities and driving an automobile is no exception.

VISION AND DRIVING

Studies have been carried on by the writer and others for the past twenty years to determine the visual limitation of drivers. Although a great deal has been learned about what is needed for vision, the exact limits at which one may drive safely have not been completely established. However, one thing is certain. A blind person cannot drive. There are several factors in vision which are important. The basic facts have been learned through research studies. To give these categorically we may first list acuity or keenness of vision which may be due to what is known as astigmatism or to the condition of the eye known as myopia or hyperopia. The latter is a problem of balance of the eye muscles. Some persons' eyes tend to pull out. Some persons tend to turn in. These conditions are called exophoria and esophoria, respectively. This vision disorder is called strabismus. This is a condition known as cross-eyedness or squint because the eyes do actually turn. Sometimes the tendency of the eyes to turn out is called wall-eyedness or cockeyedness. It is sometimes also referred to as squint.

Another condition of the eyes which may interfere with driving and contribute to accidents is side vision. Everyone realizes that danger exists at intersections. If one studies accident statistics, he will find that about 40% of accidents occur at or around intersections. Therefore it behooves the driver to exercise his most careful observation at intersections. Of course, this does not minimize the necessity for keeping the eyes open and alert at all times. While visual acuity decreases markedly away from the fovea or point of keeness of vision laterally, movement can be detected most readily at the side. Again it must be borne in mind that when the eyes move they do not see. Therefore to keep the eyes fixed ahead and then glance quickly to the side without moving the head is not entirely useless but is largely lost motion. One should turn his head completely at intersections and note the presence or absence of oncoming traffic in both directions to check before proceeding.

We find that persons tend to use one eye more than the other, the same as one uses one hand more readily than the other. The net result in this respect is that one eye does most of the work functionally when you are doing something in a routine way. Of course, in an emergency, you may possibly see as well with one eye as with the other. In fact some persons alternate from the right to the left eye while about 60% will tend to use the right eye most of the time. Probably 20% tend to use the left eye all the time, while another 20% use the eyes alternately. This is not related directly to your handedness, so if you are righthanded it does not necessarily mean that you are right-eyed. Neither does it mean that you will use your best eye. It is frequently found that a person uses his poor eye mostly. Possibly this is the reason his eye is bad. He may have overused it. Now it is obvious that if you are driving along and one eye is not working, you are practically one-eyed and can be caught from the side on which your eye is not functioning properly. There may be nothing wrong at all except that it is just a habit to look with one eye. However, you may fail to notice objects along the side of the roadway. If one has a highly arched nose or particular type of face, he may be seeing only a small part of the field of vision at any one time. Of course what we have said here applies to the one-eyed driver also who will have to exercise special caution in staying out of trouble from contacting cars at the side.

Another condition of the eyes, of course, is that of night blindness, or what is technically known as photophobia. This is literally a fear of light, but actually means that a person doesn't see as well at night as he does in daylight. As one becomes older he is more likely to become blinded by light. If you look down the right side of the road or away from the line on which the light beam approaches you will tend to withstand more of this oncoming light. However, you should know something about your condition in this respect, that is, whether you are good, bad or indifferent. The best way is to get a measurement made of these characteristics.

There are other conditions. One known as anisekonia is really a condition of the eyes in which the image on one retina is larger than that on the other. We do not know exactly how this might affect night driving except that it does produce severe headaches and anything in the way of a severe headache promotes inefficiency, at least.

Thus the affects of poor vision may be readily seen if we consider the types of defect. It is found that you will not be able to read signs quickly if your vision is poor, say 50% or 20/40 which is usually designated as the limit for getting a driver's license. You will not see as well at night if you have astigmatism or other conditions which reduce your visual acuity.

The problem of eye muscle balance is important because if you have heterophoria, under certain conditions you may have four to five prism diopters of divergence or convergence. Particularly with divergence, one may see double. If one eye looks slightly over the other, you may see two sets of headlights, one above the other. This causes a disturbance, particularly at night when you are driving in dim illumination or when you are fatigued. There-fore, every driver should, and must in most states, have a careful evaluation made of his visual limitations before attempting to drive.

Our recommendation is that some leniency be exerted in this respect. Since everyone likes to drive and needs to drive, we have recommended, and it is being generally accepted throughout the country, that while we cannot expect one to have perfect vision in order to get a license, we do expect him to get his vision up to the best possible level. If he cannot bring it up beyond a certain point his license should be stamped as a "restricted" license. This is done in several states. It means that a driver must wear his glasses at all times while driving an automobile, otherwise his license is void. It also applies to certain other conditions and may be used to keep certain persons from driving at night. Such restrictions are doing drivers a favor if by permitting them unre-stricted privileges they are endangering themselves or others on the highway. With a restricted license you may drive and enjoy yourself as much as if you have a non-restricted license and at the same time protect yourself and other people from injury. It is well to note that the defect in question may not necessarily be the fault of the applicant.

OTHER SENSES AND DRIVING

Besides vision, the senses which seem most important in driving are, in order of importance, the muscle sense, the touch or tactual sense, the sense of smell, the sense of pain in a general way, and possibly the least important with reference to driving is the sense of hearing. Of course, you understand that in modern psychology there are at least 11 senses, while physiologists maintain possibly there are 23. The other important senses are the sense of equilib-rium and the organic sense. The organic sense is fatigue, thirst, and anything of internal nature.

As we have already pointed out, it is quite fairly obvious how muscle sense and the touch sense might affect one when driving. Also the effect of smell helps to determine certain conditions of the car. These aids tend to relieve the eyes and they may center their attention on observing traffic conditions and other phases of driving. There is what is known as the warmth-cold sense. These have little effect. Pain, of course, affects one in this way. If you are wearing a tight shoe or have a severe headache, hunger pains, a muscular cramp, or disturbance of that type which is painful, it acts as a distraction and tends to limit your ability at any given time as a driver.

We admit the importance of considering the senses as suggested. However, it remains that vision is the most important sense for driving an automobile and probably will be the only one which will be incorporated in a driver's license examination for some time to come.

ESSENTIALS OF MANEUVERING SKILL

In studies we carried out a number of years ago, it was found that the maneuvering skill could be developed to a high point between the ages of about 18 to 22. While the period of best driving record, or the safest record, would not come until about ten years later including the ages from 32 to 37. This of course might be misinterpreted. It does not indicate that maneuvering is not important, but it means that one does learn to maneuver before his judgment is fully matured to give him full command of his skill possibilities. In other words, in order to stay out of trouble one may have a super abundance of skill before he develops the proper judgment at the wheel. This probably is the reason for the high death rate among automobile drivers at the ages of 18 to 24. It also emphasizes the importance of practice on every known type of skill in advance of any dangerous condition which might arise that would necessitate this skill for safely passing through the hazardous situation.

The essential skills of driving an automobile are steering, proper starting and stopping, proper maneuvering in close places which includes space perception, and the sense of touch on the brake and the clutch. Many drivers skid on gravel and slippery pavement because they press the brake too suddenly, or are unable to maneuver out of a skid after the car has once started to slide sideways. Essential elements of skill should be stressed in the various exercises given on the driving field and should be mastered with these ideas in mind.

INTELLIGENCE, KNOWLEDGE AND JUDGMENT

Psychologists tell us that there are several kinds of intelligence but with reference to driving we should take account of at least one general type of intelligence, that of mechanical ability. The fact that one may be a "shark" in mathematics does not guarantee that he will be a good driver of an automobile. Our concept of intelligence would be qualified somewhat to indicate mechanical or spatial relation type of intelligence. Knowledge of course, is not intelligence, but is superimposed upon or added to intelligence to act as a safeguard on our conduct generally. We may be intelligent enough not to take poison but if we do not know and have knowledge that a certain plant is poisonous we may eat it and thus become ill. Judgment is the result of the inner action combination of intelligence and knowledge. One cannot have judgment without knowledge and he cannot have judgment without a certain amount of intelligence. Therefore, it behooves every driver to learn as much about the thing that he is trying to do as possible. This may be road laws and regulations, driving his car, possible reactions of other people, the way accidents have occurred in the past and where hazards lie along the road, in order to keep out of trouble. He should have some kind of an evaluation given him regarding these qualities before he attempts to try his wings too vigorously.

EMOTIONAL CONTROL AND ATTITUDES

The emotions tend to serve as a balance upon our behavior. Sometimes the urge is to rush to the dance and get there in a hurry. Sometimes these subtle conditions keep us from starting early enough to give us time to get there without excessive speed. Sometimes, due to emotional disturbances or misguided attitudes, we pass another driver when we would not if guided merely by intelligence, knowledge and judgment. Therefore the emotions are a very essential factor in driving, not only as an indicator of our capacity to act in an emergency situation, but also of our tendency to develop certain attitudes with respect to people and traffic in general. Some authorities in the field have studied the importance of emotionalized attitudes. We do not care to go into the definition of attitudes except to say that an attitude is merely a feeling toward some particular thing or situation which is likely to govern our conduct. For example, if I have a bad attitude toward the movies or certain movies, it is likely I will not attend those movies; whereas if I have a pleasant attitude to movies or band music, I am very likely to be around every time such entertainment is being offered.

Emotional control must be cultivated and one should know something about his basic tendencies when learning to drive. This may save one considerable trouble and unhappiness later.

DISTANCE AND SPEED ESTIMATION

Sometimes distance judgment has been used as synonymous with depth perception. This is a gross error and should not be thought of in this way. Depth perception operates only because of the functioning of the two eyes seeing an object at different angles. Since it operates up to distances of only about 300 feet, and since a great many of our danger situations necessitate the estimation of speed at a much greater distance, it follows that we should speak of distance judgment rather than depth perception. Depth perception is due mostly to the disparagement of images along with other factors such as the presence of shadows, mist in the atmosphere, the size of the retinal image, the perspective in the landscape in comparison with other objects and a number of other considerations.

Distance judgment is very important not only when getting out of the garage, but in meeting cars both in traffic and road driving, and in allowing for pedestrians or other hazards along the highway. In other words, if one has a good, highly developed perception of vision, he can avoid getting himself tangled up in close places while on the highway by defensive driving.

Speed estimation may be considered two ways. First, the speed at which drivers are maneuvering their cars through traffic, and second, speed of cars coming up to an intersection from the side.

It may also refer to cars coming in from any angle for that matter. Many drivers are unable to judge their speed while at the wheel. This is particularly true if they go from an old noisy car which labors under pressure of 40 miles an hour to a new car which may do 80 miles an hour with scarcely exerting itself. This sense of speed is something that everyone should try to develop. Many persons do not intentionally drive fast but simply keep stepping on the accelerator until their speed is up considerably higher than they intend it to be. This aspect of speed estimation is very important and would save millions of dollars of fines to drivers throughout the United States if it were properly developed.

The second aspect of speed estimation has to do with cars which may intersect the path of the driver at any point. If you note a train coming on the track or a car coming toward the intersection and have a half way accurate estimate of speed, it is likely you will either diminish your speed and let the other car pass or you will increase your speed and get to the intersection before there is danger of contact with the other vehicle. From a practical point of view it would probably be much better to consider decreasing your speed, and if necessary stopping, because by going at a slow rate of speed you can stop, while if you are expecting to speed up to beat the other fellow you may misjudge and be unable to stop if necessary at the intersection. The act of speeding up should be reserved for the very experienced driver, who has been driving many years. If it is at all possible get an estimation of your own capacity with respect to speed and distance judgment.

COMPENSATION FOR WEAKNESSES AND DEFICIENCIES

The history of civilization will reveal to a critical reader the fact that perhaps more worthy things have been accomplished by persons who have tended to compensate for their weaknesses than by any other group. That is to say, compensation, the tendency to do some one thing better because a person lacks another ability, probably has created more historical characters than any other single characteristic. It is our observation from studying a large number of drivers that one of the important things for every driver is to know his limitations and to compensate for them. A fat man is rather clumsy and will probably never be injured by falling off a high trapeze or a tight rope. The reason is he never gets himself on a tight rope or in such other position as to endanger himself. His better judgment tells him not to do this type of thing. In a similar way every driver should know his limitations and be able to compensate, and thus be able to eliminate a large percentage of his chances of having an accident.

REFERENCES

1. Halsey, Maxwell, Let's Drive Right. Scott, Foresman and Company, 1958, pp. 307.
2. Lauer, A. R., Learning to Drive Safely. Burgess Publishing Co., Minneapolis, 1949, pp. 141.
3. Kearney, Paul W., I Drive the Turnpike and Survive. Ballantine, 1956, pp. 147.

CHAPTER XVII

ALCOHOL AND DRIVING

It has long been known that the alcoholic driver is one of the great hazards of automobile driving. It has become so well ingrained in public thinking that the trite expression "alcohol and gasoline do not mix" is heard everywhere. Almost universally condemned, there are those who will still imbide and drive.

Various figures are given as to the per cent of fatal accidents in which alcohol is the prime factor. In the 1957 *Accident Facts,* the National Safety Council gives 7% of urban accidents and 8% of rural accidents attributable to alcohol. Some students of the problem have taken a much dimmer view of the subject than others. Estimation of the proportion of accidents due to alcohol run up to 5%. In 1938 Holcomb (4) found in a study of 1,750 subjects only 24 refused to take a breath test when stopped on the street while driving. This was a random sampling in Evanston, Illinois, and of the 1,750, 12% of the normal population showed they had had alcohol. Two hundred fifty drivers in traffic accidents who required hospitalization were tested. Forty-six per cent of these drivers had taken alcohol in noticeable amounts.

WHEN IS ONE CONSIDERED DRUNK?

Earlier studies were mostly with the drunken driver. Harger (3) and others have studied the amount of alcohol in the blood to produce a condition which could be designated as drunken. It is now accepted in most states that .15% alcohol in the blood is sufficient evidence of intoxication. Below this a person is legally not intoxicated according to this view. There are studies available which show that alcohol may affect behavior at various levels, thus the range of .15 to .5% is a questionable amount of alcohol in the blood, and authorities do not agree on the effects. It is known that some are affected more than others.

While almost everyone would agree that the behavior of many persons is impaired by blood content of alcohol in this range, they do not feel it would be wise to set this as a limit for conviction of drunkenness. So much variation occurs between individuals. Some persons with this amount of alcohol, who drink habitually, would probably not be affected. Others who are neophytes with the bottle might be in quite bad shape. Then again there is the psychological affect of alcohol. Fraternities have been known to produce drunken behavior with the false spiking of punch. In other words, some persons who take a drink of alcohol use it as an excuse for behaving in a manner that might lead to the conclusion that they were intoxicated. We hear of those who become drunk by smelling a cork. Others may drink quite heavily and not be affected. Hence the effect of alcohol is dependent upon the amount a person has imbibed and his basic disposition. Persons act in various ways with a given amount of alcohol. This is generally accepted.

DOES ALCOHOL AFFECT DRIVING EFFICIENCY?

The New York Police Department report that more than half of the drivers who were killed instantly or died within 24 hours after an automobile accident in 1957 were under the influence of alcohol according to reports filed. Of 69 persons killed, 38 had alcohol in the blood ranging in amounts from .10 to .40%. Their conclusion is that finding alcohol in over half of the persons killed supports the belief that critical judgment vitally necessary to the operator of a motor vehicle is impaired by the consumption of alcohol.

Because of the difficulty in estimating accident causation in instances where the operator is found dead at the wheel, cases of this type are not counted. An analysis showed that in the majority of motor vehicle accidents the immediate cause was faulty evasive action on the part of the driver. Complete loss of control resulted in 2 head-on collisions; 20 vehicles left the highway and struck a stationary object such as a tree, light pole or bridge abutment; 10 vehicles struck elevated pillars; 2 ran into buildings; 2 struck hydrants; and in 2 parked vehicles were struck.

In addition to causing deaths to drivers, these accidents caused the deaths of two pedestrians on the street and five passengers in cars they were operating. They also resulted in injury to 29 persons in their own and other cars. Some of the basic immediate causes listed were classified as delayed perception, 6 cases, speed, 4 cases, and illegal behavior, 2 cases.

In 26 accidents in which drivers were found to have between .14% and .26% alcohol in the blood stream, a direct cause of 17 accidents was speed, 8, delayed perception, and 1, illegal driving behavior. All indicate an impairment of judgment.

ONE REMEDY FOR THE SITUATION

The commissioner directed all members of the force to be constantly alert to apprehend intoxicated drivers in order to avoid accidents. Last year 2,229 persons were arrested for driving while intoxicated. It should be pointed out that .15% alcohol in the blood or over is prima facie evidence of intoxication according to the New York legal code. Alcohol content of .10% in the blood is considered relevant evidence of drunken driving. Thus it is found in almost every instance that police and enforcement people are of the strong opinion that even .10% is a hazard in driving.

In Holcomb's study he found that among the normal population of drivers, 12% had some alcohol; about 7% had up to .05% alcohol in the blood; 5% had in the range of .06 to .14%; and slightly less than .5% had over .15% alcohol in the blood. Among drivers with motor vehicle injury accidents, slightly over half had no alcohol; 12% ranged from .01 to .05%, about 20% ranged from .06 to .14%, and nearly 14% had over .15% alcohol in the blood.

DANGER FROM DRINKING DRIVERS

Plymat (7) of the Preferred Risk Insurance Company which insures non-drinkers exclusively, at a reduced premium, is of the strong opinion that driving when drinking is equally as dangerous as drunken driving. He cites studies carried on in Sweden which show that smaller amounts of alcohol impair performance appreciably. These researchers found the threshold of impairment of driving ability of expert drivers is an alcohol concentration of .035 to .04% in the blood. Both laboratory and driving tests were given. They found fairly close agreement between laboratory tests and practical tests on the road. The impairment noted ranged from 25 to 30%. At .15%, the performance was reduced by at least 30% over the control group level.

One of the noticeable characteristics of drunken drivers cited was the release of inhibitions and impairment of the functions of judgment. Whereas coordination tests are often used to determine the effects of alcohol, Plymat contends that judgment is affected much earlier than coordination and the physical aspects of behavior. Other studies have confirmed this and we shall describe two small studies of the effect of alcohol on driving behavior.

A PILOT STUDY

Although much has been said about the effects of alcohol upon driving performance little objective evidence has been presented. The present report is that of a demonstration made before the Detroit Industrial Safety Council. It may be a better example of what may be expected in any isolated instance of drunken driving than more highly controlled studies since it was less artificial. The results are presented with all the limitations of a demonstration as described below. They are not to be considered as conclusive but are strongly suggestive of possible results which may be obtained from controlled studies.

In response to a request from the Detroit Industrial Council, the following demonstration was planned in cooperation with that organization, the American Automobile Association, the Ivory Transfer Company, and Dr. R. N. Harger (3) of Indiana Medical School. The procedures followed were originally planned by the writer. Some modifications were made due to circumstances. The American Automobile Association placed their driver testing clinic at the disposal of the project. A trained man supervised the practice of the drivers before alcohol was given them. It was intended to secure six preliminary runs to overcome practice effects, but this was not completely accomplished because of lack of time. Instead, those serving as subjects were used to assist in putting other persons through the tests between ten o'clock in the morning and one o'clock in the afternoon to familiarize them with procedures. In this way they became familiar with the operation of the equipment. It was thought that a knowledge of the apparatus would in some respect take the place of actual practice.

At three o'clock in the afternoon the drivers were allowed to partake of the drink which consisted of three or four bottles of beer or two or three glasses of whiskey as they chose. The drivers had had a good lunch at noon and took no more food until after the tests were finished which was between 6:00 and 7:30 P.M. The tests were given by four trained examiners. The test for alcoholic content of expired air was made by the Harger apparatus. An abbreviated colorimetric method was used. Even though a demonstration it was intended to control the amounts and kind of liquor taken but those in charge lost track and the effective alcohol in expired air had to be used as the sole criterion. The full action of the alcohol imbibed had not become effective in all cases and did not until about one to one and one-half hours after the tests were made. Thus the alcohol in the blood was the best criterion. On a ten minute driving errand one of the subjects seemed to handle his car quite well after spending five minutes getting it out of a close parking space. This observation was personally made by the writer.

TESTS OF DRIVING BEHAVIOR

Not all the test units of the American Automobile Association driving clinic were used for obvious reasons. It seems that acuity of vision, color vision and other sensory defects will not be affected to any noticeable extent by small amounts of alcohol. Blood pressure changes were not made since the conditions for obtaining basic levels could not be checked easily for these subjects.

Six test units were used as described below. The drivometer (Fig. 1) which measures three aspects of behavior relating to driving performance was used as follows: (a) manipulation or handling of the controls, (b) a composite measure of driving per-

formance based on an objective evaluation of the entire drivometer test considering the former two aspects of the test in relation
to the time required to complete the performance, (c) time.

Complex reaction time was measured by the American Automobile Association Reactometer. The driver keeps his foot at a
point of rest about six inches from the accelerator until one of
three things happens: (a) a red light appears, (b) a green light
appears, or (c) a buzzer sounds. For the red light he puts his foot
on the brake, for the green light on the accelerator, and for the
buzzer he sounds the horn. The time between onset of the stimulus
and the completion of the response is measured. A short time
score under these conditions is considered to be advantageous in
driving.

Strength was measured by the Smedley dynamometer and would
not be expected to decrease greatly with moderate quantities of
alcohol. It was used more as an indicator of the driver's strength.
The same is true of activity as measured by the Ream tapping
test. A total of three 10-second trials was used as the score. This
test has a very high reliability. A high score is generally thought
to be desirable for handling a motor vehicle properly.

Distance judgment was measured by the Allgaier apparatus as
modified for the American Automobile Association. It consists
in making a lateral alignment of small automobiles with a fixed
standard. The distance in centimeters of error in setting is used
as the score. A low score shows superiority.

Glare tolerance was used as a measure. In general no great
difference would be expected in glare tolerance on theoretical
grounds before and after ingestion of alcohol. The test was added
for introducing variety and motivating examinees. The AAA
glareometer is based upon the principle of reading quite legible
letters at smaller and smaller angles of arc away from a standard
light source. A high score is superior, but scores on this particular
test are not highly differentiating.

The alcoholic content index was made by an approximation
method suggested by those in charge of the apparatus, and may
not be a true index of the valid readings using the gravimetric
technique recommended by Harger who developed the test. It

was devised by one of his assistants.

The values obtained may be representative of the amount of ingested alcohol which was effective in the blood. One driver, for example, had taken very little alcohol, in fact he was somewhat dubious about drinking at all until told that he needed only take a drink or so. His alcohol index was the lowest of the group which is in harmony with the facts relating to his drinking. Data were used and presented merely for information. No attempt was made to correlate and only general observations will be given.

HOW ALCOHOL AFFECTED BEHAVIOR

It would hardly be in order to draw conclusions from this small amount of evidence gathered in the form of a demonstration. A few general observations were noteworthy. As one might expect, the effect of alcohol in the quantities consumed has little effect on vision, strength and activity. Complex reaction time, observation or attention, and distance judgment were most affected and showed about 19, 83, and 78% impairment, respectively. These losses of function are very important in driving at the levels measured, that is to say, the extremely small quantity of alcohol seemed to place the drivers at a questionable level of performance. It must also be remembered that the alcohol content of the blood was varied, being between .02 and .21% with an average of .096. The drivers also had the advantage of a slight practice effect.

The particular American Automobile Association test units employed were used because of their reliability or consistency of measurement. Unless the tests in such an experiment are quite reliable no marked difference could ever be determined from slight quantities of alcohol — chiefly because of the variation in test results themselves. While the present demonstration was not as well controlled as originally intended, within the limits of the conditions described, it was very conscientiously and impartially carried out. In some ways it was more representative of actual driving than a controlled experiment such as described later in this chapter. Those who desire to duplicate the demonstration or who may wish to carry on experiments are urged to first determine the reliability of the test units used for measuring driving performance.

Individual differences are also somewhat in evidence. The condition of the drinker — whether a habitual drinker or a neophyte — is likely to be as important as the amount and nature of beverages consumed. The idiosyncrasies of the driver himself such as the effect of a given amount of alcohol in the blood are also important factors to consider. In other words, there may be some question as to the effect of a given alcoholic content of the blood on performance. Efficiency usually decreases with the amount of alcohol in the blood as indicated by measurements of known quantities of expired air. The facts obtained from the demonstration may be briefly summarized as follows:

1. From a total of 71 measurements and alcohol indices made of 9 drivers, 48 or 68% of the more critical test results showed a mean loss of 47.4% in efficiency. The average loss on all measures made was about 28.5%. A few measurements showed some increase. Night vision showed no change.

2. Of 45 measures made on the most differentiating tests 35 or 78% showed a loss in efficiency.

3. Tests of those responses relating to attention and judgment gave a mean loss of 55.9% while those relating to manipulation showed by only a 9.2% loss. This is in agreement with results reviewed by Plymat (7). Eight out of nine drivers showed a loss on the composite drivometer score of 49.2%. Only one driver who had very little to drink showed a 22.7% gain, indicating a possible practice or other effect. Even a stimulating affect might be detrimental to safe driving. The range of loss was from 3.3 to 198.0%. A rank order correlation yielded a rho of +.746 between alcohol content as shown by the Harger apparatus and loss in composite performance on the drivometer. Correlation by the same method gave a rho of +.579 between alcohol indices and loss rankings of all tests used.

The results described have their limitations. If one were to speculate at all on what highly controlled experiments will show, it is safe to say that drivers will be found to vary enormously with given amounts of alcohol and that a driver will usually be found to be erratic in ability to drive while under the influence. It takes only moderate quantities to put some under the influence. By special effort some may be able to compensate by being very careful for a short time but care will tend to lapse. Attention and judgment, two very important factors in driving, seem to suffer most from the effects of alcohol. Manipulation suffers but to a lesser degree with a moderate amount of alcohol. The general effect of alcohol on performance is detrimental.

One case previously studied by the writer bears out the general results of this demonstration quite well. A reporter came into our driving clinic at Des Moines to experiment on himself and took the tests four times. After the first trial he drank two bottles of beer and returned some 45 minutes later. After the second trip he drank two more bottles and so on. At the end of the fourth trial the average loss on a total of nine tests used was 59.05% ranging from .9% in manipulation to 159% on distance judgment. He conversed quite well but was poor on delicate coordination and situations requiring judgment.

AN EXPERIMENT ON THE EFFECTS OF ALCOHOL IN DRIVING

This study was made in cooperation with the Iowa State Medical Society. Certain comments concerning terminology should be set forth. With respect to proof spirits, Starling in his book, *The Action of Alcohol on Man,* states that proof spirits is a designation in bad repute. It is better to use the amount of absolute alcohol as a basis of comparison. About .15% alcohol in the blood will be produced by drinking about 7 or 8 ounces of pure whiskey, or 4 pints of beer taken on an empty stomach. Since the absorption of alcohol is a function of the concentration, no definite amount required for symptoms of intoxication can be given. The intoxicant used in experiments described in this study was three doses of 2½ ounces of 94-proof gin diluted with ginger ale to 200 cc. of fluid.

As to the maximum effects of alcohol, it reaches a peak between 25 minutes and 2½ hours as reported by Himwich (cited by Haven Emerson, 2). The average time reported by one experimenter was 38 minutes but the psychological effect lagged some 5 to 7 minutes. Discrepancies seem to be a function of concentrations of the form of alcohol used, drinking habits, and other well established factors.

The concentration of alcohol in the brain is also a debated point. Miles (6) maintains experimental evidence favors higher concentration of alcohol in the brain than in the body proper. Harger (3) finds more alcohol in the blood, but the brain, liver, muscles and other organs show a concentration supporting the theory that the brain does absorb alcohol more rapidly than other organs.

Relating to the priority of alcoholic effect on the brain, that is, where it acts first, evidence would indicate that the functions of higher level mental activities are affected quickest and most markedly by alcohol. This view is also quite widely held in scientific circles although it is hard to substantiate experimentally. This would mean that mental functions are first to be affected by alcohol. Many tests of the effect of alcohol are of physical nature such as walking a straight line. Subjects F, G and L each had 7½ ounces of gin and R had 5 ounces of the same beverage. According to one authority this would amount to about 3.52 ounces of absolute alcohol ingested for the first three and 2.35 ounces for the latter subject. This was the estimate given by the doctor making the blood tests who had made considerable study of the problem.

SOME PROBLEMS

The problem of drinking and automobile driving is daily becoming more acute as the speed of automobiles increases and traffic density becomes greater. The courts are trying to solve the problem from the legal angle. They are puzzled by definitions, severity of penalties made mandatory by statutes, fixing of tickets, pathologic symptoms of nonalcoholic origin, constitutional rights of the alleged violator and dozens of other angles peculiar from the point of view of the legal profession. Plymat (7) has described the problem as it involves the drinking driver.

Traffic enforcement groups are never quite sure of a case designated as "under the influence." The medical profession has developed ways and means of measuring the amount of alcohol in the saliva, the breath, the urine, or the blood. Much progress has been made in the methods of analyzing the alcohol content in the various body fluids. These findings are all valuable and fundamentally important, yet we still have a basic question to answer, "How much must a man drink to render him a dangerous driver?" Here again is a puzzling question since some drivers are dangerous without even taking a drink. "How much alcohol does it take to reduce the efficiency of a driver to a point where he is incapacitated and should be taken off the road?" Here lies the crux of the problem. It is our purpose to present known facts relating to the effects of moderate amounts of alcohol on the human body and to try to indicate some of the obvious effects of alcohol on performance of a nature related to automotive performance.

WHAT HAPPENS TO ALCOHOL IN THE BODY

Before going into the more practical aspects, let us review some of the known facts regarding alcohol and its action on the human organism. It must be remembered that bacteria in the body create a trace of alcohol, to the extent of about .0004% in the brain, .0025% in the liver, and .004% in the blood. However, these quantities are almost negligible. The person of average size will dispose of alcohol, absorbed into the tissues after being ingested, at the rate of about 10 cc an hour. About 2% of alcohol is eliminated from the body unchanged. This amount, however, may vary from 1 to 10%. The remainder is oxidized by the body. Deep breathing, muscular activity and other forms of energy expenditure will speed up the rate of elimination and oxidation. Thus a healthy man of 150 pounds will dispose of about a pint of 188-proof spirits in 24 hours; that is, the amount of pure alcohol in a quart of whiskey. This would be approximately the equivalent of about ten quarts of 5% beer.

Alcohol after being ingested is absorbed very quickly and permeates the entire body. Intoxication is in fact the result of using up oxygen of the body. About one-fifth is absorbed directly by the stomach. The most of the remaining part, or about 78%, is absorbed by the small intestines. The effects begin after the first few minutes and reach a maximum in from two to two and one-half hours. Many tissues of the body receive more than their share of alcohol absorbed. While the saturation point of the body is 5 grams per kilogram of body weight, the brain will show an unduly large proportion of alcohol. This probably means that the effects on mental activity are likely to appear before physical effects which seem to be undesired by behavior changes. A narcotic tends to affect the centers of highest metabolic rate first.

RATE OF ABSORPTION BY THE BODY

There are many angles to the alcohol problem in relation to drunken driving. Some of the most important questions to be raised are as follows:

1. What was the concentration of the drink? Hard liquors will be absorbed much more rapidly than the light varieties.

2. What has the person eaten before or at the time he drank? Any kind of liquid or food will reduce the absorption rate but oily foods and fats will greatly retard the absorption rate or increase oxidation to prevent absorption. Milk is one of the best foods for slowing up absorption.

3. Over how long a time were the drinks spread? This has a great deal to do with absorption rate. The higher the rate the more rapid the absorption. Perhaps this is partly a matter of concentration in the stomach.

4. Is the person an habitual drinker? This is very important. The effects of alcohol may vary widely in different instances for reasons shown in Table I. The body develops a tolerance for alcohol in some way. Thus it will be seen that the absorption rate is about twice as rapid for the neophyte and that the effect lasts nearly twice as long. The concentration in the blood of the person not drinking regularly, a close correlate of symptoms of drunkenness, is three times that of the habitual drinker after three hours.

5. Physical condition and certain other factors no doubt influence the effect of alcohol on the human body.

TABLE I

PER CENT OF ALCOHOL IN THE BLOOD AFTER A CERTAIN TIME

Hours after Drinking a Given Amount	Habitual Drinker	Moderate Drinker	*Non-drinker
½	.050	.064	.097
1	.050	.102	.122
2	.048	.120	.134
3	.044	.118	.132
4	.032	.109	.128
5	.018	.092	.126
6	.010	.072	.106
7	.002	.048	.080
8	Not noticeable	.030	.055
9	Not noticeable	.020	.044
10	Not noticeable	.013	.034
11	Not noticeable	.008	.022

*Interpret as fractions of 1%. (From Emerson 2)

Note that the habitual drinker loses alcohol faster and had less to lose from a given amount.

WHAT DETERMINES THE EFFECT OF ALCOHOL ON BEHAVIOR?

Table I answers many of our questions as to the physiologic progress of alcoholic absorption. They do not go to the root of the problem and tell us the effects, for example, .05% of alcohol in the blood. We want to know what types of behavior are most important in driving an automobile. Only the high spots can be covered in the study. Among normal drivers it has been found that a safe driver must possess the following basic qualifications. He must be able to meet new situations promptly and accurately. This, of course, is a general statement. More specifically he needs all the speed of movement and activity, all the strength, all the observational and interpretive powers he has, as well as a quick shifting and wide margin of attention, good vision, a recognition of, and tendency to, keep out of danger, a considerate attitude toward other drivers and pedestrians — a humane attitude, and, finally, a cautious attitude toward any semblance of risk or danger and emotional control. He must have endurance to maintain these characteristics during a long period of driving. This requires good health, proper food, plenty of sleep, freedom from narcotic and other depressant drugs, and sound mental health.

HOW ALCOHOL AFFECTS THESE CHARACTERISTICS

There is much scientific information available and we need not review it all here. In a very general way we may say that alcohol deadens the mental activity and slows up the general powers of observation. It tends to weaken the individual as a depressant, and slow up his physical activity. Reaction time may be affected indirectly. It tends to make him oblivious to many important features of his environment (one reason for drinking) by narrowing the scope of attention and by increasing the time for the shift of attention from one thing to another. So far as we know it has little effect on visual acuity, excepting in those cases when diplopia, or double vision, occurs. In addition, alcohol is well known to result in lack of caution and realization of danger, a lack of consideration of other people, and in certain cases a decided lack of emotional control. Thus our pedestrian alcohol accident problem is on the increase — they have a disregard for danger. The driver must have endurance, and drinking not only decreases strength, per se, but invites late hours and revelry which will no doubt produce secondary ill effects. As a depressant, it is likely to lead to bad attitudes in general. The problem of alcoholic psychoses has not been considered. It is another field that is inviting to those who are interested in chronic alcoholism of the habitual inebriate.

HOW CAN THE PROBLEM BE SOLVED?

The method used in the present study was that of giving the subjects practice in advance on laboratory apparatus developed for evaluating driving performance. A description of the equipment was made by Lauer (5). It suffices to say that the equipment has been used in 12 states during standardization tests and the superior records are made by test drivers and other most proficient performers. Conversely, beginners and inefficient drivers rarely make even an average score. A previous study of many drivers showed similar general results. Thus, it had been established that the functions related to driving could be measured and that the tests were valid as laboratory evaluation devices.

The subjects used were as follows: first, a physician — nondrinker, 160 pounds, age 34; second, an engineer — nondrinker, 160 pounds, age 30; third, a war veteran — drinks some and has been arrested for drinking, 165 pounds, age 46; and fourth, a physician — nondrinker, 185 pounds, age 31. Three subjects were practiced twice in advance and one was given one practice in advance. There is reason to believe that a plateau had been reached and that further improvement offset, to some extent, the effects of alcohol as measured after ingestion.

The experiment began at 7:00 in the evening when all subjects were given a complete set of driving tests to be used as a standard comparison. This, in every case, is taken as 100%. Two and one-half ounces of alcoholic beverage in the form of gin diluted to about 200 cc. were given. After 30 minutes the blood tests were taken and the subjects given key tests to determine the effects of alcohol on driving performance. The subjects were given another $2\frac{1}{2}$ ounces, with the same dilution, allowed to rest for 30 minutes and retested. Dosages of $2\frac{1}{2}$ ounces of 94 proof gin were thus given three of the subjects at intervals of about one hour. The fourth subject did not receive the final dose as the supply of spirits was depleted.

EFFECTS NOTED

Harger (3) has established the danger zone as ranging from .05 to .15% alcohol in the blood. The condition of our subjects is shown in Table II. It will be seen that the amounts absorbed by our subjects range from .02% to .125% alcohol in the blood. The corresponding losses in efficiency as measured by the tests are also shown. A correlation of $+.58$ was obtained between the loss in performance and the amount of alcohol in the blood.

TABLE II

PERFORMANCE BEFORE AND AFTER PRACTICE COMPARED FOR ALL TESTS USED

	Subject	Efficiency Before*—Afterwards	Per Cent of Alcohol in the Blood
First Trial—2.5 ozs. gin	F†	— .69	.045
	G	— 35.5	.033
	L‡	+ 1.2	.022
	R	— 13.5	.051
	Mean	— 13.7	.037
Second Trial—2.5 ozs. gin	F†	— 41.9	.065
	G	— 72.8	.078
	L‡	+ 2.7	.058
	R	—140.1	.057
	Mean	— 63.1	.067
Third Trial—2.5 ozs. gin	F†	— 71.9†	.125
	G	—103.0	.111
	L‡	+ 0.44	.074
	R	....	....
	Mean (3)	— 57.8	.103

*Test scores made immediately before the driving performance were taken as 100%.
†F was in such condition that his friends would not let him drive home after the experiments were completed.
‡L is quite a heavy drinker.

TABLE III

COMPARISON OF MEANS OF PERFORMANCE FOR VARIOUS TESTS USED
(.094% alcohol in blood)

	Mean of All Subjects		Per Cent Loss or Gain in Performance (direction considered)
	Before	After	
Field of vision	190.50	184.20	— 3.3
Glare tolerance	59.00	47.50	—19.4
Distance judgment	34.90	41.20	—18.6
Reaction time	16.80	19.95	—18.8
Tracing	25.10	29.20	—16.4
Aiming	18.70	31.20	—66.8
Grip or strength	55.50	52.00	— 6.5
Activity (Tapping)	77.10	62.60	—18.8
Concentration test	243.00	378.00	—13.3
Contacts	78.00	69.20	—11.4
Error	0.57	0.75	—31.5
Time for trip (drivometer)	374.00	345.00*	— 7.7
Mean Loss	....	....	—19.4

Average loss in sensory group of tests, 13.8 per cent
Average loss in motor group of tests, 23.1 per cent
Average loss in judgment of tests, 24.6 per cent

*Irresponsible driver tends to move faster, reducing time for test.

GENERAL CONCLUSIONS FROM STUDY

Four subjects, three nondrinkers and one drinker, were given 2½ ounces of gin diluted to 200 cc. and then tested for effects after blood samples were taken. The results must be considered in the light of the few subjects used and the limitations of the experimental conditions described. In general, it may be said:

1. That a noticeable effect on behavior occurs somewhere between .035 and .065% of alcohol in the blood.

2. That the greatest loss in efficiency is found in abilities relating to judgment and finer coordinations. These averaged about 25% loss for all measures. Manual dexterity performance followed with about 23% loss, while sensory capacities showed only 14% loss.

3. That the noticeable effects of alcohol on functions relating to driving performance obtained through observation seem to be:

    a. Heightened variability and inconsistency in performance. Erratic behavior.

    b. Loss in tolerance to glare.

    c. Increase in length of reaction time — presumed to be detrimental.

    d. Poorer observation and lack of alertness.

    e. Tendency to hurry performance and be less cautious.

4. That the finer coordinations are affected most.

5. In general, the effects of alcohol are variable with individuals, but small amounts impair performance. Accidents taking place in which the concentration is not over .05% alcohol in the blood may easily be accounted for by the effects produced on behavior.

REFERENCES

1. Carlson, A. J., Studies on the Possible Intoxicating Action of 3.2 Beer. Univ. of Chicago Press, 1934.

2. Emerson, Haven, Alcohol and Man. The Macmillan Co., 1932, pp. 428.

3. Harger, R. N., Lamb, E. V., and Halpien. A rapid chemical test for intoxication employing breath. Jour. Amer. Med. Assoc. 1938, pp. 77-785.

4. Holcomb, R. L., Alcohol in relation to traffic accidents. Jour. Amer. Med. Assoc., 1938, pp. 1076-1085.

5. Lauer, A. R., Methods of measuring ability to drive an automobile. Iowa State Press, 1936, pp. 115.

6. Miles, Walter R., Alcohol and the Man. The Macmillan Co., New York, 1932, Chap. 10.

7. Plymat, Wm. N., Alcohol and the traffic problem. Paper given at Institute for Prevention of Alcoholism at Loma Linda, California, July 10, 1958.

NAME INDEX

A

Adjutant Generals Office, xvi
Aetna Insurance Company, xiii, 175, 182
Allgaier, Earl A., xviii, 21, 97
Allgaier Shops, xviii, 199, 301
Allstate Mutual Insurance Company, xxii, 95
American Automobile Association, v, xxiii, 19, 32, 112, 163, 175, 227, 229
American Association for the Advancement of Science, 95, 98
American Association of Motor Vehicle Administrators, v, 221
American Medical Association, 15, 22
American Optical Company, xii, 19
American Optometric Association, v, 3, 124, 128
Army, United States, v, 139, 156, 194, 209
Auto Trainer, xiii, 175

B

Bell Telephone, 5
Berman, Jack, 267
Binet, Alfred, 72
Brody, Al et al, 97

C

Canada, 31
California, 56, 73, 227
Cattell, R. B., 60, 62, 102
Chicago Rapid Transit Company, 175
Chrysler Corporation, The, 5, 9
Civil Aeronautics Authority, 107
Cleeton, Guy, 181

Cleveland, Ohio, effects of driver training, 275
Colorado, 61
Connecticut, 73, 272
Courts, F. A., 69
Carlson, A. J. on alcohol, 312

D

Dayton Power and Light Company, 5
Dennis, Wayne P., 109
Des Moines, Iowa, 121
Detroit Safety Council, alcohol study, 299
De Vries, genetic studies, 72
Driving Clinic, Iowa State College, 9, 10
Driver Evaluator, xxiii
Driver Improvement Form, 215
Driving Research Laboratory, vii, xvi, xx, xxii, 20
Drivometer, viii, 5, 6, 175
Drivotrainer, xiii, 175, 182

E

Emerson, Haven on alcohol, 312
Eno Foundation traffic studies, 200
Experiment A, effect of rest pauses, 146
Experiment B, effect of rest pauses, 153

F

Fernberger, S. W., 156
Fletcher, Edwin C., 143
Ford Good Driving League, 120
Ford Motor Company, xv, 44, 69
Forbes, T. W., 30, 34, 197, 200

*The name of Iowa State College was changed in 1959 to Iowa State University. All basic research was completed before this date as used for this volume.

SUBJECT INDEX

A

Accidents, cost of, 83
Accident, chance, xii, 26
Accident-free individuals, 61
Accident frequency, ix, 87, 187
Accident involvement, 28, 61, 87, 224
Accident-liable persons, xi, 187
Accident-prone drivers, ix, 87, 187
Accident records, vi, 4, 32
Accidents, relation to domestic trouble, ix, 27
Accidents, resulting from speed, 27, 127
Accident susceptibility, ix
Accidents, their effect on vehicles, 5
Accident trends, 83, 230, 272
Accident types, 49
Activity tests, 11
Administrators, interested in safe driving, 99
Advantages, systems of plate colors, 99
Age and accidents, 28, 32, 61, 75, 83, 224
Alcohol absorbed by the body, 307, 308
Alcohol in the body, 307, 308
Alcohol references, 23, 57, 296, 297, 305, 312, 313
Alcohol, influencing factors, 309
Alcohol, studies of, 27, 57, 296, 299, 301, 303, 306, 312, 313
Alertness, 30, 46, 149
Amnesia, 33
Amount-limit test, 4
Applied psychology, 39
Association and memory, 36
Attitudes, driving, xxi, 25, 26, 85, 101, 195, 279, 281
Attention, 20, 48, 175
Attitude tests, 102, 109
Astigmatism, 11, 18
Automobiles, differences in drivability, 285
Automobile controls, 43
Automotive driving amentia, 80
Avoiding accidents, 21
Avoiding issues, 23, 24, 26
Avocational driving, 269

B

Blackout, 207
Bad attitudes, 4, 186
Behavior patterns, 36
Before-and-after tests, 150, 165, 171
Blame for accidents, 226
Blood-pressure, 11, 149, 150, 193

C

Car size, 99, 100
Card sorting test, 150
Categories of driving ability, 108
Chart of driving traits, xvii
Character references for drivers, 214
Characteristics, changes in, 84
Compensation for deficiencies, 195, 294
Commercial drivers, 138, 187
Composite performance, xv, xxi
Community action, 220
College students, 8
Color vision, 11, 13, 124, 137
Color of licenses plates, 239, 244, 247
Control cars, color of, 115
Coordination tests, 4, 106
Coordination, value in driving, 4, 60, 149